CHOSEN
LIVING
WITH
ADOPTION

Edited by **Perlita Harris**

Published by
British Association for Adoption & Fostering
(BAAF)
Saffron House
6-10 Kirby Street
London EC1N 8TS
www.baaf.org.uk

Charity registration 275689 (England and Wales);
SC039337 (Scotland)

British Library Cataloguing in Publication Data
A catalogue record for this book is available from the British Library

ISBN 978 1 907585 63 0

Project management by Miranda Davies, BAAF
Cover photo courtesy of www.istockphoto.com; posed by model
Designed and typeset by Fravashi Aga
Printed by TJ International

Trade distribution by Turnaround Publisher Services, Unit 3, Olympia Trading
Estate, Coburg Road, London N22 6TZ

BAAF is the leading UK-wide membership organisation for all those concerned
with adoption, fostering and child care issues.

To my sister, Samantha, in my memories and in my heart,
and my sister, Wendy, with love

To my family by birth and by adoption

Contents

Foreword   xii
Hannah Pool

Introduction   1
Perlita Harris

Section 1 Who am I?   13

A small scrap of paper   14
Michelle Mother Hubbard

Coming home from the appointment (*November*, 2009)   16
Catherine Chanter

Building a sense of self   17
Gill Hardman

A Pandora's box   23
Miranda Wilkinson

I like to smile   28
Soo Cole

Striking a balance   34
Jo Burnett-Sharpe

Then and now   39
Ann Merrills

The reunion   43
Nicky Campbell

Who am I?   45
Alison Langford

A chance to be the "real" me   47
Carole Smith

She is my past and I am her future   50
Frankie Pearce

Roots   55
Therese Ryan

To be British, Vietnamese, Chinese and me   58
Jessica Emmett

Section 2 Challenges and opportunities   65

The track of self-discovery   66
Jennifer McNiven

Cuckoo in the nest   71
Annie Blackham

A tremendous freedom   75
Deborah Collier

Prepare for the unexpected   78
Sharon Figgens

Nothing to lose   84
Julie Hoskins

Seventy years ago today, Great Britain declared war on Germany and her allies   87
Gloria McLaren

Finding Joy   92
Joy Carter

Living with uncertainty   97
Shanel Cuthbert

Wife to husband   101
Jackie Rivett

Outside looking in   102
Beth Archer

Release   106
Beth Archer

Your secret   108
Cath Staincliffe

Cast on   109
Anwen Lewis

Jennifer's story 111
Jennifer Jones

My pathway to peace 116
Ron McLay

More than just a survivor 122
Viv Fogel

Finally, my choice 125
Liz Wilde

Mixed blessings 128
Liz Sibthorpe

What if...? 135
Vanessa Gebbie

Section 3 Rites of passage 141

30-minute interview (this time next week) 142
Catherine Chanter

Telling her (*Christmas*, 2009) 143
Catherine Chanter

Jacques 144
Caroline Smith

Meeting Evelyn 147
Cath Staincliffe

Our day 148
Therese Ryan

Returning to Peru 149
Milagros Caroline Forrester

Positive/negative 153
Nikky Norton Shafau

Defined by my adoption 155
Julie Beater

Swimming up the sun 160
Nicole J Burton

Prepare for surprises 167
Sarah Frances

Section 4 The meaning of family 173

My brother   174
Shenaz Drury

To have a brother   175
Rosa

Runaway   175
Rosa

Brother   176
Rosa

Mothers   177
Therese Ryan

Proud to be adopted   182
Andrew Barton

My father   183
Anna Treasure

Without question   184
Viv Fogel

My father   186
Viv Fogel

The meaning of adoption   188
Joe Jones

Adoption, family and me   190
Marie

The "Doodah" diaries   194
Deborah Weymont

In the beginning   198
Shenaz Drury

A diverse family life   200
Jenny Mohindra

Section 5 The lifelong impact of adoption 205

Write about an article of clothing 206
Catherine Chanter

The father in the shadows 207
Donald Eadie

A special gift 212
Chiquita Rajawasam

Choices and consequences 214
Bridget Betts

The things my mother might have given me 223
Vanessa Gebbie

Returning to my roots 224
Shenaz Drury

Be there 226
Pam

Never not adopted 228
Zara Phillips

Mute Bella 234
Bella Frey

Be strong, brave and proud 240
Eleanor

Useful organisations/websites 246

About the editor

Perlita Harris is Lecturer in Social Work at Goldsmiths, University of London, where she is Course Director of the BA in Social Work. An adoption support social worker by background and a registered social worker, she holds a PhD in Social Work from the University of Warwick. In a voluntary capacity, Perlita co-facilitates workshops for adopted adults who have an international element to their search for information and/or birth family, hosted jointly by the Transnational and Transracial Adoption Group (www.ttag.org.uk) and the Intercountry Adoption Centre. She may be contacted at perlita.harris2@btinternet.com.

This is Perlita's fifth book. She has edited three previous collections of writing, poetry and artwork: *In Search of Belonging: Reflections by transracially adopted people* (BAAF, 2006); *The Colours in Me: Writing and poetry by adopted children and young people* (BAAF, 2008), the launch of which was made into a DVD, *Readings from The Colours in Me* (BAAF, 2009); and *Something that Never Went Away: Reflections on adoption, being in care and searching for family members* (AAA-NORCAP, 2009). In addition, she co-authored the research study, *Pathways to Permanence for Black, Asian and Mixed Ethnicity Children* (BAAF, 2010) and has written a number of journal articles on service users' views and experience of post-adoption services.

Acknowledgements

The idea for an edited collection of writing and poetry by adopted adults came from Shaila Shah, Director of Publications at BAAF, inspired by the large number of enquiries she receives from adopted adults who want to publish their adoption life story or poetry. She was interested in how being adopted has influenced adopted people's views of the course of their life and the paths they have taken, and how being adopted impacts on individuals' philosophy of life and vice versa. I want to thank Shaila for this vision and for asking if I would edit this important collection.

I am grateful to all the adoption agencies, adoption support agencies, adopted adults' support groups and individuals who helped to publicise the call for submissions in 2009 and 2010. Thanks in particular to Adults Affected by Adoption-NORCAP, After Adoption, Adopted Vietnamese International e-group, BAAF, Family Futures, the Irish Council for Adoption Agencies, London Korean Links, the Post-Adoption Centre (London), Rena Phillips (Post Adoption Central Support, Stirling), Ruth Kelly (Health Service Executive, Ireland), Shaping Our Lives National User Network and the Transnational and Transracial Adoption Group. I also want to thank all those adopted adults who submitted writing and/or poetry which it has not been possible to include.

Working alongside Miranda Davies, Project Editor at BAAF, has been a pleasure. I would like to thank her for her feedback on the manuscript, her diligence in the provision of editorial support and for all her hard work.

A very special thank you goes to author, journalist and Eritrean-born adopted adult, Hannah Pool, for her thoughtful and inspiring Foreword.

Finally, I want to extend my warmest thanks and appreciation to all the contributors to these pages. I hope you are as proud as I am to see your insights and reflections on living with adoption in print. I thank you for having the strength, tenacity and courage to share your lifelong and ongoing journey with adoption. This edited collection would not have been possible without you.

Perlita Harris
September 2012

Foreword

HANNAH POOL

Journalist and author Hannah Pool was adopted from an Eritrean orphanage in 1974, when she was six months old. Her adoptive mother and father (both white) were American and British academics living in Sudan. Hannah moved to the UK (via Sudan and Norway) when she was seven. Hannah's book, *My Father's Daughter: A story of family and belonging* (Penguin, 2006), a memoir of her journey back to Eritrea to find her birth family, was described by the *Washington Post* as 'significant and moving'.

So much is written about adoption, and yet so little. This powerful collection of essays and poems by adopted adults shines a light on the corner of the adoption triangle that is too often overlooked – the adopted child who grows up to become an adult.

Adopted adults are lifelong members of an elite club we never asked to join. As adoption activist Zara Phillips writes, adoption has a lifelong impact: 'I would never not be adopted, and somehow this always took me by surprise.'

Most of us learn the pain of rejection before we have the ability to speak. We grow up compulsively searching strangers' faces for our own DNA, tentatively asking parents for clues about our past, instinctively worrying from an early age whether we are about to be abandoned all over again.

Simple questions throw us into a spin: What time was I born? Is there a history of cancer in my family? Where does my nose come from?

What others take for granted we long to know: How will I age? Did my father love my mother? Was I really that much trouble?

As the range of stories, views and experiences in *Chosen* shows, no two adopted adults are the same; you cannot simply categorise us as "successes" or "failures". But the thing that unites us is that, as Eleanor writes: 'We had no choice about being adoptees and living with adoption requires bravery.'

Adoption is not all that defines us. The scope and range of voices in this collection show how adoption is only one part of our identity. We are also friends, partners, colleagues. Sometimes we are consumed by the circumstances of our adoption, at other times we barely think about it. Some of us have traced our birth families, some have chosen not to, others do not have enough information to make it possible. As Jennifer McNiven writes of the tracing experience: 'Acceptance and rejection have come in varying measures, but I have gained a feeling of being in charge of my destiny as opposed to feeling I have no control over my life.'

The stories put together in this moving and important collection are the lives behind the headlines, the living, breathing embodification of each new adoption trend, each shift in government policy.

Chosen should be read by anyone whose life is touched by adoption. Whether you have an adopted son or daughter, niece or nephew, friend or colleague, whether you are a social worker or a government minister, this book will give you crucial insights on the legacy of adoption.

Like having a much needed catch-up with a fellow adoptee, *Chosen* brought back memories of my own childhood, adolescence and of tracing as an adult. At times I read through tears, at others laughter and above all, a huge sense of humility. I am proud to be adopted and lucky to know so many incredible adopted adults. Reading this collection, which is full of truth, honesty and power, makes me prouder still.

Introduction

My roots are here, I feel them deep in my memories,
in the hidden spaces of my blood [1]
(Mary Tall Mountain, 1988, p 204)

Perlita Harris was born in London in 1966. Deemed "unsuitable for adoption" due to her premature birth, a congenital medical condition and being of "full Indian" parents, she was received from hospital into the care of the City of Westminster aged two-and-a-half months and placed at the Chiltern Nursery in Reading, where her mother continued to visit her. Later, she moved to the adjacent children's home, The Rise. When she was almost five years old, Perlita joined her British foster family, with a view to adoption. Legally adopted a year later, she grew up in rural Gloucestershire with three older (adoptive) siblings. Aged 17, her *Papaji*, Salim Johnson, made contact via social services and Perlita travelled to Canada to meet him. Her mother, Phulwati, had died from breast cancer three years earlier in London, aged 42, leaving three young children. In 1987, Perlita located her mother's grave and traced her younger sister, Samantha, and her brothers who were living in Southall. In 1991 she introduced herself to Samantha, now 18, and found and visited her maternal family in India. Perlita and Sam were both diagnosed with breast cancer on 5 October 2009. Sadly, Samantha died in 2011, aged 38. Perlita has ongoing contact with her *Papaji*, her paternal and maternal extended (birth) family, and her younger brothers and brother-in-law. She also remains in regular contact with her (adoptive) mum (her dad passed away in 2009), her sister, Wendy, and brother, Peter.

This collection brings together the writing and poetry of 51 adopted adults who were born during a 50-year period spanning from 1934 to 1984, and who are aged between 28 and 77 years at the time of publication. They comprise adoptees who were born and/or adopted in England, Wales, Scotland and Ireland, those adopted privately or whose placement was arranged through an agency, and transnational adoptees who were born in another country and adopted by British or European adoptive parents, living for all or some of their childhood in the UK. The authors joined their respective adoptive family between 1934 and 1992, aged between a few days old and almost eight years.

[1] Tall Mountain M, 'My wild birds flying', in Brant B (ed), *A Gathering of Spirit: Writing and art by North American Indian women* (Firebrand Press, 1988)

Their accounts capture a broad range of adoption experiences. The adoptees range from those who joined their adoptive family at a few days or weeks old through to those who were school age, some after one or more previous placements in foster care, residential care or an orphanage. They represent people who evaluate their adoption positively, negatively or, more commonly, a complex mixture of the two; some have a close ongoing relationship with their adoptive family, others have no contact. Some have searched for a relative while others have been searched for; some plan to search while others have insufficient information to do so.

The original aims of this collection were wide-ranging: first, to give voice to several generations of adopted adults about the lifelong experience of adoption within a British context; second, to bring together writing and poetry by adopted adults who are able to reflect on their life and the paths they have taken across the life course; third, to assemble a broad range of experiences of adoption, including the perspectives of adoptees who are now in their 60s, 70s and 80s; fourth, to highlight learning and messages from adopted adults for other adopted people; and lastly, to create a resource for adopted people, members of their family by adoption, birth and partnership, adoption support social workers, and counsellors and psychotherapists working with adopted people, to help them to understand the lifelong impact of adoption.

Potential contributors were reached via a variety of sources including adoption agencies in the statutory and voluntary sector in England, Scotland, Wales and Ireland, key regional adoption support agencies, individual social workers and support groups for adopted adults, adopted adults known to the editor, plus postings on websites, listservs for adopted adults and an online forum. They were asked to submit writing under one of six themes: adoption-related opportunities and challenges; the meaning of family; the lifelong impact of adoption; rites of passage and life events for adopted people; who am I?; and my philosophy of life. I wanted to hear from people who had reflected on their adoption and how it has influenced them in the course of their life, and in the life choices and decisions they have made.

A high proportion of submissions were received from transracially and transnationally adopted adults, probably reflecting the editor's background, including involvement in the Transnational and Transracial Adoption Group, and knowledge of my previous anthology, *In Search of Belonging* (Harris, 2009). Understandably, a number of enquiries and expressions of interest did not lead to any submissions. Writing about one's adoption may not be a simple task, giving rise to a range of thoughts, questions, memories and conflicting or complex emotions. Timing of the call and deadline for submissions was critical, particularly in relation to each adopted person's adoption journey or search for information or birth family, or other pressures and commitments in their life.

Many submitted multiple pieces of writing and/or poetry, often written at different times in their life which, taken together, charted their adoption journey. Sometimes these arrived in an undigested form, unconnected to the themes requested. With submissions from over 70 adopted adults and, between them, well over 150 pieces of writing and poetry, it was inevitable that not everyone who wanted to be a part of this book would be included. Contributions were selected on the quality of writing, the issues the writing addressed and whether they added anything new to our understanding of adoption, including the lifelong impact, a novel perspective or a fresh approach to living with adoption.

Significantly, a small number of contributors have chosen to write under their first name, birth name or a pseudonym of their choice. The reasons for this are both personal and professional. They include a wish to protect one's privacy and the privacy of other family members, including children, plus a desire to ensure one is not recognised in one's professional role. Some, such as Catherine Chanter, Vanessa Gebbie, Cath Staincliff, Joy Carter and Zara Phillips, are established or emerging writers, often publishing under a *"nom de plume"*. The vast majority of contributors, however, have chosen to write under their full current name and to include identifying information in their writing and biographical paragraph.

Setting the context

It is important to bear in mind the many significant changes that have taken place in adoption policy and practice over the last century. The first Adoption Act was passed in England in 1926, introducing adoption procedures for the first time, providing legal sanction and giving adopted children the same rights as children born to their parents. The 1949 Adoption Act introduced a three-month probationary period before an adoption order could be granted, and it was not until the 1975 Children Act and 1976 Adoption Act that adopted adults in England and Wales were given the right to access their original birth certificate – a legal right adopted adults in Scotland had always had.

We have seen adoption change from a service for parents, as 'a solution for infertility' (Quinton, 2012, p 12), where privately arranged adoptions were widespread, and where there was no support for either child or parents after the adoption order, to a service for children with adoptions arranged through adoption agencies staffed by qualified social workers. This shift has been accompanied by a dramatic decline in the number of adoptions since they peaked in 1968, a widening of those children considered "adoptable" to include black and minority ethnic, disabled and older children and sibling groups, and a shift from a 'closed' model to 'greater openness' with contact with birth family (Kirton, 2009). Further, adoption has shifted away from baby adoptions, "relinquished" for adoption (a term that is not unproblematic as it implies choice), to a service primarily for "looked after" children, most of whom are older and have a complex history of abuse and/or neglect within their birth family and a complex range of needs. Seventy-four per cent of children adopted in the year ending 31 March 2012 were aged between one and four years (Department for Education, 2012). In recent decades, debates have taken place about matching and "race", with the current Coalition Government taking a largely colourblind approach under the guise of reducing delay (Department for Education, 2012a) and with the intention of bringing in new legislation to clarify how much importance should be attached to "race" and ethnicity in matching decisions. In addition, numbers of children adopted from other countries have been falling in England, as they have globally in recent years (Selman, 2012).

These changes in the profile of children being adopted are mirrored by developments in the way adoptive parents are recruited, assessed, prepared and supported, and the profile of adopters, which now includes single, black and minority ethnic, disabled, lesbian and gay parents. Today, we know from research which parenting capacities are positive for all children and recognise those additional qualities specific to parenting by adoption (Quinton, 2012). This is no longer viewed as synonymous to parenting a biological child and, together with a recognition of the lifelong impact of adoption on all parties and that "love is not enough" in adoptive parenting, there is an expectation, reflected in the Adoption and Children Act 2002, that adoptive parents will require a range of adoption support services to help them in the parenting task, as will adopted children. At the same time, we have moved away from a belief that a mother "relinquishing" a child for adoption should be able to "put it behind her and move in with her life", to a recognition of the loss, grief and trauma that many birth mothers and fathers, of both historical and contemporary adoptions, experience, and that they and other birth relatives will also have adoption support needs. The following writings span adoptive placements made over more than 50 years and it is in the historical, socio-political context summarised above that they need to be considered.

A critical look at terminology

Adopted people often talk and write about being "chosen" by their adoptive parents, a theme which comes up time and time again throughout this collection; indeed, adoptive parents may tell their children they chose them out of all the available children. However, this notion should not be accepted uncritically. While it is indeed true that the adopted person, as an infant or older child, may have been selected by the prospective adoptive parent(s), it follows that it is not uncommon for the child to be told that she or he is somehow lucky or special because he or she was chosen. These terms are loaded, problematic and frequently not welcomed by adopted adults who may feel far from lucky, special or even lovable. Further, being lucky for being chosen suggests that the adoptee should be grateful to her/his adoptive parents for adopting her/him; there is no acknowledgment of the joy, happiness and rewards that parenting by adoption gives to an adoptive parent. For those adopted from another country, being "chosen" may feel more as if they were taken as a souvenir, uprooted from their country, community, culture and language, with little or no consideration of their needs, both at the time and throughout their life. Whether or not this is the case, it is how adoption is experienced that matters.

For the adopted child, to have been chosen by one set of parents sooner or later raises the possibility that one was "unchosen" or unwanted by another set. Indeed, many adopted people speak of feelings of rejection and a deep-seated lack of self-worth. A minority of adopted people are literally physically left somewhere by their birth parents, albeit usually due to the dire socio-economic circumstances in which the mother or parents find themselves. Arguably, the birth mother and father do not have a choice about their child being adopted. Indeed, many birth mothers from the 1960s say that they did not have a "choice" about "relinquishing" their baby for adoption but were under immense pressure from family, agency staff and societal attitudes. With contemporary adoptions, where children are removed from their birth family due to significant harm as a result of abuse and/or neglect, birth parents are similarly not given a choice about whether their child is adopted.

Many adopted children and adults feel that they had no say in the plans that were made for them, that is, they were powerless and had no choice about being adopted. Things just happened to them. They left one family and, sooner or later, joined another. However, in spite of often difficult beginnings, as many of the following writings demonstrate, it is possible to develop a sense of self-efficacy – to have agency over what happens in one's life and the direction it takes. Thus, adopted people are encouraged to take responsibility for the direction their life moves in, and for how they respond to the difficult situations and range of emotions they might experience. While not denying the pain of displacement and loss of resemblance that so many (but not all) adopted people report, and the joy and difficulties that may come with reconnection to lost family members, culture, community and country of birth, perhaps it should be remembered that whatever has happened in the distant or recent past, what happens today is down to us. Indeed, we can make a difference to our lives, develop our capacity to cope with adversity and take responsibility for our own happiness.

Although we speak of "reunion" with birth relatives, this term too can be problematic. Often contact is being sought or established with relatives with whom the adoptee has had no prior contact, although arguably a relationship exists even in the absence of contact, not only in a biological sense but in the mind and imagination of the adopted person and/or birth relative. The term "reunion" may be misleading in a second sense, in suggesting that this is a happy or joyous event that both parties want in equal measure and feel equally prepared for. The reality is that the sought after person may have always thought of the adopted person or, on the other hand, may not have known that they even existed. Thus, the sought after relative may suddenly receive a request for contact from someone whose existence she was unaware of or had no intention of searching for. Further, rather than thinking of "reunion" as a one-off event, we need to think in terms of making contact and developing a relationship as a process that can take years, even decades, as one negotiates different expectations, issues and difficulties that the emerging and evolving relationship throws up. We also need to be mindful of the emotional impact of searching and establishing contact on all parties, including the surfacing of long-standing grief for birth mothers and fathers. The accounts in this collection address all of these "post-reunion" issues and more.

Finally, the language we use to refer to the parents to whom adopted people are genetically related – natural, real, birth, biological, blood, original, first – each reveal underlying values and attitudes about which parent, birth or adoptive, is more valued or important, and the terms are limiting or one-dimensional in different ways. In this collection, "birth mother" and "birth father" are the preferred terms used. At the same time, it is recognised that these women and men have given (and may continue to give) adopted people a great deal more than merely birth.

Listening to adopted people
For the contributors to this anthology, sharing their adoption experiences through poetry and other writing is an act of empowerment, demonstrating

their ability to think and speak for themselves about their experience of adoption. When reading these pages we should remember that each person will revisit their adoption story at different points in their childhood and adulthood, revising it and adding to it, as his or her understanding develops and new information is incorporated or obtained regarding the sequence of events, the involvement of other people, family members and agencies, and the feelings, perspectives and actions of others. In doing so, understandings may be developed and a fuller and more rounded picture created. Thus, adopted people are active participants in creating their respective adoption story and no story is ever complete or finished. There is always room to add to it. By looking back across their lives, these writers show us how their adoption story has evolved and developed over time. They reveal the continued day-to-day impact of adoption on their lives. By listening to adopted adults and how they understand and experience their adoption, I hope we will be in a better position to understand, help and support them, whether as parents, family members, social workers, therapists or other professionals.

The structure of this collection

The book is divided into five sections. There are over-arching themes in each section and cross-cutting themes that readers may want to look out for. Some sections are longer than others, reflecting the topics contributors more commonly chose to write about. A few contributions were written in the past; the vast majority were developed specifically for this collection. You will find both similarities and differences between the ways in which people have written about and understand their adoption and its continued impact on them. Importantly, it should be remembered that these writings are a reflection of the author's thinking about adoption and their emotions at the time of writing. Thus, their understandings of and ways of living with adoption may have changed significantly, as may their sense of connection to and being rooted in their birth and/or adoptive family or birth community/ country. A biographical paragraph telling you a little about the contributor accompanies each piece, providing a context for understanding their respective experience of adoption. Where the author has more than one poem or piece of writing in the book, their biographical paragraph can be found alongside the first piece.

Section 1, *Who am I?*, focuses on questions of identity and belonging. Adoptees, including two late-discovery adopted adults, tell us about their evolving sense of self-identity. They reflect on the different elements and experiences that make up who they are, and how they have viewed their identity at different times in their lives. Thus, we gain an insight into some of the events and experiences that may disrupt or add to previous understandings of one's identity, such as accessing information held in one's adoption records, learning one's birth name, seeing someone who resembles you, tracing birth relatives or re-connecting with one's community of origin. While the process is not always easy or without pain and struggle, suggestions are made for other adopted adults, such as weaving together the different strands – birth family, adoptive family and own family – into one's sense of self and making use of a counsellor skilled in adoption issues. What is conveyed most strongly is that this is a journey of self-discovery, a journey which, for everyone, will be different. It is also an ongoing journey, with no end point or final destination. It follows that adoption offers adopted people the freedom to question and to explore their identity, to embark upon an amazing journey of self-discovery.

Section 2, *Challenges and opportunities*, gathers reflections on the challenges and opportunities that adoption brings, and the different ways contributors have found to think about adoption and to address some of the difficulties they have encountered. They offer us insights into the lived experience of adoption and how it affects on them on a day-to-day basis. The challenges they write about include the stigma of adoption, the impact on self-esteem and belonging, a fear of being sent back and not feeling "good enough", feelings of rejection and shame, feeling displaced, alone and unlovable, difficulty in trusting and loving others, and difficulties in "post-reunion" relationships. In addition, several transracial and transnational adoptees highlight the lived experience of 'everyday racism' (Essed, 1991) and confusion over racial identity. Sometimes, the challenges identified are reflected in self-harming and addictive behaviours.

At the same time, the writers reflect on a range of opportunities they view as going hand-in-hand with the experience of being adopted, such as a better material standard of living and higher education, and suggest that adoption might offer a freedom to be whoever one wants to be. Thus, it can be seen as offering both opportunities and constraints when it comes to identity and who we become:

There were clear benefits to being adopted. I could grow up to be anything I wanted, and I suppose I did. (Jennifer Jones, p 115)

Others highlight the increased insight, empathy and self-awareness they have developed as an adopted person, while some suggest being adopted and overcoming adoption hurdles has given them an inner strength and determination.

The contributors offer advice for accepting one's adoption and moving forward as complete humans, rather than living as a wounded person. These tips range from healing at your own pace, forgiving yourself, learning to take care of yourself and sharing your story with other adopted people, through to receiving counselling. The contributors write about the different ways they have found to live with and make sense of their adoption including writing and creative activities, stand-up comedy, and reframing and rewriting one's life script. In doing so, they offer adopted people pearls of wisdom, encouragement and hope:

It's not how you start, it's how you finish, and I am far from finished. (Joy Carter, p 96)

Section 3, *Rites of passage*, focuses on the common rites of passage in a person's life and how adopted people negotiate them, as well as some that are peculiar to adopted people. A rite of passage can be understood as a ritual event or ceremony that marks a person's passage from one social status to another. They have three phases: separation, transition and reincorporation. Thus, in the final stage, one assumes the new identity and re-enters society with a new social status. The contributors to this section write about a wide range of events, including the passing of the legal adoption order, birthdays, having biological children, the death of a birth parent, the death of adoptive parents, the first meeting with one's birth mother, visiting one's country of birth, connecting with one's religious and cultural heritage, and bringing birth and adoptive family members together. What is conveyed is that for adopted people, there are no blueprints or guidelines for how they should do these things, how they should feel, behave or respond to the situations they find themselves in:

I have had to dig and excavate, for as an adoptee, nothing can be assumed or taken for granted. (Sarah Frances, p 168)

Instead, the complexity of thoughts, actions and emotions are laid bare, including the grief, sadness and/or happiness that accompany many of these rites of passage and life events.

In Section 4, *The meaning of family*, contributors encapsulate the meanings they attach to family and reflect on their family and family relationships. The section opens with two people who write about the loss of a brother – an adopted brother who committed suicide and a brother whose placement disrupted – and their continued thoughts about him. Several writers raise poignant questions about the language commonly used to describe family relationships in adoption:

Some call you my "real mother". Who is more real? The mother who carried me nine months, gave birth to me, and went through the heartache and sacrifice of giving me up, or the mother who has loved and looked after me since I was five weeks old? (Therese Ryan, p 179)

and about the duration of these relationships, the "invisible threads" that connect people together:

Does a mother ever cease to be a mother? Was there a moment when I stopped being your daughter? (Therese Ryan, p 180)

Together, the contributors reflect on a range of family relationships and interpret family broadly, to include, for example, mothers and fathers by birth and by adoption, unrelated adopted siblings, wider adoptive and birth family, partners, close loving friends, and becoming part of a lesbian and gay "family". Important issues are raised, such as whether adopted people are able to take for granted family relationships, the appropriateness of letting go of negative and uncaring family members, and rewriting one's script from a script characterised by loss and separation to one defined by connection and family:

I have a family. I have roots and I belong. (Deborah Weymont, p 196)

Several adopted people write about their feelings about their adoptive family, expressing love for their adoptive parents and feeling loved unconditionally by them, while one person writes about being estranged. Together the writers demonstrate that family is about so much more than those to whom we are related genetically. Further, they demonstrate that being adopted offers adopted people a unique and invaluable perspective on the meaning of family.

Section 5, *The lifelong impact of adoption*, focuses on the myriad ways in which adoption impacts on the lives of adopted people throughout their life, and on the lifelong impact for birth and adoptive parents, birth siblings and other family members:

Adoption is not just a concept; it is a profound and life-changing experience for all those whose lives are touched by it. (Bridget Betts, p 221)

They draw our attention to a wide range of issues including several which are touched upon elsewhere in the book. They reflect on childhood feelings of rejection and abandonment, of feeling different and wanting to belong, through to sadness and grief. They explore their search for identity including joining communities of adopted people or visiting their country of birth, and the longing and continued thoughts and questions about their birth mother and/or birth father in adulthood, irrespective of their age. There is comment on how adoption may be played out in significant relationships, particularly the adopted child/adult–adoptive mother relationship. Through these writings we gain a sense of how adoption impacts across and between generations, reverberating across families and into the future generations. There is the realisation of how completely different one's life might have been if one had not been adopted. Several writers point to the rich lived experience that comes with adoption, pointing out that our experience of adoption shapes who we are and how we see ourselves, and as such, adoption is a gift, a bitter-sweet gift, that adopted people should be proud of.

We are privileged to have this opportunity to enter into the world of adopted people. The salience of what adopted people are able to tell us about their memories, experiences, thoughts, insights, questions and feelings about living with adoption cannot be overstated. Within these pages the complexity of the adopted person's lived experience of adoption is laid bare. Their words may not always make for easy reading, especially where their loss, grief and struggles with self-love and self-identity are so blatant and stand unmasked. Yet I hope you will find this collection informative and illuminating, for these contributors' words are replete with insights, wisdom, encouragement and hope.

This body of "service-user" knowledge adds to our understanding of adoption. I hope it may guide us all in our thinking and actions, whether we are personally and/or professionally connected to adoption. For adopted people reading this collection, I hope you will see that you are not alone and your experience of living with the lifelong impact of adoption is shared with many other adopted people. This book is for you.

References
Department for Education (2012a) *An Action Plan for Adoption: Tackling delay*, London: DfE

Department for Education (2012b) *Statistical First Release: Children looked after by local authorities in England (including adoption)*, 25 September; www.education.gov.uk (accessed 5 October 2012)

Essed P (1991) *Understanding Everyday Racism: An interdisciplinary theory*, Thousand Oaks, CA: Sage Publications

Kirton D (2009) *Child Social Work Policy and Practice*, London: Sage Publications

Quinton D (2012) *Rethinking Matching in Adoptions from Care: A conceptual and research review*, London: BAAF

Selman P (2012) 'The global decline of intercountry adoption: What lies ahead?', *Social Policy and Society* 12:3, pp 381–97

WHO AM I?

A small scrap of paper *Michelle Mother Hubbard*

Coming home from the appointment (*November*, 2009) *Catherine Chanter*

Building a sense of self *Gill Hardman*

A Pandora's box *Miranda Wilkinson*

I like to smile *Soo Cole*

Striking a balance *Jo Burnett-Sharpe*

Then and now *Ann Merrills*

The reunion *Nicky Campbell*

Who am I ? *Alison Langford*

A chance to be the "real" me *Carole Smith*

She is my past and I am her future *Frankie Pearce*

Roots *Therese Ryan*

To be British, Vietnamese, Chinese and me *Jessica Emmett*

A small scrap of paper

MICHELLE MOTHER HUBBARD

Michelle Mother Hubbard was an extra-marital child born in the mid-1960s, hence being placed for adoption. Her birth parents (Irish mother, Jamaican father) each had their own separate spouses and families. She was adopted at the age of three months by (white) English parents who went on to adopt a mixed-race boy, giving Michelle a brother. After years of searching, Michelle successfully and miraculously traced both birth parents (father in 1988, mother in 1996). She is a freelance poet and storyteller with so much to write about... a never-ending story! Michelle's last successful self-published book, *The Irish-Jamaican*, is a celebration and creative documentation of her history, culture, identity and families. Michelle is a proud mother of three and grandma to four. She is known on the poetry scene as Mother Hubbard.

I was born
Onto the mahogany
Of a social worker's desk
I was a small scrap of paper
(Birth) marked CONFIDENTIAL

They placed me into her in-tray
Wrapped me in bright red tape
Tucked me away tightly
In a dark grey filing cabinet
Held by the arms of the system

I was given a box full
Of emotions to play with
But they were all broken

Breastfed by the bosom of a typewriter
That trickled out a steady flow of words
Nourishing my file as it grew daily

Six months worth of documents later
I grew from a small scrap of paper
To a large bulging folder

Eventually I was weaned off
The bitter taste of the system
And finally fed with a solid sweet family
To sustain my healthy growth

Coming home from the appointment (*November, 2009*)

CATHERINE CHANTER

Catherine Chanter is a teacher who has led education provision for young people with mental health problems in a variety of settings including mainstream schools, Pupil Referral Units, the Tavistock Clinic and adolescent in-patient services. She has worked as a Family Group Conference Co-ordinator, seeking family-based solutions for children on the edge of care, and sits on her local adoption panel. Catherine grew up knowing she was adopted, but her adoptive parents never felt able to share what they knew of her story. She undertook the search for answers on her own, eventually discovering her wonderful name, her Irish heritage and her birth mother in Canada, who, like Catherine, is a poet. Catherine has had work broadcast on BBC Radio 4 and a novella and collection of short stories published entitled *Rooms of the Mind* (Cinnamon Press, 2011). She has a Masters in Creative Writing and has just completed her first novel.

The one thing I did not expect was a name.
It had never occurred to me that I would have been given
a name.

That she loved me enough to have named me.
A beautiful name. An Irish name. A unique name.
My name.

That I was not anonymous. What will you do now?
Laugh out loud, dance through this town holding hands
with my name.

Building a sense of self

GILL HARDMAN

Gill Hardman was born in May 1945 in Orpington, Kent and adopted at seven-and-a-half months. Her birth mother and birth father died in 1957 and 1985 respectively. Although contact has been made with birth relations, this has now stopped. In Gill's adoption she was physically secure, emotionally less so. Both her adoptive parents died in the late 1980s but she keeps in regular touch with their son, who is seven years older than her. Gill lives in Twickenham, London. She contributed to *Bye Bye Baby – The story of the children the GIs left behind* by Pamela Winfield (Bloomsbury, 1992) under the pseudonym "Jane".

A constant awareness of my adoption has woven its way through the fabric of my life. My sense of identity has evolved as ignorance of my origins has become partial knowledge. With a little mature reflection, this has enabled me to appreciate the benefits that adoption has provided and to feel a good deal nearer to knowing who I am.

I was born in 1945 and adopted in 1946, aged seven-and-a-half months. Until the passing of the Children Act 1975, I had no idea that any information about my birth parents even existed; I had assumed my adoption was an indication they had both died. Certainly nobody ever suggested otherwise. I knew when my birthday was and I knew I was adopted, but that was it; my adoption seemed to be a taboo subject. The nearest my adoptive parents ever came to giving me information about my birth family was when I was 28 and requested it. I had two small children of my own by then and I wanted to know what my and their heritage was. The information I was given, in a written letter, was about my maternal grandfather's status and included an unpleasant comment about my putative birth father, so I didn't pursue it any further. (Since obtaining my original adoption file, it has become apparent that even in 1946 my adoptive parents knew my birth mother's name and many other details about her and her family, but in those days all parties were sworn to secrecy.)

In 1975, having assumed until then that, like my adoptive parents, I was thoroughly British, I discovered my mother was Anglo-Irish, with an American grandfather, and my putative father was American-Jewish of Lithuanian origin – a GI posted to the UK during the Second World War. This information had a huge impact on me. Before, even wondering who my birth parents were had felt like a terrible betrayal of my adoptive parents. Since 1975 I have enthusiastically followed every lead in an attempt to build up a picture of my birth mother and her family and, where possible, of the man she claimed was my father.

As I delve into my memory of childhood, I can only give a general impression of how my adopted status affected me then. At secondary school, I remember feeling the need to explain that my mother and father were my adoptive parents. I felt guilty doing so, but I think I was trying to fumble my way through a fog of confusion because, subconsciously, I felt the truth was being withheld, whereas I felt a need to be honest. I didn't feel I belonged and yet maintaining loyalty to my adoptive parents – to try to actually be their daughter – seemed to be the main imperative, which I found so very difficult. I felt an obligation to them, as though my existence would somehow be in doubt were it not for the umbrella of their respectability. Without any sort of dialogue between them and myself as I grew up, there was no way of satisfactorily untangling my inner turmoil.

In my early childhood I began to build up a sense of self, mainly as a result of the love and attention given to me by my adoptive mother's elderly second cousin ("auntie") who was given the main task of caring for me (she lived in our house). Our household consisted of my adoptive parents, their son (seven years older than me), two elderly female relatives and several rather eccentric lodgers. This gave the home a rather fragmented feel, more of a boarding house than a home. In many ways, it was a potentially positive environment for me to grow up in. My adoptive mother played the piano and introduced me to music and duet playing, for which I shall always be grateful. However, apart from my "auntie", who patently adored me, there were few signs of demonstrative love from my adoptive parents – my adoptive mother was particularly awkward with me – and I sensed that they regarded me as perplexingly sensitive. I was once asked by someone working in our house whether I realised how lucky I was not to be in a children's home; this threw me into yet more confusion about my status in the family. There were few displays of emotion at home, no raised voices and certainly no shouting; extreme emotions didn't seem to be part of the lingua franca. I remember once, after being teased about something for the umpteenth time, I threw a spoon in my father's direction. It hit the ground and the very tip crumpled. Thereafter, this spoon was laid at my place at mealtimes and I was reminded that it was my "temper spoon".

When I was 11, my adoptive parents sent me to a small girls' boarding school, which was a disastrous decision. I was utterly miserable; I felt completely abandoned by them and it was probably then that any possibility of my ever grafting onto the family withered. In the 1950s, my boarding school operated on very old-fashioned lines, especially socially, and there was little real care or comfort to be found. Having sensed rejection once, this was a double blow, particularly as my pleas to be removed from the school were brushed off. My unhappiness had a deadening effect and impaired my ability to focus on schoolwork. I got by somehow, sustaining myself with music, acting and daydreaming about the future, but at home I felt more and more like a misfit: solitary, fearful, unconfident and sensitive. Where there might have been a relationship with my adoptive parents there was a vacuum. The lack of opportunity for any discussion about my adoption was, I suspect, the reason why I developed a habit of self-censorship, which in my teens manifested itself as paralytic shyness.

During my five years at boarding school my lovely auntie's health had been progressively deteriorating and she died (aged 80) when I was 16. As this happened during term time I was not allowed to go to her funeral, so for years I was unable to grieve for her properly. I am now able to fully appreciate the emotional and psychological nurture she gave me as a child.

I was told that further education would be unaffordable, so I left home and worked in London, sharing digs with friends until my marriage in 1966. There was never any confrontation with my adoptive parents, no bust-ups. On this last occasion, everything was arranged politely, without objection – or much comment – from them. (I kept in regular touch with them until their deaths in the late 1980s.) My focus, thereafter, was to escape my past and build a new future with my husband and, hopefully, to have children. I did not realise, at the time, how malleable I still was.

Things went well and I blossomed. Being the mother of three small children suited me perfectly. I gradually built up some confidence and felt hopeful for the future, but after 13 years my marriage turned violent and abusive. I realise now that what identity I had developed by then was either as a wife or mother, and once the doubts about my marriage crept in the old insecurities returned. My lack of confidence and self-worth meant I became fearful again and looked to myself for the solution. Whatever the failings of my adoption, violence had never been a part of it and I am confident that both my adoptive parents would have been horrified had they known about it.

With the benefit of hindsight, I can now appreciate the knock-on effect it had on my children. Instead of extricating myself from a dangerous situation, I stuck it out for years, misguidedly thinking I was doing the right thing by "keeping the family together". It is probably nearer to the truth to say that I couldn't bear the thought of the longed-for family being torn apart. Although no violence or abuse was aimed at the children, for some extraordinary reason I didn't seem able to appreciate, at the time, how the damage to them as observers was just as bad; the long-term effects on them linger on, years after my divorce. I recently asked them how they felt my adoption had impacted on their lives. Their reply was that they felt the roles had somehow got reversed and they felt responsible for me. I feel bad this burden landed on them. My son felt I would never be truly happy until I had fully completed the "quest". (Ironically, I feel the same sort of role reversal in relation to my birth mother, who had a tragic life and who has been all but eradicated from her own family history.) For many years, the failure in my marriage put a brake on my attempt to build up my sense of self and my confidence plummeted.

In the late 1980s, I made contact with my mother's first child (my half-sister) and she, in turn, approached one of our birth mother's sisters; I had always feared a negative response. However, I did eventually visit this aunt. She gave me lunch and after a seemingly amicable couple of hours, handed me a few childhood photos of my mother and told me, rather formally, that my birth family would not recognise me. I was shocked and upset and made my escape soon afterwards. Since then, all I've been able to do is build an ever-expanding, richly "embroidered" family tree; fear of rejection deters me from making another approach.

A slight sense of detachment has often enabled me to view life objectively, but at times of crisis, it frequently gives me a terrible sense of not belonging, of always being an outsider. Despite having a friendly and affectionate nature, it is only within my own family that I feel I truly belong. There have also been one or two incidents in my life where the truth has been turned on its head, to my disadvantage. Having my motives and actions misconstrued, or being lied about, ties in with, and aggravates, my acute sense of not being heard – the concealment of truth, again.

Since my divorce 17 years ago, I have been able to see myself as a survivor and not as a victim, which, in turn, has enabled me to build up my confidence and view all the components of my life in context, from a mature vantage point.

Over the last 35 years, I have done extensive research into my birth, and – more recently – my adoptive parents' families, to work out how I can weave their histories into my own. My mother's story is particularly poignant and follows a familiar pattern. Unmarried when she had her first child, she was forced to give her up at birth. Not surprisingly, she went to pieces and two years later produced me. Tragically, she died of cancer, aged 37, and was buried in an unmarked grave in Florida, where she had emigrated. I have fewer details about my putative father; he died before I could contact him. My adoptive mother lost her own father when she was only four and then, in her 20s, her fiancé drowned in a yachting accident. My adoptive father lost his two (pilot) brothers in flying accidents in the space of a year in the 1920s, after which his own father eloped with another woman, leaving him, as the sole surviving child, to care for his mother. So there was a lot of underlying sadness in all these lives. I find it easy to understand my birth parents' plight against the backdrop of World War II. Latterly, I have tried to be more understanding of my adoptive parents, too. I am able to take a more sympathetic view of them but find it harder to understand their shortcomings as carers. Given the imperative for secrecy in relation to illegitimacy and unmarried mothers in the 1940s, it may be that they represented the norm. I cannot be sure. The information I have about my birth family is interesting but their stance makes it hard to take things further.

Curiously, it has only been as an adult that I have felt a pang when people refer affectionately to their mothers, fathers or grandparents. As a child, I never knew what I was missing. As an adult, I know only too well how much demonstrative love needs to be the watchword in family relationships, whether adoptive or not. The close relationships I have with my children make me realise what I missed as a child.

Apart from my family, my other main passion is music, which has been like oxygen to me and has lifted my heart when life's realities made me howl. A keen sense of humour has also frequently provided the perfect antidote to painful situations.

I have sometimes been regarded as over-analytical and earnest by people who cannot comprehend why I would want to find out about my birth family. I should be thankful for what I have rather than what I lack seems to be the message. Yet to me, the need to know why I am as I am does not conflict with an appreciation of the good things in life. Trying to define who I am has been an emotional and very time-consuming task; I sometimes fear it has diverted my energies from pursuing other enthusiasms and even seeking a fulfilling career.

Where possible, I would advise adopted people to incorporate both birth and adoptive families into their own heritage, while being very cautious before contacting birth relatives. My adoption was not a good experience emotionally but I am absolutely certain, knowing what happened to my birth mother, that I would have been a great deal worse off had she kept me.

Researching can be very therapeutic; finding information solves many unanswered questions and the process itself is intellectually rewarding and fulfilling. In my case, it stimulated an interest in social conditions in British society, both past and present, and has led me on to write. Nonetheless, research doesn't answer all the questions and won't necessarily lead to emotional fulfilment.

I am disappointed I cannot verify that the man my mother named is my father, but there is very little I can do. I traced his daughter some years after his death, but without enough to prove that he actually is my father, the relationship seems rather tenuous. Even a DNA test would be inconclusive without a living male relative in common. I have no alternative but to live with that question mark.

I have a wonderful growing family of my own, with seven grandchildren. My family identity is in relation to them, far more than to my birth and adoptive families. Gradually, my sense of individual identity is building up as I manage to cobble together a patchwork of what I see as my own attributes. I am probably an amalgam of my genes, my experiences of adoption, my thoughts, my life experiences and my roles as wife, mother and grandmother.

I shall always find it difficult to discern which attributes are innate and which the result of my environment; I'm sure this applies to everyone, whether adopted or not. Having no way of knowing what my parents looked like as adults, or of knowing what their personalities and characteristics were, I can only look to my children for clues. I think my idealism and affectionate nature are innate but my lack of confidence is still a work in progress, and what I might have been had I not been adopted is anyone's guess. My determination, stoicism and refusal to be defeated have enabled me to face problems with pragmatism and optimism. I still occasionally sense the echoes of that sad little girl within me, but the determined survivor inside can now incorporate and reassure her.

A Pandora's box

MIRANDA WILKINSON

Miranda Wilkinson was born in London during the summer of 1971 to a white British mother and black African-Caribbean father. Miranda was relinquished at birth and adopted by white parents who went on to have their own birth child 16 months later and adopted another mixed-race child four years after that. Her family moved from Hoddeston in Hertfordshire to Leicestershire and then to a sleepy village in the heart of Wiltshire until they settled in Reading when she was seven. Miranda is mother to a 20-year-old son who has just flown the nest to study law at Greenwich University. She has devoted her career to child care and child protection and is currently employed as a Team Manager in a Duty and Assessment Social Work team based in the West Midlands.

'Coloured, coloured, coloured…' This chant regularly rang through my ears as children joined hands and skipped in a circle around me in the playground at primary school. Even though I was only five years old at the time, I remember thinking it was odd that these children thought I looked like a rainbow (the image that came to mind when I heard the word coloured) because I could clearly see that I was brown and I often wondered why they could not. As it happened, I had been distinctly aware of my "brownness" from an extremely early age because I was different. Different from my mum (Chrissie), different from my dad (Peter), different from every face I had ever seen in the picturesque but entirely "white" community that we lived in, and different from my little baby brother, Toby, who arrived 16 months after I had been adopted, the birth child of my adoptive parents.

I always knew I was adopted, even though for many years I did not fully understand what this actually meant. I was regularly told that being adopted made me special because I was wanted so much, but I didn't feel special. I felt wrong, I felt different and most of all I felt alone. This was despite my parents often telling me how much they loved me, showering me with warmth and affection and telling me I was chosen; I was not an accident that happened to them by mistake. They used words like *unique* and *precious*, but what I felt was more *different* and *odd*. Although I didn't know it then, this early realisation that I was different would have a life-long impact on my sense of self. I remember understanding fully that I couldn't make the brown go away, even though there were many times I wanted to. My brownness became an everyday problem to me because it made me wrong, deficient somehow, and

I became scared that this glaring deficiency would surely be seen by everyone around me unless, of course, I hid it and so hide it I did. I hid it by becoming "useful" in order to distract people from looking at me and towards looking at what I did instead. It seemed to work, but I remained terrified nonetheless. Terrified that people would see right through me and find out I was a fraud, that I was really nothing more than a fake. I was also terrified that if my parents found out what was happening to me in the playground they would surely want to give me back, so I never said a word.

Thankfully they worked out what was happening for themselves and, to my immense relief, did not want to give me back. They challenged the staff, whose response was to inform them that they were perfectly within their rights to move me to another school, adding, however, that they were happy for my brother, Toby, to remain in the school. We were both removed immediately and went to a school much further away, but one at which the Headmaster, Mr Burgess, was a white man who had married a black lady and who had, at that time, two mixed-heritage children. I remember feeling such a sense of relief that I was no longer alone and Mr Burgess to this day remains a significant influence on the way I perceive and interpret the world around me. I remember with such clarity the day he taught me the *Sticks and Stones* proverb.[1] I can picture where his desk was in the room, the fireplace behind him and the chair I sat on as he taught me the words. I remember where the door was and most of all I remember both the kindness and passion with which he spoke to me. He told me that whenever someone made a comment about my skin colour, I should think about how hard most people try to get a suntan and I should feel very lucky to have a permanent one; these people were just jealous of my beautiful brown skin. Why I found it easier to believe him than anyone else I still do not fully understand – maybe it was the emotional distance between us – but the powerful life-altering lessons he taught me I have never forgotten and they have, without doubt, helped me through many a difficult time.

When I was six years old my parents adopted another mixed-heritage baby, Barney, who also had brown skin, and I loved him. He was so much more interactive than the brown knitted doll my mother had been forced to make me, having been unable to find a brown-skinned doll in the shops. Then when I was seven we moved to Reading where, for the first time, I began to see faces that looked just like mine. People didn't stare as much (well not at me as an individual; as a family, we always elicited attention when we were out as we were rather an unusual sight), the kids in the playground didn't tease

---

[1] 'Sticks and stones will break my bones, but names will never hurt me.'

me and I wasn't alone any more. I made friends, the best of whom, Ceri, remains my closest friend to this day. She, along with the never-ending love and support of my parents and extended family, helped me to realise I could be accepted for who I was just because I was me and that what I looked like made no difference at all. Ceri once told me that if I was green with yellow spots she would still be my friend, and over time I learned to believe her, but there remained a powerful voice inside telling me I was not good enough. This voice motivated me to continue to find ways of being liked that often, as it turned out, had the opposite effect, resulting in feelings of increasing self-loathing and despair. I did, however, survive adolescence and puberty, though it was far from easy on me or on my ever-loving and supportive family and friends.

At 18 years old, I was fortunate enough to be accepted as a camp counsellor on the Camp America programme. Before settling into the camp in New Jersey, I had the opportunity to stay in a neighbourhood called Jamaica in Queens, New York City, with the family of a friend of mine back in the UK. The inhabitants of Queens are predominantly black African-Caribbean. I walked through the streets, black faces all around me, for the first time ever one of a majority, yet I was once again overwhelmed by the fear that I would be found out; that these people would somehow be able to see right through me and would know I was a fraud. Surely they would see I wasn't really black but rather, as I had come to believe, a "coconut" – black on the outside but white as the pure driven snow on the inside. I was consumed by a completely irrational fear that it would only be a matter of time before someone shouted 'fraud' or 'fake' at me and I would have to explain why I was *pretending*. I was struck by the realisation that had I been in a street full of white faces, I would have been perfectly at ease and completely confident, even if I was being subjected to stares and barely disguised whispering and pointing (as had often happened in the past). Walking down those streets, I was consumed by the feeling that I was a proverbial sore thumb, a fish totally out of water. As a result, I lost all confidence. My head lowered, arms folded, my heart raced and I made no eye contact with anyone at all. It took several days before I began to relax and I realised then that I didn't fit in anywhere – with anyone. I felt alone and disconnected, as if I didn't belong.

While this feeling has never fully gone away, it was once again at the forefront of my life when I met and subsequently married my black African-Caribbean husband. We shared many things in common in our lives, but as we got to know each other it became clear that our upbringings had literally been worlds apart. One quite simple example that comes to mind is music. Many a time a song would come on the radio or in a shop and he would say, 'Oh, this is such a good tune,' snapping his fingers and belting out the words in his own inimitable fashion. I would, more often than not, be left standing there, completely blank, having no knowledge or recollection of the song in question. He would encourage me, enthusiastically saying, 'You know this song, it was massive. We played this all the time.' Yet I didn't know, I never knew and it made me feel like an alien. When songs I did know from artists like ABBA, The Beatles, Marti Webb or The Carpenters came on I became animated and he would have the blank expression. Sometimes he would look at me in such a way that left me literally feeling like I had landed from another planet. He would tease me about it and say that I was 'Sooo Caversham' (an upper-middle-class area of Reading, Berkshire where I lived with my family). At first I could laugh and share the joke, but as time passed it stopped being funny. I no longer found this amusing, instead it made me feel different – different and deficient in the same way I had felt as a child in the playground all those years before.

The time it hit me hardest was during a visit to my mother-in-law on the beautiful Caribbean island of St Vincent. Spending time with her was one of the most wonderful and emotional occasions of my life. She was the archetypal "big black mamma" and I loved her from the minute I saw her. I loved being around her and even when I couldn't understand a single word she was saying I loved listening to her talking, joking with me and chastising me, even when I wasn't wholeheartedly sure whether she was being serious or not. The confusion that followed was immense. For the first time in my life I had experienced a glimpse of what it might have been like to have been raised in a "black" family. In a family that looked like me, where I didn't feel different and I did fit in. But in reality I knew my birth mother was white and single and had I remained in her care my upbringing might actually have been remarkably similar to my upbringing with my adoptive parents. My feelings for my mother-in-law also made me feel immensely guilty – guilty for even thinking about what it would have been like to be raised in a black family, guilty and ungrateful and selfish. I became consumed by self-loathing and I chastised myself for all the emotions I was experiencing. I reminded myself what my life could have been like had my parents not been so wonderful. I reminded myself how much I loved my family and that actually, even with the knowledge and understanding I now had as an adult, I wouldn't change a thing about my past. So what was my problem? It is a question I am still grappling with. I have not yet found the answer.

Along with his wonderful black African-Caribbean mum, my husband also came with another life-changing element to his identity: he was a Muslim. Before we met, I had never given religion much thought, but he swept me completely and utterly off my feet and I would (and indeed did) do anything for him. Although it was a complex and confusing issue, the bottom line was that to be together he needed me to become a Muslim. So, after two years of marriage, I accepted and took on his beliefs and my already confused identity changed beyond recognition. Sadly, our relationship ended after ten years. There were many reasons for our separation and we both had our part to play. Looking back, I cannot help but wonder whether my deep-rooted desire to fit in somewhere, to be accepted as part of a group where I did not stand out like a sore thumb, motivated me to take on this massive, life-changing thing. The visible identity, which the wearing of a *Hijab* (headscarf) and *Abbayah* (full-length dress) gave me, meant my skin colour was irrelevant. I was accepted. We dressed the same, we looked the same. We spoke a similar language and followed the same doctrine. There was a comfort and security in that beyond my logical comprehension. With our separation, however, a new conflict emerged as I no longer felt "connected" to Islam in the same way I did when we were together. I remained paralysed by indecision and uncertainty for a long time. I did nothing in haste, but in 2010 I finally found the courage to try just being "me", and I haven't looked back.

Another quite recent discovery I have made is that youth evidently afforded me the ability to put many of my "issues" to the back of my mind, hidden from consciousness. With age it seems that there is an ever-growing capacity issue and an ever-reducing amount of space available for my issues to remain hidden within. The logical answer, of course, is to stop hiding them away, to get them out and just deal with them. For a long time I worried about this potential Pandora's box and questioned whether I was really ready to open it. Writing always has and continues to provide a safe (and unresponsive) outlet for emotions that are totally beyond me, because words on a piece of paper do not and cannot judge or question or hurt what is already a fragile and sensitive sense of self. As it has turned out, however, words were just not enough and when I turned 40 last year everything changed, almost overnight. I realised with utter certainty that time was not infinite and that it was quite literally running out. I understood that if I did not do something to try and answer the perpetual question, 'Who am I?', I would be condemning myself to a life in which I remained paralysed by fear that the answer is the one thing I have dreaded all my life: 'Nothing and no one'. So I have, at last, initiated a search for my birth family and it is with both apprehension and nervous anticipation that I have begun a journey of self-discovery that frightens me beyond all written explanation.

I like to smile

SOO COLE

....

Soo Cole was born in 1971 in Hong Kong and is British Chinese. Since the age of ten she has been practising martial arts. She recently completed a BSc in Sports Science/ Sports Coaching at the University of East London and plans to do a Masters degree. Soo lives and works in London. Soo's writing is dedicated to her adoptive mum: 'For my mum who passed November 2008. You taught me to always try my best because even if I did not succeed no one could say I had not tried. With love from your daughter.'

....

Before I was adopted my birth certificate states that I was called Wai Man. I was born in 1971. The exact time and place where I was born and the names of my biological parents are not known. My adoptive parents were told very little – just that I was taken to a baby home in Hong Kong when I was less than six months old. They first came to see me when I was around six months old and at the age of two years, a day before Christmas, I was legally adopted.

I like to smile, it increases my face value

My mother told me that she chose me because I was smiling. Apparently I smile all the time! My closest friends tell me that when we first met I smiled and it made them feel welcome. In times when I have felt different, my smile has made me allies, broken down barriers and kept me going. I believe I have a lot to smile about.

My parents told me I was adopted as soon as I was old enough to understand. At nursery school other children would ask me why I did not look like my parents. I told them it was because I was adopted (a big word for a four-year-old to say) and would explain that my "real" parents could not look after me so I had other parents. When some people find out I am adopted they feel sorry for me. My parents told me I was special, that they had chosen me, which is why I feel grateful to have been adopted. Of all the children in the baby home they had chosen me! Being adopted as a baby, I have no recollection of my biological family, no memories of who they were. I think I am lucky.

My "real" parents are the ones who love me

Both my parents are English. If I looked in the mirror it was obvious we looked different, but I do not feel different to them. My handwriting resembles my mother's and some of her values are now mine. She told me I should always tell the truth and she had a strong sense of justice and fairness, something she instilled in me. My parents told me I should always try to do my best; it would not matter if I failed as doing one's best is all that can be asked of someone. I may not look like my parents on the outside but on the inside I am a lot like them. Years later, a good friend from Hong Kong told me there is a Chinese saying that 'The one who loves you is your real parent.' I love that my parents chose me.

Stand by me

Initially, when my parents first adopted me there was resistance from some family members who did not agree with adopting a "foreign" baby. My parents stood their ground, telling them if they could not accept me into the family then they (my parents) did not want to know them. Visiting those relatives when I was younger could be a little uncomfortable, but over time (sometimes quite a long time), some gradually came to see me differently. This experience made me conscious of being made to feel welcome and now I am very aware when others feel left out. I recognise that when my parents adopted me it was not easy for them. They made a decision and stood their ground. I admire them for that.

Travel broadens the mind

My father's job meant that we moved to several different countries when I was younger. We finally settled in the UK, in a small town in the East Midlands, when I was ten years old, so I could get a good education at secondary school. The area we moved to was predominantly white and generations of local people had lived and worked there – people who had known each other for years – so we were a little unconventional in more than one way. At school the children of minority ethnicity could be counted on one hand. I stood out. The friends I made at school are some of my best friends now and although my upbringing was different to theirs, I feel accepted by them.

To have experienced different cultures in different countries helped open my mind. People are different in the ways they speak, eat, think and behave. I see this as a good thing, maybe because I *am* different. When my parents went to Hong Kong they fell in love with the country and the people, which influenced their decision to adopt there. Whenever they would speak of Hong Kong, I would listen to their stories. It was like travelling back there, to that time with them. It means a lot to me that they love the culture, people and country so much. It made me want to go there for myself.

My journey

My own journey has been about trying to discover who I am. Growing up, I did not know any people who looked like me. I related to what was inside people more. I am an only child and as a child I had a lot of time on my own to be in my own world. I loved reading books that captured my imagination. When I was ten years old I discovered mini-biographies and read about the Native Americans, Nelson Mandela, Steve Biko, Mahatma Ghandi, Martin Luther King, Elvis Presley, James Dean, Marilyn Monroe, Albert Einstein, all of whom inspired me in some way. I was trying to find people I could relate to, it did not matter what they looked like or where they were from. I was starting to form ideas about who I might be.

Daring to be different

I had experienced a small amount of racism in the other countries we had lived in. I encountered racism from older people, not just children at school, and I did not understand how adults (who I thought had all the answers) could say some of the things they did. My parents told me to ignore them, as they were ignorant. My friends would get angry at people who were racist towards me, but I just wanted to understand why they were saying what they said.

Most people assume my parents are Chinese. Many non-Chinese people have asked me about my name; it is an English surname and begs the question, 'Is your mother Chinese?' When I reply, 'No,' the assumption is that my father is Chinese, despite my English surname. When I reply, 'No, my father is also English,' the common response has been confusion, annoyance, sometimes anger and sometimes questioning, such as, 'Are you sure?' When I say I am adopted, it sometimes clears things up, but occasionally the confusion remains. I have had some extreme reactions from people, including anger, pity and bewilderment, but it usually includes a mini-interview afterwards.

This experience has made me realise that no matter how I would like it to be, I am different, I see the world differently. I do not assume connections like other people do and when I fill out a health form, when they ask if there is any history of heart disease, I answer 'No' because whoever designed the form also thinks differently from me and assumes that there is a blood connection between my parents and I. I have also realised that some people have never met someone like me, so learning to deal with the situation helps them gain a new experience and understanding. The way I deal with it changes how they relate to me.

Same same but different

When I was younger I knew little about my ethnic background. As I got older, I noticed people would make assumptions about me and my upbringing; they often assumed I had turned my back on my "Chinese roots", which was sometimes met with disapproval. At that time, I did not really know about Chinese culture and did not understand why people were proud to be Chinese. How could I be proud of a culture I was not brought up in and did not really know much about, and why did they expect me to be proud?

At university, I found myself joining the Chinese Society. This was the first real contact I'd had with Chinese people. Initially I was resistant, but I was also curious. I had concerns about not being able to speak the language and not fitting in. These worries were dismissed by the Society who insisted they would help me learn. Their enthusiasm was infectious and I was curious as to why they were so proud of being Chinese and wanted to share their culture with me. Being at university, away from home, the Chinese Society became my family and my first introduction to Chinese culture. It was a big learning curve towards understanding how I felt about my ethnicity. Beginning to actively learn more about my ethnic roots helped me to understand myself more and also helped others empathise with me. Previously, I had felt as though some people looked down on me for not taking an interest in Chinese culture or for being too westernised. After gaining such an interest and learning some of the language, I had a greater understanding of why people thought that way of me but I also found that, on the whole, people's assumptions about me changed. I was given credit for being interested in and learning about Chinese culture despite not having been brought up with it.

My best friends include some of the friends I made through the Chinese Society; I visit and stay with them when I go to Hong Kong. My parents have met them and know them well too and so, for me, there is some feeling of resolution between my Chinese background and my adoptive family. To me, family is where I can be myself and people still like me for me. A saying that has stuck with me since primary school is, 'Be the kind of person you would like to know.' This advice has helped me along my journey of self-discovery and, together with martial arts, helped me to continue to learn about myself – a journey I see as life long. I do not know much about my beginnings, but I see my adoption as a point of reference from which I can expand knowledge about myself, through understanding the culture I came from, the people and the language. The sum of my life experience to date has made me who I am today.

Karate Kid

Part of finding out about myself began when I started martial arts. I went to see *The Karate Kid* with my mother – a film we both really liked – and afterwards, a couple of friends and I decided to do karate. This was the beginning of my interest in East Asian culture. Since then, martial arts has become a big part of my life and for the last 12 years I have been training at the Shaolin Temple in London. As well as learning a martial art, it has been a way of learning about Chinese culture. It has aided my personal growth physically and psychologically. Many of my friends are Chinese, or have an interest in martial arts or Chinese culture, and this has become a significant part of who I am today. My teacher is a Chinese martial arts master and has helped me learn more about Chinese culture. I have since trained for, entered and won competitions in *san shou*, a form of Chinese full-contact fighting. One of my proudest moments is when my parents came to watch me in my first competition, where I won the national title. My "kung fu family" met my parents and it was a great moment for me.

Over the past few years my knowledge of Mandarin has improved and this has allowed me to go to Hong Kong and China and communicate with people there. When they ask about my roots, which often happens when they hear my accent, their response is usually favourable and I am made to feel accepted. I realise a lot of the problems I experienced as a child were due to a lack of understanding, and by learning to communicate, I am able to break down many of the barriers I experienced from preconceptions and racism.

I learned from you

Not long ago, my mother passed away and it was the single worst experience of my life. I became a different person, but it has brought my father and I closer. I may not have been blood related to her, but I felt as if part of me had been taken too. When she was alive it felt as if we had a strong, almost psychic bond. After she passed away, I had dreams about her, and I often talk to her. I have never dreamed about my biological mother.

My parents have dramatically shaped who I am today. My mother taught me honesty, integrity and to have strong principles. She was not afraid to stand up for what she believed in. From her I learned that it is fine to cry at sad films and that nature is a wonder to behold. I wear my heart on my sleeve and believe in the power of dreams. My father gave me the courage to be bold and try new things and learn from my mistakes, to be independent and not to suffer fools. When I feel misunderstood, or people think I am quirky, I always know my parents, family and friends love me and understand me, which to me is what family is about. To me, family transcends biology. I do not really think much about my biological family as I was too young to remember them. Neither do I have a longing to find them. Sometimes I feel curious but not enough to do anything about it. Finding out about Chinese culture has helped fill that gap. My life has been what I have made of it, along with a few curve balls to keep me on my toes. The past is the past, the future uncertain and it is what happens now that counts – at least, I try to live by this and be the kind of person I would like to know. This journey gets better and better.

Striking a balance

JO BURNETT-SHARPE

Joanna Burnett-Sharpe was born in Hounslow near London in the summer of 1976. She was adopted by English parents at six weeks old. Her Sri Lankan birth mother returned to Sri Lanka very soon after her birth. At the age of 17, Jo began searching and found her but has yet to receive a response. Jo is an actress working in theatre and television. She is a panel member at the Intercountry Adoption Centre (IAC) and a speaker on IAC preparation courses. Jo married in 2009 and lives with her husband in south London, a few miles from her adoptive family with whom she remains close.

For as long as I can remember I always knew I was adopted. There wasn't a particular day I was sat down and told. My parents simply wove it into everyday life from when I was tiny. 'The grass is green, the sky is blue and you're adopted.' It was a fact of life rather than a drama.

I was shy. Painfully shy. The kind of shy that forces you to retreat into the back of your head and hide. Even as a child in a pushchair I'd dread new human contact. I'd be merrily playing with my toes when a huge smiley face would force itself down to my level and coo with awkward questions... 'Now who's this little angel?'; 'What's your name, sweetie pie?'; 'Shall we count your toes... one... two...?', by which time I'd have folded up in a ball of tears, hoping they would drown me. Adults were gross intrusions on my being. My parents were exceptions and I clung to them with all my might. Mum in particular was a security blanket and because she didn't go to work she was my constant. The few times she had to leave me with other people resulted in me crying uncontrollably. I was lost. I felt as if I'd been abandoned all over again.

As I grew into a more robust toddler there were one or two exceptions. These were the magic people, people who possessed the power of "quiet". One such person was Stephan. He was a gardener. A tall man with skin so black it shone blue, an afro that sat like a crown on his head and a gleaming machete to tame the gardens. He never looked at me or asked anything of me but let me be. He might have uttered a few soft words; a remark about the beauty of leaves in frost or the sweetness of a sun-warmed blackberry. I'd follow him and sit near. Occasionally he'd extend a hand containing a piece of fruit or a nut, his gaze never shifting from his work. I loved these moments, someone allowing me to be myself in their world, with no demand for a response in return. I felt free.

Primary school turned me around and placed me in the wider world. After tears and a sit-down protest, I was dragged into school where I met a few like-minded, quiet beings. The first layer of shyness fell off and I quickly made more friends. I was more than happy to tell people about my background: 'I'm adopted and I'm originally from Sri Lanka and I'm English like my mum and dad,' I would cheerfully retort. I'm not sure that I knew what "originally" meant but as long as adopted, Sri Lankan and English were mentioned I felt it summed me up. I knew my skin was brown and that's how people look when they're from hot countries. I still thought I might grow up to look like my blonde Sindy Doll. There were several other adopted children in my primary school, so I imagined the world was about half adopted and half not.

It was a huge shock to move on to secondary school and find out how unusual my background was. I'd be picked up from school to cries of: 'He's not your dad. He's white and you're Indian' or even, 'You're a Paki! They can't be your parents.' I was devastated. I couldn't work out how they knew. It had never crossed my mind that my parents were white. My skin felt tight and I wanted to scrub off my brownness. I became obsessed with skin colour and scrutinised everyone. I could have graded everyone in my class from dark to light.

As I approached my teens I noticed how some of the boys would chat to me. I remember one saying how cool I was and the reason we could be mates was because he would never fancy me because I was a Paki. I started to dread the summer because I'd tan even more. I stayed out of the sun as much as possible and invested in some foundation a few shades lighter than my face. I was pleased with the pasty look, although thinking about it I must have looked like an ill ghost. I ignored the other Asian girls' attempts at friendship. I jumped headfirst into my London accent and delighted in tarty gothic clothes. Anything that put distance between my fragile sense of self and the Indian subcontinent was a plus. Although I was rejecting my racial background, I had a fascination with my birth mother. I often thought of her and wondered who she was, what she looked like and whether she thought about me.

I had limited information from social services. I was born in the UK and my adoptive mum gave me the details she had about my birth mother: her age, height, hair colour, eye colour, her qualifications and hobbies. I also had a piece of lace and a pendant left to me by my birth grandmother when the adoption papers were signed. I loved these things. They connected me to my past with the essence of a fairytale. I could have been anyone and ended up anywhere. It sometimes troubled me to think that I might not have met my parents but I revelled in the infinite possibilities.

I wanted to meet my birth mother. Initially the driving force was curiosity, but it quickly gained its own momentum and the safety of my girlish imaginings disappeared. At 17, I had access to my adoption papers which documented the circumstances of my adoption. My birth mother was described as flying round the world with work so within the space of ten days, I could have been born in any of four countries. She was single, travelling with her parents, deeply religious, and conception was due to a gang rape. The reality crushed me. I couldn't justify my existence and my identity became intrinsically linked to violence. I think I would have fallen apart if I hadn't had such a strong relationship with my family.

After the initial shock and grief from the concrete facts and the shattered possibilities, questions began to flow again. How did my birth mother cope? Was she OK now? Does she have children? Does she look like me or do I look like the male side of the family? That was a tough one. I needed to look like her. I began writing to the address in Sri Lanka given to me by social services. I'd mentally explored the fact I might get a negative response, or no response at all, but the emotional truth was impossible to predict. From the moment I dropped the letter into the postbox, I realised I'd given away the core of my control. It was up to my birth mother to respond. The wait was unbearable and the response never came. I sent many letters and continued to wait. My adoptive mum and I decided to go to Sri Lanka where I would be able to explore my roots and maybe try to make contact.

The country was hot, people were smiley, cars were old, colours were bright, air was sweet, and I felt sick. Everywhere I looked there were faces like mine. I was grateful for my Topshop jeans and Metallica t-shirt. At least I wouldn't be mistaken for a local. I hoped to blend in as a western tourist but the unusual combination of a Sri Lankan looking teenager and an English woman made us the focus wherever we went. Waiters, local workers and generally anyone we came into contact with would politely ask where I was from, where my mum was from, what language I spoke and was I Singhalese or Tamil? I squirmed with burning frustration. 'She's my mum and we're English!' I would bark before walking away to avoid puzzled expressions.

On one occasion I tried to relax by having a dip in the pool. Staff stopped momentarily and glanced at me. A few nudged their colleagues but most just paused, then went on with their business with an air of disdain. My stomach knotted. I realised all the other guests were white. Scantily clad bikini bodies were expected from them but not from me. I ran for my towel and wore long sleeves the rest of the week. My last shred of confidence had drowned. I had no idea who I was in this foreign country. Racism in Britain was easier to deal with than this. I wanted to go home.

The rest of the trip was spent trying to make contact.
We found the address.
My adoptive mum went round.
The people who answered said the family were away.
My adoptive mum left our number.
My birth grandmother rang.
She said they were at a wedding a hundred miles away.
She said my birth mother was married with children.
She invited us there.
We travelled.
We sent notice that we'd arrived.
The address didn't exist.
We rang.
They didn't answer.
My world crumbled.
We went home.
We rang again.
Someone answered.
It was my birth grandmother.
She said she wasn't the person we spoke to in Sri Lanka.
She said my birth mother never married, never had more children and lives at home.
We were all confused.
I was hurt.
I wished she'd write.
A letter arrived.
It contained two blank sheets of paper.
I felt old and hollow.

I didn't know what to do or what to think.
I was consumed by grief.

Once the initial shock and grief had lessened its grip, I realised I had choices. I could let the need to find the missing part of myself control me. I could bury it and hope it never came back to haunt me. I could hope to find a balance between the two.

I moved away to college and spent time living and getting to know myself. I remained quite closed to influences from Asian cultures. I pushed the English part of me through the clothes, music and friends I had. If anyone could wave a magic wand, I would have still chosen to be white. Then I decided to become an actress. I loved performing and saw it as a creative outlet that allowed me to become any character I chose. I soon discovered I would be judged and given roles largely based on my appearance. I would have to justify myself, explain where I am from and often play people from the part of the world from which I originate. I also faced the daily rejection of working in an oversubscribed profession – not the ideal set up for someone struggling to find a secure sense of herself.

My first job was with an Asian theatre company which brought huge dread. I was straight into wearing traditional Indian costume, speaking with an accent and, at times, in a different language. I didn't have the cultural knowledge the other cast members had but they didn't have my mixed heritage. I was forced to peel off some of the identity rejection layers I'd built up. Frightening but liberating. I remember looking as I fixed *bindis*, painted henna and attached nose rings to my costumed self and for the first time enjoyed the darkness of my eyes. My confidence began to grow.

It's more than 18 years since I went to Sri Lanka. I have been lucky enough to have a supportive family offering unconditional love, brothers whose experiences are equally complex, friends and now a husband, all of whom have embraced the diverse mix that I am. I continue to write to my birth mother and hope one day I'll get a response. Although this hope remains, it doesn't define me. I know I could turn up on her doorstep or hire someone to secretly take her photo, and I could regain a sense of control, but at what cost? I've learned how important it is to own your history and I would hate to force her to see me or steal an image of her when she's already been through so much. My desire is for her to want to acknowledge me. I understand this may never happen and it has taken me into my 30s before I've faced this. It comes with sadness and I treat it as a bereavement.

My identity is an ever-growing part of my life. My sense of self has developed and become strong but only through patience and nurturing self honesty. If I were advising someone who has experienced adoption I'd encourage listening to yourself and trying not to make hasty decisions governed by pure emotion. There's a balance to be struck and I'll always strive for that. My past has created me and that past is an intricate weaving of my birth family, the family that raised me and my new life in marriage. I look to the future with an open heart and trust that my strengths will carry me through the inevitable challenges that lie ahead.

Then and now

ANN MERRILLS

Ann joined her adoptive parents at two weeks old. Her adoptive parents gave her, as an only child, a very solid middle-class upbringing, but sadly they lacked emotional warmth. Her adoption was kept a total secret but, aged 27, she found out herself by going to the Records Office. Ann traced her birth mother in 1988 and had limited contact with her in the few years before she died. Ann then traced her birth father's family in 2004 and now has regular contact with this large extended family. Ann is married, lives in the West Country and sits as an independent member on Wiltshire Council's Adoption Panel.

Through the looking glass... Identity lost
Life is unreal, relationship cost.
Research completed, Identity found
Life is different, emotions unbound.

I was adopted in 1948. The journey in search of my identity has taken some 60 years. At this stage of my life, I can look back with gratitude that I have been fortunate enough to find my roots – to have been in touch with members of both birth families – and I can only feel the greatest empathy for those for whom such a discovery is, for whatever reason, not possible. I have also been particularly fortunate in that the relations I have met have been incredibly accepting, especially given that for both sides, to learn of my existence was, for some, an immense shock.

My journey has also been society's journey; attitudes towards the issues and processes of adoption have shifted seismically in the last half-century or so. We have moved from the dreadful disgrace that was heaped upon those who were sinful enough to have children outside marriage, to a society with a much greater degree of tolerance. The shame of illegitimacy is, however, still internalised. Even though I was never told I was adopted, that sense of somehow not belonging and feeling inferior was inherent in my upbringing and can still sometimes be triggered.

At the time of the post-war baby boom, there were plenty of unwanted babies for "good" parents to adopt. Assessment procedures were minimal: my parents took me at two weeks old, less than five months after the loss of their own baby. Modern social workers would throw up their hands in horror, but this was still the age of the stiff upper lip and counselling was unheard of. This was a time when it was completely believed that a baby had no memory of any sort. Adoptive parents assumed they were being given a blank sheet.

In 1948, total anonymity was guaranteed to birth parents when they relinquished a child. The corollary of this was that adoptive children had no right to access their birth records; this was only available after legislation in 1975. Coincidentally, it was around this time (at the age of 27) that I found out for myself that I was adopted. Up to that point, I had lived in total ignorance but one day, when I happened to be in London, I went into St Catherine's House, where birth records were then held. I simply looked myself up in the Adoption Register – and there I was. At some level I had always known but it was still an enormous shock. It affected me much more deeply than I initially realised, especially as when I went through the necessary interview to access my birth certificate, the main thrust of the "counselling" was to let sleeping dogs lie. There was no assistance to go searching – and it took me until I was 40 to take the step of tracing my birth mother. Attitudes were beginning to shift and some basic help and counselling began to be available.

Nevertheless, little was known about "reunion" and the enormity of that step. Thanks to a skilled intermediary, my birth mother and I eventually met up and in the three years before she died, I heard how I came about. She had been 33 – a teacher – and my birth father 55 when I was conceived and, unsurprisingly, he was married. They met early in the war, during the black-out, on the railway station where my father ran four bookstalls, and subsequently had an illicit relationship; he told her he had four children. In the event, when I finally plucked up courage to go looking some 16 years later, I found out I was the youngest of seven, and that I had five half-brothers and one half-sister, and a huge extended family. I was just in time to meet two of my brothers who have since died. My life still feels like one big jigsaw and I am still finding more pieces to fit in.

It really has made a difference to my perception of self; it somehow makes much more sense when you know your genes. I can fully understand how my parents felt they were protecting me by weaving a web of fantasy around my origins. Only the other day, an adoptive cousin told me her mother had been told my birth father was high up in the Army. In fact, he was a sergeant and had been captured in the First World War and was in the Home Guard in the Second World War! Another cousin was astonished some years ago when I told her I'd met my mother. She said, 'But you can't have. She died at your birth!' Sadly, secrecy is a terrible basis for any relationship and when I look back, I have no memories of a close and loving upbringing, though I was given every educational opportunity in life and for that I am very grateful.

'You'll never find peace until you find the pieces.' I'm not sure where I garnered that aphorism, but I know I do now feel much more integrated, much more whole, definitely much more at ease with myself, but it has taken many years and very skilled counselling. However, I have been lucky with the people I have been fortunate enough to discover. Tracing your birth relations is definitely akin to opening Pandora's box – you cannot shut it again and you have to be prepared to deal with rejection. For the people contacted, it can also be very traumatic. My sister, in particular, now in her 80s, has, I know, had to reassimilate her memories of her father and reappraise her experiences of her parents' marriage. Luckily for me, she had always wanted a sister!

The journey of finding the pieces ought not to be quite so hard and long for today's adoptees. Secrecy is no longer acceptable and shame is no longer integral; illegitimacy is an outmoded concept. Now, a *Child Permanence Report* is required for each child being put forward for adoption, and as much information as social workers can gather around birth circumstances and family accompanies that child, together with life-story work. Hopefully, these children will find this map useful along their journey of self-discovery, but the risks and demands of "reunion" will always be there and the need to process and assimilate challenging histories will always be the difficult lot of an adoptee. Society has begun to acknowledge how perilous and precarious this journey is; the Adoption and Children Act 2002 recognises the need for life-long support. Potential adoptive parents are now much more aware of the issue of identity and the need for contact with birth families wherever possible and appropriate.

Now, too, it is generally accepted that the name/s the child is given at birth is part of his or her identity and adoptive parents are encouraged to retain them. A little while ago, I was in a gift shop which had those coasters with first names and their meanings on them. I was reading them, but couldn't actually decide which I was. I have always been known as Ann, 'from the Hebrew meaning "graceful"'. She is 'industrious and practical and can turn her hand to anything. A lady of many talents.' But, my birth mother had called me Frances (after my birth father, Frank), 'from the Latin for "from France". An honest, caring, loving person who holds traditional values dear.
A discreet and special lady.' Actually, my original birth certificate says Frances Elizabeth, which my adoptive parents changed to Elizabeth Ann, so maybe I am really Elizabeth, 'from the Hebrew meaning "oath of God". She is confident and poised, well organised and efficient. She has her life under control.' If only!

I do feel that my life has really all come together in recent years. I now know I was named Elizabeth after my birth grandmother, and I have recently discovered that, strangely enough, my birth great-grandmother was called Annie. Incidentally, my birth mother was Alice...

The reunion

NICKY CAMPBELL

Nicky Campbell is an award-winning radio and TV presenter. Born and adopted in Scotland, he enjoyed a happy middle-class childhood, rarely thinking of his birth parents until a chance meeting with a private detective led him to his birth mother. This brief account of their first meeting is taken from his memoir, *Blue-eyed Son: The story of an adoption* (Macmillan, 2004). Nicky is also a dedicated patron and supporter of BAAF. He is married with four daughters and lives in London.

Eleven came around and eleven went. I'd already had two pints of Guinness by this time. In fact this mother and child reunion was still an hour and a half away. Stella was horrendously late. Punctuality has always been a big thing for me and this minor transgression seemed almighty at the time. It disconnected me from her. I felt let down. Maybe I was being rejected again. I had another pint.

Every woman over 60 who entered the lobby got the full treatment – the once-over and the expectant stare. I must have come across as some louche gigolo preying on unsuspecting widows.

I'd just about given up hope when a dishevelled and chaotic looking woman shambled through the door and walked gingerly towards us. She apologised profusely. She hadn't been able to sleep for nervousness and had taken a sleeping pill which had knocked her for six, hence her lateness. It was her epidural I guess.

The Hollywood soundtrack stayed determinedly silent. There was no outpouring of emotion. Just awkwardness. My first impression of my mother was that she looked like… she looked like an old woman in her late 60s or early 70s. Think of your parents – they are timeless. You remember them as younger, as middle-aged and as older, as they are and as they were. The millions of mental snapshots of their lives as you have known them merge together as one in your mind. Now imagine meeting your mother for the first time as she looks or might look at 70.

I kissed her as I would a distant aunt. She kissed me for the first time since the social worker had taken me away 30 years before. As we sat down tentatively I saw her looking at me and looking away so as not to stare. I looked at her and looked away. She told us about the accommodation she was living in. Her sister was there too and it was very comfortable. They had their own little flats within the building and were well looked after. I looked at her. She looked at me. I looked away. As I spoke it sounded like someone else's voice saying strange things like, 'It's a really nice hotel this' and 'Well, it's really good to meet you at last.' I wasn't myself. I didn't know who I was. I needed a leak. Three pints and 30 years came cascading out. It was a huge relief and it was wonderful to be alone. The moment seemed endless. Going to the Gents had been like walking into a cathedral from the searing intensity of the Mediterranean sun.

Then, as I turned to wash my hands, I caught sight of myself in the mirror. TV presenters and mirrors are on pretty good terms but this was an altogether different experience. I had a Stephen King moment. I saw my reflection in the mirror but it didn't look anything like me. I saw new and different things about my face. I saw some of the features of the stranger that was my mother. There was something very frightening about it. It wasn't me. It was him. Who was he?

Who am I?

ALISON LANGFORD

Alison Langford was born in 1936 in the north-east of England as the result of an affair between her mother (white British) and a married man (unknown). She went to her adoptive family when she was five months old. She employed a tracing agency four years ago and has found that she is part of a very large family. Alison is in touch with five cousins and has been warmly accepted by them. One dear old lady of 96 remembers Alison's mother with affection, which is very special, and she has been given some wonderful old photos. Alison has lived in Surrey ever since her adoption and has been happily married for 48 years, but has no children. It was therefore doubly important for her to find her roots. This poem was previously published in an issue of the Surrey Adoptee Support Group newsletter.

I wondered where I came from
To whom did I belong?
No father named
My mother shamed
But I had done no wrong.
In childhood games
I wondered why
I never felt the same.
No siblings, too, to talk it through
Plus a new rootless name.

When starting work
The questions asked
Upset me till I cried.
What illnesses and problems were
And when my mother died?
On marriage I acquired a name
That had some real meaning.
But still no blood relations
For whom I'd have strong feeling.

When no child came
I thought that this was going to be my lot.
Although I'd much to thank God for
I thought that He'd forgot

How much I want identity
Not just a blob in space.
A real place in history
To join the human race.
Imagine my delight
When at last I had a plan
To search for my relations
By whatever means I can.
I'd left it rather late to try
As I am growing old.
Some folk are not alive now.
The clues are going cold.

However, with the help of Jane
And website information
Cousins I've found
Joy all around
With many generations.
So now at last I've found the past
Believe it if you can.
And I am just a tiny cog
In a gi-normous clan!

A chance to be the "real" me

CAROLE SMITH

Carole Smith was born Theresa Mary Hill on 11 September 1942 at St Albert's House in Slough, Buckinghamshire, England. She was the fifth child of 12 known children. Placed in a Catholic foster home three weeks after birth, she then joined her adoptive parents and was adopted legally in 1945. Two of her birth siblings were also adopted. Carole learned of her adoption in 1968, but was unable to trace until years later. Her efforts to find family failed until her husband, Brian, hired an investigator in 2004. In 2005 Carole and her daughter, Colleen, had a reunion with five siblings. There has been consistent contact since then. To date, Carole has been in touch with nine siblings and located two uncles and their families from her mother's Irish side of the family. Carole lives with her husband in British Columbia, Canada.

I was legally adopted two-and-a-half years after my birth, although I was with my adoptive parents from three weeks of age. I learned of my adoption when my parents were going through a divorce in 1968. My dad was sorting through his papers and came across my original Birth and Baptismal Certificate. He said, 'I thought you should have these.'

I was 26 years old and did not know I had been adopted. My dad never wanted me to find out. Even relatives were sworn to secrecy. He felt emigrating to Canada would protect me from my past. He had grown up in a large home where he was fostered. He never knew that his favourite aunt who brought him treats was in fact his mother. When he was told aged 16, he ran away, lied about his age and enlisted into the Army. Later, he brought his mother to Canada and she lived with him until her death. I was devastated when he spoke quickly of the reason my birth parents gave me up for adoption: I was one of eight children, my father had deserted the family and my mother was unable to care for me.

Throughout my life I have always felt the need to explain myself in finite detail. Each time I talk about "me" I add more, hoping people will understand who I am. Since finding my relatives in 2004, I have experienced a life crisis and have sought out a counsellor, through Adults Affected by Adoption – NORCAP,[2] which specialises in helping adoptees deal with loss. I hope this

---

[2] See under 'Useful organisations/websites'.

time to try and focus on an area that lies deeper within, as I really wanted to give voice to the little girl who has been invisible for so long.

I experienced a passionless adoption and lived in a house where I was alone most of the time. I was threatened and abused by our tenant from the age of three. I was made to abide by the adage: 'A child should be seen and not heard.' From my earliest memory, I knew I had no voice. I was not "seen", as I was taught "not to draw attention to myself", as this was vanity. I was the invisible child, brought out at special events. I believe God gave me a special gift, a singing voice, but I was only allowed to use it when it didn't disturb anyone. None of my adoptive family came to any school concerts or events at which I sang. Few knew this little girl. Relatives back in England commented that 'I resembled a sad little Jewess' and I seemed to be an 'old soul'. When I was to move to a better school one of my teachers at my old school commented to my mother, 'Do you think changing schools will make a difference?' I was a "no hoper". I was being moved because the other schoolgirls kept beating me up.

I never thought I belonged to this family. Being adopted seems to represent a second chance but even when stories of children being adopted were brought home, neither parent expressed any thought or emotion. They remained silent. So, when my father came to my home (at age 26, I had been married for ten years and had two children and an abusive husband) and handed me my adoption documents that proved when I was born and where I came from, I found I had to swallow this information deep within me. It seemed I was expected to show no distress or cause any fuss. Just disappear. Stay invisible, be quiet. I was, however, devastated.

I could not (was not allowed?) to express my distress to anyone. The fact that I had been adopted seemed to be an inconvenience to others. My natural mother had given me away, I never had a second mother, nor did there seem to be a chance of being a sister to my siblings. Plus, now I was no longer a member of my adoptive family. I was not their blood. They had done their "duty". (A story I heard was that my mother adopted me because I would be her "ticket to heaven".) I no longer existed to them.

What is identity? Who do I belong to? Am I connected to a family or disconnected from a family by the stroke of a pen?

I received my adoption records and papers in 2008 after a long and complicated search. I felt like I was having to explain, to justify who I was and fight for the right to be me. However, I have been gifted two precious things for doing so: the signatures of both my birth mother and birth father.

I never found relief from the grief and sense of loss through counselling. When, in 2008, I read the book *The Primal Wound* by Nancy Newton Verrier,[3] it touched a nerve that seemed to awaken a very hidden emotion. It explained the connection between mother and child and the truth about the development of the real self. It was the first moment I believed there was hope for the "hidden child" within me. Maybe she could surface and the days of performance and trying to please others in the hope of being accepted could stop. It explained how I felt as a child and the effects of being adopted that mark my entire life. I didn't know how I would finally find freedom from these things, but I had found an answer that was real. To me, even though I was over 60 years of age, I felt I had a chance to be the real me.

I had believed I would have an identity as a daughter, a wife, a mother. Then, as an adult, I thought my career would define me. It appeared these would, but if I became ill, or was not able to "perform" as expected, I quickly lost that identity. I was not valued in my family. I felt like a burden to everyone. I was damaged goods. My perception was that society, family and friends treated me as though I was not there. People were afraid when told the truth about the bad things family members had done. It made them uncomfortable. They preferred I remain silent.

I believed that, given a chance, I would find the answers I needed to survive, to "live the life" I was given and have the courage to live it. It has been a long journey and there have been some very difficult times. However, after tracing my siblings in 2004, my daughter and I went to Europe to meet them in 2005. My daughter said that if she had not seen everyone for herself, she would not have believed it. I was one of 12 known children. Two of us were adopted and did not know about each other until we were adults (me at 26, she at 55). My siblings knew about us but did not know where to search, as our original names had been changed through adoption. In future, I hope it will be easier for siblings to trace an adopted sibling without encountering red tape or negative attitudes.

If anyone is still questioning the necessity of a child knowing his or her roots, may I remove any doubts. The moment I heard, 'You have a sister and she is alive and wants to have contact,' a thick wall of defences came crashing down. The hole in my heart started to heal, regardless of what I was to discover upon being reunited with nine of my 12 siblings. I went looking for my family tree and I found an orchard.

----

[3] Published in the UK by BAAF, most recently in 2009

She is my past and I am her future

FRANKIE PEARCE

Frankie Pearce was born on 11 December 1966 in Edgware Hospital, London, as a mixed-raced baby born to a British white woman. She was then transracially adopted at nine months to a couple who were unable to have children, changing her name to Frances Tarrant. Frankie had a difficult adoption, which has left some scarring in her life, though she feels she has come a long way with her self-esteem and self-confidence. She made contact with her birth mother, who herself had a very difficult abusive life which affected her mental health, leaving her unable to care for the children she had borne. Unfortunately, the developing relationship between Frankie and her birth mother has since broken down and they are no longer in touch, though she still remains in contact with her half-sister, niece and nephew. Frankie currently lives and works in London.

Becoming a mother and having my own family has helped me with my adoption experience. Being a parent gave me a physical connection with another human being through sharing the same genes. This in turn gave me a tremendous sense of belonging. I started to feel I was a real person within a family, being more than just a relation awarded by the courts to two complete strangers, as stated on a legal document.

At three months I was being fostered and before I turned one I was adopted by the same family. By the age of eight, I was fully informed of my adoption by my adoptive parents. Before then I had already felt a sense of difference between myself and my parents and the rest of the extended family, such as cousins and grandparents. Maybe this was due to never feeling any real bond with my adoptive mother. I remember her being cold towards me and very impatient, as though I was an annoyance to her. When I was about five, my colour difference became very apparent to me. I would look down at the skin on my arms, point out the lighter shades on my wrist and say, 'Look, I'm turning white like you' or, 'If I scrubbed harder would I be white like you and Dad?'

I used to put a lot of my life struggles and unhappiness down to being black and adopted. I'm not very confident and in some situations, where I feel outside of my comfort zone, I become very quiet and unsure of myself. I found it very hard being black and growing up within a white family in a largely white area. No one understood the confusion going on inside me. I was visually black, but inside I felt and thought white. I hated my biological father who had given me this colour. I would think, if it was not for him, my life would be different and I would not have to endure constant name calling from other children and sometimes adults. I would have fitted in. I would have been accepted. I had a face and skin colour that resembled no one. I grew up feeling like a walking, talking jigsaw puzzle, with holes. Who am I? Where do I come from? Why am I black? Where does my skin colour come from? After years of on-and-off searching for my birth mother, I finally found her five years ago. I discovered that I look very much like her when she was younger though, of course, a darker version. I then got in touch with my elder half-sister with whom I share our mother's looks. My birth mother and half-sister are both white, but that didn't matter to me. What was important was the fact that I could at last put a face to the title "birth mother" – the woman who was responsible for my existence. This finally started to give me a sense of connection.

The feeling of disconnection, which I often experienced while growing up as an adopted child, was now replaced with some roots and history, giving me some background about myself. Yet, the holes on my black side still exist. Unfortunately, I don't think there is any way of filling them. I have given up trying to trace my father. With the little information about him that I have, I don't believe I will ever be able to track him down. I wish I could because I really would love to know about my history and my black ancestors, and how I came to be here, in this country, as a black person. Also, when I get asked the dreaded question, 'What country are you from?' I always reply the same way, 'Erm... I don't know because I am adopted.' This leaves the person who thought they were asking a non-intrusive question, feeling a bit awkward and not knowing what to say next. So, I just try to give them a very, very quick run-down of my adoption and say I do not know what country my birth father came from. Sometimes, I have had people really staring at my face, trying to guess what country or continent my features originate from.

To have got myself to this point in life, accepting me for who I am, has taken some hard work and I still have some way to go. I have moments where I suffer from self-doubt. Even now, within my own family with my own biological children, I still wonder if I truly fit in or if I'm accepted. I know I should not be thinking this way about my own family. Sometimes these feelings just creep up in my mind and at times I seem to lose control over them. I know I get insecure and I am aware I can need a lot of reassurance at times. This is hard work for my partner who is very patient with me. He could tell me he loves me, but in my head I could be wondering, 'Why? How could you want to love me?'

At present, I am in my bedroom crying because I know I push people away and I feel alone. This feeling will last for a while until I feel brave enough to go back downstairs to rejoin the rest of the family. I hang back because I'm scared of being ignored if I say anything. This is what usually happens to me when some silly negative comment has been made to me. I get defensive and withdraw into myself. This is when I start to feel I'm no good, an idiot and a waste of space. I try and push these words into the back of my mind, along with the thought that one day everyone in my family will leave me. Then another part of me will tell me to, 'Shut up. Why would they? You're a good mum. Stop being an idiot, these thoughts will pass.' I guess I will always have a battle going on inside my head when I find myself in a situation I do not handle well. If I had not had counselling, these thoughts would have stayed in my head for hours or days, instead of a few minutes.

I have grown into an adult who holds a very low opinion of herself. I was unwanted by my birth mother and chucked out of my home by the time I was 17 because my parents found me too much to deal with. By this time they had given me a nickname, "Black witch"; slightly nicer than just being called, "It", by my adoptive mother. I felt rejected by everyone for one reason or another. I felt ugly, stupid and worthless. It was not until much later on in my life that this started to change.

The first process was to change my surname back to my birth name. This gave me a feeling of divorcing my adoptive parents. I then moved from the suburbs further into London with my three small children. Now I was able to walk around town without racial comments being hurled at me, which in itself was amazing. By this time though, I formed a new friendship with a woman who I had met in a school playground while collecting my son. She was slightly older than me and also a single parent with three children. At the weekends, she would go out clubbing. I was really happy when she asked me if I would like to go with her one Saturday. The only thing was the clubs were open until six in the morning so stimulants would be needed. I had previously dabbled in drugs, so it was nothing new to me. For the next few years at the weekends I would be totally off my face on drugs while the children were being looked after by their dad. I would return on Sunday once I was back to normal. I look back on the drug-taking now and think I was an idiot. I could have died. You don't know what you are putting into your body. I was in so much pain once because I took a pill which contained rat poison. I admit I was selfish and inconsiderate, especially being a mother. But I don't regret it as going clubbing gave me confidence. The people who went to these clubs did not care who I was, where I came from, what job I did or do. Everyone was there for one thing: to have a good time.

I made some really important friends from those days, who are still in my life now, and I consider them a part of my family. It was the first time in my life that I felt accepted for who I am; I started to feel wanted by people. Of course, along with the highs of drugs come the downs, and depression set in. So much was going around inside my head. I stopped my weekend clubbing when I started work. I also had a new relationship which made me very happy, so I didn't need the club scene as much, but there were still thoughts in my head that would not leave. Anti-depressants were not solving the issues but were masking them. I felt I had to do something more. In the past, when I was 17, I had touched on counselling and had found it really helpful. I decided in order to move forward I needed to receive counselling again.

Speaking to somebody who was outside of my life was a great relief. Having counselling helped me to understand why I think the way I do, how damaging it is to me and how to change those thoughts. It helped me to accept the fact that I was abused emotionally as a child, and to acknowledge that the way I was treated was not right and not my fault. If you have been unfortunate enough to have suffered difficulties in adoption or fostering, and you have not considered talking to someone about it, I cannot begin to tell you how helpful counselling is. Even though I still have moments with my insecurities, I have learned how to deal with any negative thoughts that enter my head and I can see my strengths. I no longer feel angry or upset about my adoptive parents, especially my mother. I now believe she was not well in herself and suffered terrible insecurities which she passed on to me.

If you do decide to go for counselling, make sure you go to someone who specialises in adoption or fostering. Someone who may not be trained within that field may not understand why you think, feel and act the way you do. I once had a series of sessions with a counsellor who could not understand why I kept wanting to talk about my mother and how she had treated me. This experience put me off going to see another counsellor for a while. As I was still suffering from depression, which was getting heavier and heavier in my head, I was advised to go to the Post-Adoption Centre (PAC).[4] I had my first meeting with an amazing counsellor who worked with me to change the negative views I held about myself.

Being a black counsellor, I was able to open up and be honest with her about how I felt about myself as a black person. I was able to tell her I had a fear of black people because they didn't accept me. I explained to her about my

---

[4] See under 'Useful organisations/websites'.

three children who are mixed race, how they seem to embrace their colour and are proud of their skin, living within the culturally diverse West London area. They have never had to suffer the racial name-calling I endured as a child. She told me how important it was for me to accept, acknowledge and embrace my colour, which I feel I have done with her help and through my children. She got me to take part in a weekend programme about changing my thought patterns, letting go of the past. I found it very enlightening and it was brilliant to meet up with other adopted people, sharing and listening to their experiences. It is amazing to be able to discuss how you think and why with like-minded people who have gone through similar experiences. This programme taught me one thing: to stop playing the victim and move on. Let the past go, leave it where it is – in the past.

To some extent I have done this. I have let go of some of the memories that stopped me from enjoying my life. I have stopped blaming social services for placing me within an inappropriate family, who would not be accepted to adopt a child today. I no longer feel my whole existence was ruined by adoption. I could have experienced similar insecurities with my biological parents. My adoptive parents made me into the person I am, someone who is a fighter. I look back at the little, black, confused and unhappy girl. I see her in her bedroom, not knowing what her part is in this world, longing to be accepted and wanted. She is my past and I am her future. I look down on her and try to reassure her that what she is going through will make her a better person. One day she will have her own home, a partner, her own family, close friends and a cushy office job in London. Yes, there will still be tough times, but all this will help me to cope with those moments. I will feel rich in love from family, friends and a trusting, loving partner. This will make up for all the love I've missed.

Roots

THERESE RYAN

Therese Ryan was born in Castlepollard Mother and Baby Home, County Westmeath, Ireland. She was adopted when she was five weeks old and grew up in Sligo where she lives with her husband and three children. She has had some contact with her birth mother but has yet to meet her. She has, however, met her half-sister. Therese's writing has been published in the magazines *Force 10* and *SHOP*.

I am ten years old, on an errand in town for my aunt. In the grocery shop I hand her list to the man behind the counter, telling him who it's for. He leans down towards me and says, 'Well, you must be a Ryan anyway with those big brown eyes.' I feel warm and safe inside.

I envy my friend's big family. They look alike. There are hordes of uncles, aunts, cousins. Familiar features reappear: the long eyelashes, the pointed chin, the easy walk, the tone of voice. They can trace themselves back generations. They visit grandparents in the houses their parents grew up in. They know who they are.

I look to other people to tell me who I am. I am the person I think other people want me to be. Somewhere inside I feel I am nothing. I wear different personas to hide the emptiness. I am the good child, the dutiful daughter, the tireless wife and mother.

I like to be a part of groups. I take on the identity of the group. They confirm who I think I am.

My children's homework is to draw up a family tree. We write down the names of grandfathers, grandmothers, uncles and aunts. My husband and I never met our grandfathers just as my children never met my adoptive father. We struggle to recall grandmothers' maiden names, grand-aunts and uncles. The children write names in boxes on the sheet. There is nowhere to write the names of my birth parents, my children's grandparents. This sheet demands tidy answers. I want to say to the children, 'This isn't all. It isn't this simple.' I say nothing.

Real history is in the omissions. I imagine another family sitting at their kitchen table drawing up their family tree, unaware of their older sister. Did my birth mother think of me as she spelled out the names of her parents, aunts and uncles? Was I so deeply hidden that no thought of me filtered into her consciousness? A secret hidden among the branches of the family tree. Who was I back then?

I am 34 years old. I hold my original birth certificate in my hands for the first time. My name is Jacqueline. There is a dash where my surname should be. A dash also for the name of my father. I am confused. This is the gateway to my past but I am a stranger to myself.

On that other family tree I would be called Jacqueline. Maybe I was named after Jacqueline Kennedy who, with her young children, visited Ireland for a month in the summer of 1967, the year I was born. I imagine the women and girls in the mother and baby home crowded around a radio, listening to a reporter describe the glamorous outfit Jacqueline wore to the state dinner: a bright full-length gown of chiffon and a white ermine stole. I was Jacqueline for less than five weeks. My parents weren't told my name when they adopted me. They named me after St Therese of Lisieux, "The Little Flower", to whom my father had a great devotion.

Jacqueline. I write it, say it aloud slowly. I like how the initial sharpness gives way to a lingering softness. Still, no matter how often I say it, the name does not fit me. I love the name Therese. We grow into our names. Jacqueline was my name in my other life.

My first moments alone with my newborn daughter. I sit and watch her sleeping. Panic. I do not see anyone I know in her. Where have we both come from?

As she grows, I recognise my features in hers. She reassures me that I am real, I exist. I wonder who else shares these brown eyes with us, the shape of our eyebrows, our slight build. I love when people say, 'She is the image of you.'

I start my search for my birth mother. I want to know where I have come from. I want to know who I look like, who my children look like. I gather shreds of information like gems. My birth name, my birth mother's name, the county she was from. I need to know who I really am. Can shame travel across the placenta?

I cannot look within myself. I am afraid of what I may find. The real me is unlovable. My head disputes this, but the heart knows the truth.

I cling on to my adoption story. It covers the emptiness I feel inside, becomes my identity, makes me feel different – special. Maybe it is better to retain the magic and mystery of not knowing where I come from. Reality is ordinary.

I am a detective gathering clues. Huge gaps are slowly filled in with tiny patches of information. My birth mother agrees to have some contact. I have half-siblings. My birth mother and I write to each other through a social worker. I wait for the photographs she promises to send. When I see them, surely I will see part of myself. I study the photographs of her and my half-brothers and half-sister. I don't recognise these people. They are someone else's family.

I want to construct a new identity for myself. A self that is acknowledged, worthwhile. Then I can become the person I was meant to be. I want to leave behind this old me.

I think if I meet my birth family I will finally know who I am. I will be someone different then, a better person. Years pass by. There is no meeting.

My birth mother refuses to tell her family about me. I am invisible. A ghost from her past come back to haunt her. I do not exist.

I find a photo of myself as a child in my school uniform. Long curly hair. A mischievous grin. Dimpled chin. It is like looking at my youngest daughter. I am her. She is me.

The journey to find my birth mother leads me back to myself. Only I can say who I am.

I speak to my half-sister for the first time on the phone. Her voice is familiar. We are easy with each other. She welcomes me. I relax into myself. This woman I am is good enough.

My sister sends me a photograph of herself. We are alike: our slight build, curly dark hair, brown eyes, sallow skin.

I am an oak tree sending out my own roots.

To be British, Vietnamese, Chinese and me

JESSICA EMMETT

Jessica Emmett is an artist, illustrator and designer. She was born in Hong Kong in 1982 after her Vietnamese birth parents fled there after the Vietnam War. Her birth mother was granted relocation status in the US and felt she could not bring up a newborn baby there, especially as her birth father was out of the picture. Jessica was given up for adoption after five months and placed in foster care. After 12 months, she was adopted by a British couple living and working in Hong Kong. They later adopted her sister, a Chinese-Hong Kong adoptee. Jessica grew up in Hong Kong in an expatriate community before moving to North Yorkshire in 1998. She completed her Photography & Media Arts undergraduate and Masters degrees in Manchester and stayed there for eight years before moving to Oxfordshire where she lives with her husband. Jessica is in the process of tracing her roots.

To be British

I was born, adopted and grew up in Hong Kong. My (white British) parents were living there at the time. Hong Kong was one of the last major British ruled territories outside the UK before the handover back to China in 1997. I find it hard to explain what it was like to be raised in a British expatriate community.

Few of the expats I knew spoke Cantonese – only enough to pay for things and get taxis home (or, in my case, some novel swear words). Most expats seemed fine with this self-made isolation and had little desire to speak the language. Having gone to an English-speaking International school and having English-speaking friends and no push from my parents to learn Cantonese, it was easy for me to follow suit. With hindsight, I would like to try and learn Cantonese, and one day I will.

Food was a major part of the British expat life. We used to go to eat at the Hong Kong *Harry Ramsden's*, where you could eat your weight in fish and chips and drink British beer. We used to have roast dinners every Sunday and during the week we would mainly eat western foods. We often had shepherd's pie, pork chops, mashed potatoes and baked beans. Once I left home I tried to avoid these foods at all cost. Occasionally, we would go out for *dim sum*, or my mum would make Chinese/Asian food at home.

Life as an expat was complicated enough. What happens when you start to bring adoption into the equation? I'm a Vietnamese adoptee while my younger sister is a Chinese adoptee. It was sometimes odd to grow up in an East Asian country and be isolated from my own Vietnamese community. However, it would have been impossible not to take in some Chinese culture from just living in Hong Kong.

When I lived in Hong Kong I never really questioned my "Britishness". In 1998, when I was 16, the family moved to the UK. I made the mistake of thinking that having been raised as British and often visited the UK, I would easily slip into life here. We moved to a very small village in North Yorkshire with only a handful of neighbours. My Hong Kong friends would joke that I was moving to live with the sheep and cows, and it wasn't far from the truth. I see why my parents picked that house; it was (and still is) the dream house they had always wanted. For me it was devastatingly opposite to Hong Kong in every way. If people thought I was a difficult teen in Hong Kong, I was made worse by this move.

I was a "tomboy", and still am to a degree, so when my parents suggested I go with my sister to the local girls' grammar school I was horrified. My two years at that school were probably the most difficult of my life. Let's put it this way: I was a rebel with bad grades who was taught in my liberal Hong Kong international school that you didn't need to be book smart to achieve things. This new and strict school didn't know what to make of me – students and teachers alike. It was the first time in my life that I had experienced feeling "different", a minority. I was often introduced as 'the girl from Hong Kong'. This was the first time I had experienced racial slurs on the street and blatant mistrust from locals. After fall-outs, friend changes and almost rejecting Britishness altogether, I found a small group of friends who seemed to like me. They helped me through some rough times.

After my terrible experiences at grammar school I went to university. I often asked my friends what it was to be British. They struggled to explain. In many cases they told me it was frowned upon to show national pride, that being British had negative connotations outside of sport and that the very thing I was brought up with, the Empire, was just the image a modern UK was trying to shake off.

I thought doing British things might be the key to being British. I did things like drink tea, which I've never liked much; watched football/sport, which I never took to; watched old TV and sketch shows, which I could never relate to; drank alcohol (under age), which I did for two years under large amounts of peer pressure before realising I was super intolerant; and hung out in pubs, where I would be horribly nervous about going to the bar because of the staring. I desperately wanted to do the things my friends liked but worried that since I couldn't, I might never be truly British.

I tried to take another approach. I was starting to learn about the UK through my photography degree. Learning the history of art in the UK was giving me a good sense of the culture in terms which were accessible to me. I finally felt I was connecting.

I feel much more settled now, but it has taken a long time. What really helped was living in Manchester for eight years. I can happily say I'm a northerner or a Mancunian or, more occasionally, a Yorkshire lass. I moved to Oxfordshire in 2008 and I've adapted more quickly this time.

I went from "Empire" British, to almost rejecting Britishness completely. Now, 14 years since moving to England, I can confidently say: 'I'm British.'

To be Vietnamese

Out of all my cultural identities, being Vietnamese is probably the least developed. Throughout my life I have had very little exposure to Vietnamese people or culture. I know about the Vietnamese history that is related to war and pretty landscapes in photography books.

My birth mother was a refugee "boat person". I also know that she was once in a "camp". Sometimes we would drive past the Hong Kong refugee camps and I would wonder if my birth mother was inside (even though I knew she was in the US). When I was younger, I occasionally sensed that the local Hong Kong people resented the Vietnamese refugees. I didn't understand the reasons why but sometimes comments were made when people learned I was Vietnamese.

In 1997, when I still lived in Hong Kong, many of my good friends were going on the school trip to Vietnam. I went, realising that once I moved to the UK there would be few opportunities ever to go to Vietnam. We did sightseeing of war-related tourist traps and museums. I didn't feel a sense of connection in the way I thought I might. It was only when we volunteered at an orphanage for a week that I felt any link with the country of ethnic origin.

When I first moved to the UK I had little interest in what it was to be Vietnamese. In 2006, I decided to enter a competition which involved taking old BBC archive footage and turning it into a short, personal documentary.

I saw they had several clips about the Vietnamese boat people. I won the competition and my prize was two days work experience at the BBC in London. A day was organised for me in the BBC Vietnamese department. It was amazing! It was the first time I had talked to Vietnamese people who had lived in Vietnam, who were refugees and knew other Vietnamese people in the UK.

In 2003 I joined the Adopted Vietnamese International (AVI) group,[5] becoming active in the group in 2008. Since then, I've been flung into the Vietnamese adoptee community. I have been lucky enough to make some top friends and even work alongside a few. I have been inspired by the great work many Vietnamese adoptees are doing in the adoption and academic fields. I was lucky enough to meet a group of UK Vietnamese adoptees for Tet (the Vietnamese/Chinese New Year) in February 2010.

While I'm writing this many of my Vietnamese adoptee friends are in Vietnam for the reunion marking the 35th anniversary of the end of the Vietnam War. I couldn't go due to a lack of money and the fact that I didn't feel a "need" to in the same way that I have a need to return to Hong Kong. There are a lot of places I'd rather visit in the world. I feel guilty and that I should care more about visiting Vietnam in the way that many Vietnamese adoptees do. I definitely want to go in the future, but in my own time.

I know I'm very early on in my Vietnamese journey, especially as I'm currently tracing my roots. For now, I'm very happy with my little Vietnamese culture. I can confidently say: 'I'm Vietnamese.'

To be Chinese

Ironically, even though I was born and grew up in Hong Kong, I have always hesitated to call myself Chinese, feeling that I've not had any claim to the title.

When I first started in my international secondary school I hung around with the Chinese girls in my class. Everything seemed fine until I started to spend time with them outside of school, where they often forgot that I could not understand when they spoke Cantonese. It didn't bother me because it didn't feel deliberate or nasty, but I realised I was out of the loop. I continued to talk to them in school but naturally moved to a new set of friends. It was disappointing that language was a barrier to knowing them better.

---

[5] See under 'Useful organisations/websites'.

Living in Hong Kong, it was fairly normal for people to assume that I could speak Cantonese. Prior to the handover, if I explained I was adopted and could only speak English, occasionally local Chinese (strangers) could be quite rude. When I was younger, I was told many locals resented anyone East Asian who only spoke English. It was about local people getting educated in western countries, then returning and refusing to speak Cantonese in favour of English, as a sign of status. I returned to Hong Kong in 2008, after ten years of being away, and was glad not to experience any such resentment.

Moving to the UK was when my "Chineseness" was really tested. Unsurprisingly, Chinese and Vietnamese people whom I met were convinced I was Chinese even when I explained that I was adopted and Vietnamese.

Like my parents eating British food in Hong Kong, I went on a mission to eat as much Chinese/Asian food as possible after I moved. I picked to go to university in Manchester partly because of the large Chinese community and Chinatown, with shops that sell imports of my favourite sweets and foods. I wish I'd been able to connect with the Manchester Chinese community more, but as in Hong Kong, I felt isolated from the community.

After my Masters degree I decided to stay in Manchester as it was the first place since moving that I'd felt was home. I was applying to get onto a programme and art residency. One of the stipulations was that I was an "artist of Chinese descent". I struggled with this phrase for ages. I felt frustrated because, if anything, I felt more Chinese than anything else. I doubted if being born in Hong Kong or living and growing up there was enough to fulfill the "descent" part. In fact, it was fine for me to apply. On the scheme, I connected with many wonderful British-born Chinese artists and sometimes felt a fraud, even though everyone knew about my Vietnamese background. They joked that I was more Chinese than they were. The project was good for me.

In 2008, I started working with adoptive families and adoptees from China and Hong Kong. This set me thinking again about being Chinese. I started to ask questions about Hong Kong and its relationship to China. I think Hong Kong is the perfect example of what it feels like to be transracially adopted. In simplistic terms, Hong Kong was originally Chinese but then leased to Britain for 99 years. Under British rule and many different cultures and migrants later, it flourished into its own unique international identity. Now, after the handover back to China, it is reconnecting to its Chinese roots, but it still retains its ties with British/international history. Therefore, I think it will always stand apart from mainland China.

Recently I've changed my self-given title of "Vietnamese adoptee" to "Vietnamese/Hong Kong adoptee". More specifically, I can say with confidence: 'I'm Hong Kongese' (or what some expats call "Honkers").

To be me

I have always been pragmatic about adoption, but as you can see, coming to terms with being British, Vietnamese and Chinese is pretty complex, to say the least.

Adoption is a big part of who I am today, partly because I've chosen to work in the adoption field. When I first started to look at adoption in my artwork I was hitting creative brick walls. I talked to my tutor about it. He said, of course I was struggling, I was trying to tackle the whole of adoption and attempting to explain it all in one artwork. He said it was impossible. He suggested that I break adoption down into smaller, more accessible pieces and just look at one issue at a time. I don't think he realised the extent to which his advice influenced me in so many ways. I now take adoption one step at a time, at a pace I am comfortable with.

Now, at 30 years old, I have a very strong sense of self. I'm open to the possibility that my ideas about adoption and cultural identity are still developing and shifting my sense of self, but I can confidently and happily say: 'I'm me!'

CHALLENGES AND OPPORTUNITIES

The track of self-discovery *Jennifer McNiven*

Cuckoo in the nest *Annie Blackham*

A tremendous freedom *Deborah Collier*

Prepare for the unexpected *Sharon Figgens*

Nothing to lose *Julie Hoskins*

Seventy years ago today, Great Britain declared war on Germany and her allies *Gloria McLaren*

Finding Joy *Joy Carter*

Living with uncertainty *Shanel Cuthbert*

Wife to husband *Jackie Rivett*

Outside looking in *Beth Archer*

Release *Beth Archer*

Your secret *Cath Staincliffe*

Cast on *Anwen Lewis*

Jennifer's story *Jennifer Jones*

My pathway to peace *Ron McLay*

More than just a survivor *Viv Fogel*

Finally, my choice *Liz Wilde*

Mixed blessings *Liz Sibthorpe*

What if...? *Vanessa Gebbie*

The track of self-discovery

JENNIFER MCNIVEN

Jennifer McNiven was born in 1948 in the south west of Scotland, of Scottish birth parents. Her birth mother was living with her sister at the time. Afterwards she returned to work and Jennifer's care was divided between her mother and her aunt. Her aunt had one child and had lost another, and wanted to adopt Jennifer, but her mother was against it. Jennifer was taken to an adoption society in Glasgow and subsequently adopted at two-and-a-half months by a couple living in Edinburgh. She has traced her maternal and paternal birth family, but only has sporadic contact since her birth father died a few years ago. Her birth mother had already died by the time Jennifer tried to trace her. Jennifer lives in Edinburgh, where she was educated and eventually married. She has two grown-up children.

I was born and adopted in the late 1940s – very much part of the post-war bulge. At that time, there was an enormous stigma attached to having a child out of wedlock. The choices available to a woman or girl who found herself in that position were few and stark. If she was lucky, a family member might step in to bring up her child, or even to formally adopt him or her. In those circumstances she might have some contact with the child. As a mother myself, I think the decision to have to give up a child would be one of the most awful decisions one could ever have to make. Sadly, many mothers were advised or even coerced into putting their child up for adoption. They had little say themselves. Their voices were silenced.

I discovered some years ago that after I was born, both of my grandmothers sat down and put their heads together and decided I should be adopted. I can't know what their motives were, but I would like to think that they made their decision in favour of the best outcome, as they saw it, for all concerned. I would think that matters of expediency also came into their decision, with many complicated issues playing a part: different religious faiths, possible class differences and plain economics.

At the time of my adoption there were many babies born to mothers who, for one reason or another, couldn't bring up those children as their own, but equally there were numerous couples who found themselves unable to have children of their own. Those were the days before easily and cheaply available contraception, before abortion became legal and before assisted conception.

In my experience, the standard adoptive family of the 1940s and 1950s was pretty much like mine: two adoptive parents, father in employment and at work, mother at home looking after the house and one adopted child. Apart from a desire to adopt, and a visit from a professional person to assess the home and check it was suitable, adoptive parents did not receive guidance on how an adopted child might differ in his or her needs from a biological one. The screamingly obvious need that was not recognised was the need to know where one came from in order to gain a sense of belonging. In my case, the minimal information that was available was denied because I was told I didn't need to know. Enlightenment about such things came long after the 1940s and 50s.

The positive side of being adopted

Being adopted did often confer advantages which might not otherwise have been available if a child had been left in his or her birth family. The child's standard of living might have been much better and he or she might have had better access to education which would benefit them in later life. This was the case for me, knowing the circumstances of my birth family and the opportunities available to them at that time. As a child, you do not reflect on your life and what you are doing, nor do you compare yourself with those unknown to you. You live for the present and accept your life is the norm. Apart from being adopted, of course. That sets you apart from your peers. It is only with maturity that you examine what your life was like and what it might have been like had you not been adopted. I am grateful for those advantages which being adopted gave me.

The negative side of being adopted

Being overly compliant/lack of security

I was one of the group of adopted children who aimed to please and to conform to parents' expectations. In effect, the Adoptee became the Adaptee. Why was this? At the age of seven or eight I was told I was adopted. At that time one of my best friends was the oldest of four children, and I spent a lot of time at her house playing with her and her brothers and sister. I was exposed to and became a part of a family setting, which seemed to represent a real and *proper* family and only highlighted for me what I felt I was missing.

'Why can't I have brothers and sisters?' I asked my mother.

'Because you are adopted,' was the answer. 'Oh, and you don't tell people that, by the way, it is none of their business. They don't need to know.'

Adoption = Stigma was the message I heard. There was something shameful about being adopted and it set you apart from other people. So, suddenly, I felt I had to be complicit in keeping the secret; otherwise I would incur the wrath of my mother.

'So, where did I come from?' was my next question.

'We chose you,' came the answer.

To my child's mind, it seemed logical that if I had been chosen, then I could be "unchosen" and this gift lay entirely in my parents' hands. After all, my childlike mind reasoned, you have been abandoned once already by your "real" mother, the person of all people who should keep, protect and love you. I thought if you were part of a real family then you were always part of that family – in effect they were stuck with you! But as an adopted child your place was much less secure. This was because you didn't really belong. You weren't a natural part of that adoptive family. So in effect, you could be sent back, especially if you didn't meet expectations in terms of behaviour or academic achievement. These thoughts I had as a child were compelling and contributed enormously to my chameleon-like behaviour. I desperately tried to fit in, to please and to conform at the expense of developing my own sense of self. Only as an adult did I realise how little I knew about myself.

Feeling lonely and not belonging

Being adopted was an isolating experience. My adoptive parents were in their 40s and there were no other children around within my immediate or extended family. The family comprised mostly maiden aunts, albeit kindly ones, so I was brought up surrounded by adults. I never felt I really belonged in my adoptive family but then neither have I felt a genuine part of my birth family whom I have met.

I believe the feeling of belonging comes from being unconditionally accepted for who you are, rather than how you match up to expectations, which was what I felt I had to do. The accumulation of shared experiences and shared lives also plays a big part. One cannot catapult into either an adoptive family or birth family out of the blue and expect to feel at home. New relationships have to be built and this doesn't happen overnight. I only felt a genuine sense of connection when I had my own children.

For me, a summary of the negative feelings and experiences associated with being adopted would include being excluded, alone, not being quite good enough, fearful, and having to keep secrets, plus low self-esteem. I have to concede that perhaps I might have felt most of these things because of the way my mother brought me up. Perhaps she simply treated me in the same way she would have treated a biological child.

The way through

What have I done about the negatives I associate with being adopted? The first thing I did was to trace my birth family. I waited until both my adoptive parents had been dead for some years, as I felt disloyal. After all, they had brought me up and I knew my mother would have viewed me as ungrateful and dissatisfied with what I had.

Still, the time came for me to do what I needed to do. I was married with my own family and felt there was a degree of duty to my children, in case there was some dreadful genetic inheritance lurking in the shadows. On the other hand, there was the excitement of setting out on a journey to gain knowledge, if nothing else. I set off down the track of self-discovery.

I was fortunate to be able to find a lot of information quite quickly. This led to contact with a birth relative who told me my birth mother had emigrated to Australia, had married and had a family. I made contact with them (although my birth mother had died by then) and have still to meet them in person. However, the journey to this point has been enriching and enlightening in many ways. Now I know so much about my birth family, which has helped me understand the complexities of life 60 years ago. Acceptance and rejection have come in varying measures, but I have gained a feeling of being in charge of my destiny as opposed to feeling I have no control over my life.

Amazingly, I also found my birth father. I thought this would be impossible as I had no name and none of my maternal birth family knew who he was. When I met him he was a delightful and welcoming 82-year-old man, who suggested a DNA test to check we were related! For the few years he lived after our reunion we were able to get to know and understand each other, to some extent. Before we met, he said he wouldn't mind if I had two heads as it wouldn't make any difference to him. This went a long way to making me feel accepted without qualification for who I was. At last, I felt the unconditional love which had been missing from my life.

I have been more than fortunate with the fathers I have known: first of all, my adoptive father, who was a kindly and accepting man, even though he was somewhat distant from the actual business of bringing me up; secondly, my birth father, who accepted me with open arms despite the fact that he had to reveal to his own older sister that he had fathered a child in his 20s; and finally, my "stepfather", who welcomed me into his Australian family without a second thought and who was able to tell me what a wonderful person my birth mother had been throughout their life together.

More recently, another positive effect on my life has been my involvement with Birthlink.[1] I originally contacted the organisation when I wanted to search for my birth family. After that, I became a general volunteer, progressing to becoming a volunteer searcher and then a director of the charity. It is nice to be able to help others involved in the adoption circle.

My conclusions

As Sir Francis Bacon wrote in 1597: 'Knowledge itself is power.' I believe that finding out about your origins helps you to understand who you are. Yes, it is a journey into the unknown, but if you set off on that journey with an open mind and are prepared for anything, good or bad, you will only benefit in the long run. Gradually, you will have a new sense of identity. For some people just finding out information is enough; for others, there is the need to meet up with the people who have helped create the reality of their existence. There is no right or wrong thing to do.

Believing that those who shaped our lives, be it birth parents or adoptive parents, have done the best they could under the circumstances in which they found themselves, and given the resources they had available to them at the time, goes a long way to reconciling oneself to the fact of being adopted. We are complex people whose lives have been shaped by birth family and adoptive family and the circumstances under which we were brought up. If we can integrate the myriad strands that combine to make us who we are, then we can go forward as complete human beings.

[1] See under 'Useful organisations/websites'.

Cuckoo in the nest

ANNIE BLACKHAM

Annie Blackham was born in 1949 not long after the end of World War II. Both her birth parents were white British and in the military. Her birth mother was 18. She came from a large family where there was already a baby in the house, and told no one she was pregnant until she went into labour. Annie was taken from her at birth. The adoption was arranged privately, possibly by the hospital almoner who knew her adoptive parents. She was ten days old when she joined her new family in a town 15 miles away. They had tried to adopt a baby girl before but her mother had reclaimed her. Annie does not think she was a good substitute. Only since her 50s has she come to terms with her childhood and appreciated the advantages her adoptive parents gave her. She has never lost the deep loneliness of being the cuckoo in the nest.

I was a solitary child, very self-sufficient, always making dens for privacy and reading my beloved books. The secret of my adoption gave me plenty of scope for fantasy. I was a princess who would one day be recognised, a twin who had been separated at birth.

I was the cuckoo in the nest, the outsider, a miniature observer of the duplicity of adults and a listener to their lies.

'Doesn't she look like her father?' I often heard. The smiling concurrence used to grate on me for although my dad was my most loved person, of course I didn't look like him. Different blood, although we were both small and freckly, fair and quiet.

From a very early age, probably two onwards, I loved being outside. I didn't mind the weather. I was always wanting to get away, to be in control of my own environment. I'd ride around the quiet road on my red tricycle, sometimes meeting the boy who lived at the bottom of my garden – over the fence, of course. I used to love listening to his family talking, just chatting normally, occasionally arguing but all open. Our family wasn't like that – everything was quiet, undercover, muted. 'What will the neighbours think?' was the unspoken tenet.

My mother was an extrovert, full of boundless energy, sporty, very bright, larger than life, bitter about her lack of education. After having passed on to grammar school, she had had to leave at 14 to look after her ill mother, not unusual in those days and she was an only child. My father was from one of the most respected families in the small town and a teacher at public school. A well-spoken old English gentleman, kindness itself but totally out of his depth with his volatile wife.

Their natural son, my adoptive brother, was years older than me and we never really knew each other, both almost only children. He was quiet, conformist, always making things in his bedroom, *Meccano* and later radios. I remember he wasn't a strong child, suffering from ear problems that necessitated him inhaling *Vick*-scented steam during most of the winter. Even now he listens with his head slightly tilted, his good ear towards the speaker. A lovely man.

They wanted a girl and they got me. A shrivelled, skinny orphan, rescued from a hospital cot at ten days old. No father's name on the birth certificate and a different name to the one I was brought up with.

I failed to thrive for the first few months and as my mother was suffering from nervous trouble, my father looked after me as best he could when he wasn't at work. I was supposed to end her depression at not being able to conceive but instead just exacerbated her sense of yet another lack of fulfilment. We never did bond.

So, maybe those first ten days with no mother gave me the realisation that there would only ever be me to rely on. Perhaps this is the cause of my failed marriages – I have low expectations to start with and then when the husband fails to come up to scratch, it's easier to be without him. I can trust me.

My fulfilment came from two things: reading and travelling. When I was a child the travelling was limited to the local park, then the fields and the canal and, as an adult, travelling anywhere, anyhow, whenever I could.

When I travelled I met people who I could have an honest relationship with. There's no pretence with a stranger on a canal bank. You're just two people meeting and passing the time of day. There was Jim from Betchuanaland. He must have been a traveller. He told me stories of Africa and taught me to drink canal water. There was the Egyptian family who moved into the area. I was fascinated by their darker skin and flashing eyes.

When I was at home life was relatively normal for that era: church on Sunday, Sunday school in the morning, best clothes, white gloves, sweets to keep me quiet during the sermon; back for Sunday dinner and then off to grandparents for high tea.

My mother's parents lived in a small house near the railway station and I spent a lot of time there. My grandmother was one of the first certificated teachers in England. She always retained a disciplined air but was great fun. She was a fine needlewoman and made hats at home. People often came to try them on – I remember the hat pins. She also recited poetry at soirées and won poetry competitions. She used to read poems to me before bedtime. I can still remember some of them. She was a good-looking woman with long black hair which she rolled around her head in a sausage. Sometimes she used to let me brush it for her. I loved helping her on wash day, wielding her dolly peg in the copper boiler in the corner of the kitchen or turning the mangle with the ever-present danger of squashed fingers.

Grandpa was mostly at his allotment, growing rhubarb to keep him regular and great blowsy peonies for Grandma. I used to hide under the plants and savour the smell of his baccy. They didn't have much money but were decent, respected folk. Grandma was a good woman but she died when I was seven or eight which didn't help her only child, my mother.

I did belong to Grandma and Grandpa. Grandpa lived for another 20 years and we always had a special relationship. He lived with us for a while. This was hell for him and my mother – they never got on – but it was what you did then. What would the neighbours think if he went into a home?

My dad's family lived on the other side of town in a big five-storey house with lots of land around it. His mum had died on his ninth birthday after the birth of his sister. Grandpa had remarried and his new wife and her sister helped him with his seven children. This was the posh side of the family. You wore your best clothes and had your best manners. The house was a grand place. My mother was never happy there and so I usually went with my dad. We'd often go into one of the gardens with my grandpa and pick raspberries or enjoy the wonderful flowers. The greenhouse was full of the fragrance of tomatoes and the smell of sun on wood. My great-aunt kept bees and chickens in the orchard down the lane. It was a wonderful place for a child like me – I could so easily get lost in this environment, with people pottering nearby but not interfering. I wished I could spend more time in the big house but my mother was a jealous woman and although she didn't particularly want me around, she didn't want me on my father's side either.

We sometimes had Christmas in the big house, with all my father's brothers and sisters and their offspring. I envied my cousins who lived there: all those people to love them and all that space. My great-aunt would cook the most amazing Christmas dinner and we'd all sit round a huge table together. My dad was so different with his own family. His siblings seemed to be very close and were always laughing and happy to see each other.

After the most enormous high tea the children would perform a little play to entertain the adults. The youngest aunt would supervise but I was chronically shy and hated every minute of it. I'm sure my mother was mortified by my lack of talent as she was a games player and excelled at everything from cards to Scrabble.

That side of the family was terribly kind to me but that was just it: I was never family to them but someone to be kind to. My youngest aunt had me to tea after school sometimes and I would pretend I lived there too.

So with all this drama and contrast in my life I suppose I've always had good material! After reading, writing seems a natural occupation and if I can do both when I'm travelling I count myself truly fortunate.

A tremendous freedom

DEBORAH COLLIER

Deborah Collier was born on 6 January 1963 and joined her adoptive parents at 14 days old. They have always been completely honest with her about her adoption, telling her all they knew about the circumstances of her relinquishment. Years later, when Deborah accessed her adoption records, she found that everything her adoptive mother had told her was correct, even down to the name of the social worker who had approved her parents as adopters and used to visit her as a baby. Deborah was comfortable being an adopted child and content with her parents. She has now reached a stage in her life where she feels she wants to give back and ensure the well-being of children currently being adopted; she joined a local authority adoption panel in 2009.

My adoptive mother told me I was a happy baby and used to wake her up in the middle of the night wanting to play. My character from birth was naturally ebullient. I am the sort of person who sees her cup as half full and not half empty. I think life is too short to be unhappy and I make the most of it. My philosophy of life has proven to be an antidote to being relinquished by my birth mother as an infant. It has often enabled me to make behaviours that may result from being adopted work in my favour.

I find I strive to excel. I attribute this to being adopted. I have a need to prove I am "good enough". I am quite happy with this behaviour because it means I can achieve quite easily. While some people may find it difficult to summon up willpower to complete a goal, I know I will always finish what I start. For example, when I was eight, I decided to enter a sponsored swim that was two weeks away. I did not know how to swim at the time yet had complete confidence that I could learn to swim in that two-week period. I taught myself to swim and then swam two lengths of my local swimming pool to the amazement of my parents. As an adult I have worked hard to gain promotion and now have a job at management level.

In my romantic relationships I have the ability to disconnect very quickly when the relationship ends. It is like I have a switch in my head I can just turn off. I think this is a coping mechanism I developed to prevent me feeling the loss of my birth mother as a child. This behaviour has been beneficial, saving me from heartache over the years. While a psychiatrist would say I have an attachment disorder and perceive this as negative, for me it is positive. My girlfriends grieve for several months when their relationships end whereas I very quickly get on with life.

I have a strong desire to make my own choices and decisions in life. Being adopted means I did not have choice as an infant and other people made decisions about my future. This has intensified my sense of independence. I am independent financially and emotionally. This can make boyfriends feel unwanted because I don't "need" them in the way many women need a man in their life. They must be extremely confident to be with someone as self-reliant as me. The path I have taken is to remain single.

I am transracially adopted and have a dual heritage. Throughout my life, I have been subjected to people asking me questions about my ethnicity and parentage. While tiresome, at times, this has encouraged me to always tell the truth and be open. Most importantly, my adoptive parents set a positive example and were always honest with me. My mum recently recounted an incident that took place when I was two years old. A neighbour, Dawn, was chatting to me as I sat on the back doorstep. I told her I was adopted and went on to explain what that meant. Dawn was astonished that I understood I was adopted but my mum had explained adoption to me in an age-appropriate way from infancy. I cannot remember a time when I didn't know. Being asked very personal questions about myself by strangers and the way my parents dealt openly with my adoption has shown me that 'honesty is the best policy' and my veracity has been strengthened. I joined a local authority adoption panel as an independent member in 2009. I have been able to use my life experience as a transracially adopted adult to contribute positively to help children going through adoption today.

A challenge for me as an adoptee is not knowing my birth family history and what my exact heritage is. I have a white British birth mother and a black birth father, possibly from Guyana. I knew my birth father was black Caribbean but didn't know his country of origin until September 1997 when I traced my birth brother. He had a limited amount of information in his adoption file about our birth father. I was 45 when I met a birth relative, my brother, for the first time. Until then, I didn't know which of my traits were down to nature and which were due to nurture. Adoption had cut me off from knowledge of my inherited characteristics. I was open to trying different things to see what I was good at, both at work and in my personal interests. I didn't place limits on myself. As an adoptee I had no preconceived ideas about myself based on the life stories of relatives. This gave me tremendous freedom. My adoptive parents did not assume I would share their interests or career paths and I was able to discover what I enjoy. Accessing my adoption file, meeting my birth brother and using the internet to do genealogical research provided me with an opportunity to increase my self-awareness.

Adopted people do face challenges that can be distressing, but I think we often develop increased self-awareness and empathy as a result. I have tried to make the best of my adoption-related behaviours and make them work in my favour. I have been proactive and gained knowledge about my heritage. I joined a local authority adoption panel because I want to give back. I consider my adoption a success and I am happy within myself.

Prepare for the unexpected

SHARON FIGGENS

Sharon Figgens was born in 1965 in Lambeth Hospital, London, to a 14-year-old girl who had to give her up for adoption. She named her baby Christine, after her best friend who had stuck by her when everyone else turned their back. Christine was given to her new parents when she was six weeks old and was legally adopted and renamed Sharon nine months later. She is white, adopted by white parents. She grew up in Stanford-le-Hope, Essex, as an only child and had the best parents anyone could wish for. Now aged 46, Sharon is still very close to her parents and although she moved to Nottingham in 2001 with her two boys to remarry, she still relies on them for support, both financially and emotionally. Sharon cannot imagine life without her adoptive parents and will always be grateful for the wonderful opportunity they gave her.

I was born on 27 December 1965 in Lambeth Hospital, south London and was named Christine Ann Alcock by my birth mother. I was immediately taken away from her and put into a foster home on the Isle of Dogs. Six weeks later I went to my new mum and dad. In September 1966 the adoption was finalised and my name legally became Sharon Ann Pearce. I grew up in Essex.

My mum and dad are two of the most wonderful parents any child could wish for and I grew up knowing I was one of the most wanted children on the planet. My mum, at the young age of 14, had serious problems with her womb and after she almost died, my grandmother gave permission for her to have everything removed, leaving her unable to have children of her own.

Once they had decided to adopt, my parents started the procedure which was to last years. It was heartbreaking for them, being told one minute they had a child on the way, then to be told the birth mother wanted to keep the baby or some other event would take place and everything would fall through. On their third attempt they found me and, after they tried unsuccessfully to adopt a baby brother, I was raised as an only child.

Being an only child I never wanted for much. I had everything I needed and two parents who loved me very much. I had lots of aunts, uncles, cousins and we were a very close family. We went swimming early every Sunday morning for years and I went to lots of dance classes and performed in many shows to which my parents came. I was brought up knowing I was adopted, but do not actually remember being told. My parents were very open with me about everything and as I grew up and started asking questions, always answered as best they could. I knew my birth mother was only a child herself when she had me and therefore never really needed answers as to why she gave me away, which is probably why I never felt the longing to trace her. Being only 13 when she fell pregnant to a man in his 30s, who I understood went to prison, I assumed she would have grown up and forgotten all about me. She would have a husband and probably more children who would not even know of my existence.

My parents were fairly strict in some ways, like when I was a teenager I had to be home from the youth club at half past nine, when most of my friends went home for ten. I sometimes used to think to myself, 'I bet my "real" mum would let me stay out till ten,' but obviously I realised as I got older that it would probably not have been the case.

Finding out about my birth mother was never an issue. I was interested in adoption and liked to watch TV programmes about it, but sometimes it used to annoy me when adopted people would say things like, 'I don't know who I am' or 'I have no identity'. I would think, how can you say that? Of course, you are your own person. My birth mother is just that, a biological person who gave birth to me, she is not my mum, she doesn't really care. Think of your adoptive parents and how much they care about you and how much you are wanted by them.

I only knew the pain of how hard it must have been to try and adopt a child, the pain of parents unable to have their own biological children. I even participated in egg donation a couple of times to try and help these parents achieve what my parents had.

However, as I got older I did start to wonder more about my birth mother. It was when I had my own children and people would say how the boys looked like their father, or his uncle, or his brother, etc. I used to get upset, as maybe they looked like someone from my birth family. Then I started to think I would just like to see a photograph of her. I had no desire to meet her, or to upset her life or mine, but I was intrigued to know what she looked like. Occasionally, I would look at adoption websites but would never register. I just couldn't bring myself to upset anyone, including my mum and dad. I didn't want them thinking I wasn't grateful for my upbringing because I was. They were and are my mum and dad and always will be, and I love them both to bits.

In some ways, I wish I could end the story there, but you never know what's going to happen in your life. I always thought everything was best left alone. 'What you don't know can't hurt you' as some would say. Yet, everything did change when an envelope arrived out of the blue on my parents' doorstep, franked by Tower Hamlets social services.

I was 35 by then and living around the corner from my mum and dad. My husband and I had split up. I will never forget the day my mum came round and handed me an envelope. She hadn't opened it but she knew what it was about. She gave me the envelope and said, 'It's about your mum. It's up to you what you want to do with it.'

She left almost immediately, leaving me on my own to digest what she had just given me. Tentatively I opened the envelope. It was from a lady called Barbara Prynn and she had written to my parents on Jean's behalf... Oh my god, her name's Jean... I had an Auntie Jean myself. Jean did not want to cause any problems for me or my parents. All she wanted to know was if I was safe and well.

I thought things over for a few days, without really discussing it with my mum or dad, and eventually plucked up the courage to phone Barbara. I felt sick as I dialled her number; my stomach was in knots. I got through to her straight away and told her who I was. She was very pleased to hear from me and was delightful on the phone, telling me a little about Jean, who she had already met. I decided I would write a letter to Jean and send it to Barbara to give to her. There were questions I wanted answered, including medical history. I was fed up having to tell people I had no medical history and after I was paralysed by Guillaine Barré Syndrome at the age of 21, which thankfully I recovered from, I had wondered more and more about what hereditary conditions there may be in my birth family. There were funny things I wanted to know, like whether she was short (I'm only five foot one) and if she had tiny feet (mine are size two).

I set about writing to Jean and enclosed a couple of photographs, one of me and my best friend, Alison, and a couple of me and the children. I thought she would want to know what I looked like as much as I did her. I thought it would be nice for her to see the photos when she met with Barbara the following week.

After the meeting Barbara called me and told me I looked just like Jean. She said Jean arrived with her best friend, Christine, who I was apparently named after, and the pair of them couldn't believe their eyes when they saw me. Jean had written me a letter which Barbara forwarded to me. It was addressed to 'Dear Christine' and in it she told me she was one of nine children and that she had four other children of her own: three boys and a girl. She had been married twice, the first time to an abusive husband with whom she had three children, and then had her youngest son with her second husband. She was not much older than me really. The shocking part was the brief medical history. She had already had three strokes before the age of 50.

We wrote to each other for a year or so and in the meantime I went on holiday to Fuerteventura with my children, my best friend and her family. While there I met a gorgeous Canadian man, Andrew, who was there with his children and who was also going through a divorce. Four months later I made the hardest decision of my life and left Essex to move to Nottingham to be with Andrew, leaving my wonderful parents behind.

After I had moved it felt easier to pass my address on to Jean to write to each other directly. It just didn't feel right giving my address out when we lived so close to each other. She was probably only about 25 miles away and to my astonishment when I received her address, she lived around the corner from my great-aunt and uncle. I later found out that there were rumours that Jean's baby had been adopted by my great-aunt's niece, but this was dismissed as it wasn't deemed feasible they would give me to someone so closely connected.

Approximately four years passed with us writing to each other. We didn't communicate that regularly but kept in touch, until the day came when I decided I was ready to actually meet her, and I invited her and her husband, Brian, to come and visit us in Nottingham.

She was thrilled but as the days grew closer my nerves started and I couldn't sleep. It's very hard to explain to someone what it feels like never having seen anyone that you are actually related to. The day arrived and I was a wreck. I'd cried all night with anticipation of what she would be like. I mean, I had seen a couple of photos and I had spoken to her on the telephone, but to actually see her in the flesh was something I couldn't describe. Finally, the moment arrived and she was in just about the same state as me. Andrew had to go outside and help Brian coax her out of the car. As she walked through the door we just grabbed each other and hugged for what seemed an eternity. She was just a slightly older version of me.

After a short while we both wondered what it was we were so scared of. I felt like I'd known her for a long time and since that day we have met a few more times. When she came to visit the next time she brought her daughter, Nina, and her two children and one of her sons, Matthew. We all got on really well and the funny thing was I am the only one who looks like her.

The years rolled on and we would write to each other occasionally, then I received an invitation to her youngest son Brian's wedding. It threw me into turmoil slightly and I phoned her. She said Brian had specifically asked that I be there, but I hadn't met him or the rest of her family and I didn't want to be the centre of attention. I couldn't imagine walking into a room full of her family and friends who had never seen me before, especially as I look so much like her, so my husband and I decided we would go to London and meet the majority of them before the wedding.

On 1 May 2010 my husband and I made our way to London. I didn't have any nerves about meeting them. I had heard so much about Christine, my namesake, and how she had been there for Jean all her life. Every time I looked at her I just wanted to cry. We sat and talked for a while but I had heard enough at the time. She had photographs of her own mother and my great-aunt together; they all knew each other, so the rumours were true. All those years I had been so close to her and yet a million miles away. Christine told me how Jean had been ostracised by everyone. None of her friends were allowed to associate with her, but Christine's father used to take her to visit Jean when she was put in St Christopher's, a home for pregnant teenagers, and then at Lambeth Hospital. She gave me some flowers and a card, which she asked me not to open until I reached home.

I really struggled to open the card and still find it difficult now. Christine just said how lovely it was to finally meet me as the last time she saw me, etc... I can't even type it. However, as the day of the wedding finally arrived I was sicker than I've ever been in my life and my husband had to call and pass on our apologies since there was no way I could travel. I feel dreadfully guilty I didn't go, but maybe it wasn't a good idea, perhaps it would have been too emotional.

I could write a book on this subject, in fact I feel at the moment like I am watching a movie. All my life I grew up knowing the heartache of parents who could not naturally have children and then the pain of trying to adopt a child and I never really gave a thought to the biological mother. Now I have seen and heard the tragic story of a young girl, a child, who had no choice in the matter, who was put into a home and then had her baby taken from her. She then spent the rest of her life wondering what had become of me. She was open with all her family and her children, all of whom knew of me.

Perhaps it would have been best not to have known, but now I do I just want to find out more, no matter how upsetting it is. My thoughts of never wanting to find out when I was younger have certainly changed as I've got older, but I do keep my two lives separate. I talk to my mum more about it than my dad, but it's not something we openly discuss very often. I think it would be too hard on my parents if they realised how much I know. However, I would never say leave well alone to other adopted adults now; everyone's circumstances are different and in my case things worked out fairly well, but you have to be prepared for the unexpected and if you can't take the upset then maybe it's best to leave things as they are.

Nothing to lose

JULIE HOSKINS

....

Julie Hoskins was born on 6 August 1969 in Taunton, Somerset and was fostered at ten days old by her adoptive family. She was adopted at the age of five months in January 1970. Her birth mother was 15 when she fell pregnant and 16 when Julie was born; her birth father was 17. She still lives in Somerset and has been married to a dairy farmer for the last 21 years. She has two teenage girls and works full-time as a school librarian. In 2007, she was traced by her birth mother. Julie is currently writing a book (in her spare time) on this experience.

....

From an early age, I am told around eight, I knew I was adopted. I don't know how much it really meant to me then. I just understood that my mother did not give birth to me. They were my parents, they looked after me, I knew no others, so why should it bother me? I can remember school friends being much more curious than me. I didn't see what I would gain by knowing who my birth parents were. My view at that young age was that they didn't want me, so why look for them?

As I grew up as an only child, I often wondered what it would be like to have brothers and sisters, but realised this was not possible due to my circumstances. I knew my mother had had four miscarriages before deciding that adoption was her only option. Looking back, I really don't know how she coped. At the time my parents had no car, only a motorbike, and had to rely on family to get them to and from hospital. It would have been awful as my mum was one of six children; it would have been so difficult for her seeing her siblings producing children and not being able to have her own. I realised as I got older and found out more about the process involved in adopting a child just how much they must have wanted me. The checks you have to go through were tough then; I am sure they are even more difficult now. I never doubted they were my parents and that they loved me.

I now realise that because of my positive experience of being adopted, I never felt the need to trace my birth family. I had the family I needed: parents, cousins, aunts and uncles, all of whom were very supportive. I've been told key life events often lead to adoptees tracing their birth relatives. I married and had two children and it never crossed my mind. When we decided to have a family my husband and I discussed the possibility of not being able to have our own children. I felt strongly that, if this happened, I did not want to try fertility treatment, we would adopt. I still find it hard to understand why so few people adopt. I guess it is not an easy or quick option. I admire any parents who go through the adoption process.

Even in 1969, when I was adopted, it was highly unusual for babies to go straight to their prospective adoptive parents. This was my birth mother's wish. I know now she never wanted to give me up but, in 1969, being only 16 years old, she had no choice.

I was traced in 2007 by my birth mother. It was a very difficult thing to deal with. I remember when I first received a letter my father said, 'Don't upset her. Without her giving you up we wouldn't have had you all these years.' I had never thought of my adoption like that. As a parent, how could you carry a child for nine months, go through the trauma of giving birth and then give your child away? It has made me realise the sacrifice that lots of young girls and unmarried mothers made in the 1960s and 1970s, when adoption was at its highest levels.

At first I was angry about being contacted, but when I calmed down and thought more about the situation, I realised I had nothing to lose, only a lot to gain. I found out about the circumstances of my birth from my adoption file at County Hall. The saying that there are two sides to every story is right. Finding out that I was really wanted and not given away lightly changed my views about my birth family. I began to think about the true horror of giving away your baby and wondering for years what had become of her.

To start with, I think I was afraid of how I would cope with having another set of relatives. I won't say it has been easy. The thing that has changed me most is the joy I have given to so many people just by meeting them and being me. It's odd that all of these people knew of my existence for years. I had never moved out of the county I was born in, so have lived close to my birth family all my life without knowing it. My parents were told not to tell anyone my original name; I'm guessing I could have been easily traced with this information.

Over the past five years I have forged a firm friendship with my birth mother. Being an only child, I have never felt such a connection with anyone else. There is no mistaking that we are related, I think some people think we are sisters as the age gap is so small. We look alike, dress alike and even act similarly, despite having grown up apart. The main reason the relationship has worked so well is everyone has thought about everyone else's feelings throughout all the meetings. My parents have been great. I think they were less surprised than me when the initial letter arrived; they always knew it would happen. It took 37 years and a change in the law, but Maggie, my birth mother, is so happy with the way things have worked out.

This is an extract from an email from my birth mother:

> Like we keep saying, life is for the living and building memories, if I died tomorrow, I have had all the wishes in life I could ever have imagined. Finding you has been like winning the lottery, and every day is such a better day since I have found you.

Adoption has worked for me, I have great admiration for anyone who has adopted a child in the past or is thinking of adopting in the future. I do look at life differently now – I take each day as it comes and try to make the time to meet up with people I like and love. You never know when they will no longer be with you.

Seventy years ago today, Great Britain declared war on Germany and her allies

GLORIA MCLAREN

Gloria McLaren's birth parents were Canadian of English and Scottish descent. She was born in a maternity home in Clapham, London, in December 1934 during a trip to England. She was fostered by a lady in Battersea for the first six years of her life, during which time she was happily evacuated to the countryside for 18 months. Gloria was then adopted by her foster mother's brother-in-law and his second wife who had just given birth to a son. Gloria did not want to be adopted and was very unhappy despite a few good times. She eventually married and had two wonderful children. After her husband died she went out to work to support them. She found out she was far from stupid and retrained as an art psychotherapist and became an NHS department manager. At last, Gloria was happy and fulfilled. She is now retired and does historical research for her local U3A (University of the Third Age) group.

I was four years old and standing in my cot, listening to Ada shouting up the stairs to Kit in the top flat and Kit shouting back. It all sounded so exciting, I thought it must mean we would be having a party.

Ada was the nanny hired to look after me. She and I lived downstairs and her brother-in-law, Joe, and his second wife, Kit, lived in the upstairs flat. It was Kit's birthday. She was 34, two years away from having her only child, a boy, and two years away from adopting me.

Who am I? There are three of me by nationality and three by upbringing. Nature or nurture, which am I? I am English, Scottish and Canadian; born in Clapham, London, to Canadian parents of Scottish extraction. I have red hair, green eyes and a flaming temper. My name is Gloria and I am unique.

My parents came to England with "Uncle Bill" who owned businesses in Canada and England. I do not know why I did not live with them after I was born. For the first four years I lived with Ada. During this time "Uncle Bill" and my parents scarpered back to Canada and safety. My father and "Uncle Bill" visited me but I do not recall ever seeing my mother. "Uncle Bill" arranged a passage to Canada for me and a place to live out there but the British government would not let me go; all children's passages abroad were stopped after the sinking of the *SS City of Benares* in 1940.[2]

So I stayed with Ada who now received no remuneration as money and food could not get through to England from Canada, but she kept me. We had a very hard time. Kit and Joe did what they could to help, but I got two very serious illnesses.

Then, when I was five years old the government decided to evacuate my school en masse to Devonshire. I arrived in a small, beautiful village to spend the next 18 months with a lovely family. This was my first experience of real family life and I was so happy. It was wonderful. I loved my new family and the little thatched cottage in which we lived. Try to imagine my rage, my disappointment and terror when, one evening, I was told I had been adopted by Kit and Joe and would be collected by Kit the next day and taken to live with them in a London suburb. Kit had written in a letter that she now had a little baby boy and I could play with him "like a dolly".

Unfortunately, I knew babies were nothing like dollies. They were squally, noisy, smelly things that didn't know how to play. Also, I had never really liked or trusted Kit. I don't know why since she had taken me out, fed me and helped me to get over an illness. Anyway, my feelings were proven correct. Plus, I did not like the faceless suburb I was to be relocated to.

We didn't get off to a good start. During my absence something had gone wrong with Kit and Joe's relationship and they were now sleeping apart. Joe was on war work, so often worked long hours while I was left alone with Kit and the baby.

A health visitor came to check on me but I hid my face so she could not see the tears. I was frightened that if she did, I would be beaten and sent to a "home" once she left. She never pushed to find out why I hid my face and didn't speak. I don't know why Kit had become so violent; I don't remember her being so before. Did she have post-natal depression? Or was it a combination of war stress, her cataracts that she refused to have operated on and becoming pregnant while adopting me? Perhaps it was all just too much for her, and she seemed to get little support from her husband. He was a gentle man who could be highly irascible at times. He lived in the kitchen and Kit and the baby and I lived in the dining room. The front room was neutral ground for when we had visitors.

---

[2] The ship was carrying evacuees from Liverpool to Canada when it was torpedoed by the Germans on 14 September 1940. Of the 260 passengers who perished, 77 were children.

School, along with church, was a place of refuge for a while, but six was an awkward age to change schools. My education was in advance of that at the local infants' school so I spent two years in the bottom class of the junior school. That got a bit boring after a time, but I loved school and my teachers. My artistic skill seemed to please Kit. When I was caught stealing someone else's paints, she didn't punish me but gave me money to buy my own. I was amazed and grateful. I still use that box which is one of my few treasures. However, I was not allowed to ask questions and got into a great deal of trouble after one of her friends laughingly commented what a strange, serious child I was with the odd questions I asked. Kit told me I was stupid and shouldn't talk to adults because it embarrassed her if they laughed at me. So I learned that I was stupid and not to ask questions. Oddly enough, I was top of the class in all school lessons. Since I couldn't ask questions, I learned to rely on books and developed a love of reading. When it came to the 11+ exam, although I passed the mocks with flying colours, for the real thing, sat at the posh grammar school with its posh pupils, I couldn't even remember my name. I panicked. How could a stupid idiot like me go to a posh school like that? So I must not pass the exam.

The adoption took away my self-esteem and with it a certain amount of my self-confidence, although if I didn't stop to think about whether or not I could do something, I would dive in and do it. Looking back at pre-adoption days, I believe I probably had a lot of confidence and self-esteem, and I trusted people. The adoption destroyed my trust and I have never really regained it. How can you trust when your whole life as you know it is suddenly taken away without any warning or prior discussion?

Also, the first two "upbringings" had treated me as a person in my own right. Now I was a skivvy and a babysitter. Teaching me I was an idiot really screwed me up because I was the opposite: I had the highest IQ in the school and the headmistress wanted me to go to university. I couldn't understand how a woman in her position could be so unintelligent as to think an idiot like me could do that. Yet I don't think I would have survived university life for long. I would have had the same type of breakdown that I eventually suffered at art school. Difficult as I found life at home, it seems I could not survive away from it. The twist between what I could apparently do and what I thought I could do meant that I threw away many chances in life on account of not wanting others to find out what an idiot I really was. I also shied away from intelligent, good-looking men.

Being made to wear clothes from the second-hand shop, when my adoptive brother had new ones, didn't help much either. Later I discovered I had a talent for designing and making my own clothes. Unfortunately, I didn't realise for many years that these clothes became a shield behind which I could hide my idiocy and boring lack of conversation. The shield became a defence through which others could not reach. This affected my ability to make friends. Although I have done much work on these effects, deep down they are still there. This has often led to me hurting people who have cared for me; I can't believe they really care, so eventually I do or say something to upset them and I walk away, not understanding what I have done.

My adoptive relatives always forgot my first name. This made me think they forgot me. I didn't count. I was only the adopted one. I still feel upset when someone forgets my name. It's getting better now as most of my acquaintances are elderly and forgetful like me, but I take great care to try to remember people's names for fear of hurting someone. Joe had ensured that my birth name was hyphenated with theirs. This created a double-barrelled name which was too much for most adults to say, so my name was dropped, but I signed all my paintings with it and I have now reclaimed it via deed poll.

I have always found it very curious that I was allowed to have an education while my brother was not. I passed art exams and was allowed to travel to the next town to college. I didn't do well there – the strain of keeping up with the intelligent, well-dressed students eventually proved too much – and the breakdown meant I had to have time out. I don't know what Kit and Joe thought about that.

I feel adoption needs a lot of thought on the part of adoptive parents and agencies. You cannot expect to transplant a child from one existence to another, often completely different environments. Any gardener knows that a plant would not survive such cavalier treatment. I went from being rather spoiled and petted, taught to think of myself as something very special, to a nobody-come-dog's-body and maid of all work. Naturally I was rather resentful of this. No doubt, if both Kit and I had had someone to talk to about how we felt, how things were progressing, the resentment and misunderstandings could have been avoided. I hope the situation is different today. I suppose during the war years the adoption of a child was of little concern compared to the greater concerns of war. Perhaps at that time everyone was doing what they believed was for the best and sometimes we cannot expect more.

Adoption has left me with two great problems that I have never completely resolved. One is a lack of understanding of loving and being loved. I think this must be something you learn from parents, but for the adopted child the obvious reason for feeling unloved is a belief that they are unlovable, which is why they have been adopted. This affects all relationships including the relationship with one's own children. The other issue is one of belonging. Belonging is mostly taken for granted but when you are not sure you belong in a family group you never feel quite sure that you belong in any group. This also has a deleterious effect on all relationships. Where do you belong? To whom do you belong? In my case, what ethnic group do I belong to? I have become aware of how this has affected me and my relationships and, in some measure, I have dealt with it.

I was widowed at a fairly early age, with two children to support. Luckily, I got work in the therapy department of a local mental health hospital and was able to train as a therapist myself. Without my adoption experience and my art therapy training, I would not have had the knowledge to be able to help abused young children to come to terms with all they have been through, and to work with adult survivors of childhood sexual abuse. My training and my work was a very great help to me and, through me, to others whom I was able to help.

Finding Joy

JOY CARTER

Joy Carter is an established stand-up comedian, writer and presenter. Hers has been a remarkable journey. She and her twin sister, who sadly died, were born into the Biafra war in Nigeria. Joy was miraculously found alive and later adopted by white missionaries. In the UK she then battled racism, bullying and identity issues to become a performer. Now a confident woman, she uses her unique comedy, writing and her amazing story to encourage people around the world. She regularly appears on TV and radio and gives inspirational talks. Joy will soon publish her first book, *Priceless*, which explores the journey of identity relating to fashion and culture, plus a collection of poems written over her lifetime. Joy Carter is a woman on a mission of the heart.

I was born into the Biafra war in Nigeria, some time in January (my date of birth is a little vague) along with my twin sister. At the time of my birth, a Save the Children Fund nurse was driving along in the bush and an old lady ran into the road and waved at the nurse to stop. The nurse pulled up her jeep and followed the old lady down into the dense bush. Then, suddenly, she disappeared. Where she had been stood the nurse found twin baby girls, one dead and one alive, so she picked me up and took me to the local hospital.

Two years prior to my birth two young white British people met in Lagos (after working there as missionaries and professionals for some years), fell in love and decided to marry. My adoptive mother to be had already given birth to a son. As the war raged worse and worse the couple decided to do something to help. They went to the local hospital where they were asked to look after a baby because the hospital couldn't cope with the 50 other babies the war had injured. So, the nurse handed them me. A few weeks later the couple decided to adopt me. Two years later no one had come forward to claim me and on the advice of the Foreign Office all British people were recommended to leave and return to England. My mother had given birth to a second child so I had two white brothers. I am of African heritage but as I came with no documentation, next of kin or any information, that's all I know – my parents' story and the story from Enid Johnson who arranged my adoption in Nigeria.

This was the beginning of my story. Little did anyone realise what lay ahead. Overcoming the trauma of adoption has given me a valuable insight into understanding the inner healing process and a unique chance to help others who are suffering with "unseen scars". I found that adoption left me with emotional and psychological scarring from the beginning. My parents tell me that when my brothers and I were learning to speak I chose not to; in fact, by the age of five they were concerned I wouldn't speak at all. My parents would constantly tell me that they loved me but deep down I always felt I was not good enough and second rate compared to their "natural" children. I would always be testing their patience as I wanted them to confirm the lie in my head that said, 'They don't want you any more.'

I approached the complexities thrown up by my adoption like my parents and school advised: I ignored them – with terrible consequences. Little was known about adoption then and schools and parents were left with no resources or understanding. On the outside I was an extrovert, living a life of extremes and excess, eager to please, funny even if upset and immaculately dressed. No one would ever suspect that inside I was secretly destroying my life fibre, piece by piece. I coped until I hit a situation that would trigger me to instantly fall apart, and the outward shell would break up to reveal the inner Joy as the poor, broken-hearted, hurting, malnourished and self-harming person I really was. My friends marvelled at my glittering performance of "perfection" but secretly I longed to be the normal whole and happy girl next door. Everyone taught a "turn the other cheek" mindset when dealing with bullies. This reinforced my belief in my non-existence and emotional bankruptcy. At school I chose to wear my favourite clothes on days when I knew a confrontation with the bullies would happen, believing, 'If I am going to get a beating I may as well look fabulous!' It worked but I had no way of dealing with the growing hurt inside. Little did I realise the hurt was a volcano of congealed agony waiting to explode in a massive disaster that would bring me to the brink of death. The volcano was triggered by the sudden death of my elder brother, my "perfect blue-eyed boy", who was everything to me. The ages of 17 to 24 saw me live life without hope in sheer self-destruction, followed by 12 long years to heal.

I believe my behaviour was the result of being adopted in my formative years and not being able to get any professional help to understand my past and present problems. Consequently, I have found self-belief a real issue. I was always looking for things to justify my identity. I would cling to people, father figures, jobs, fashion, anything to give me some idea of who I was. In many ways I was like a chameleon; I made myself fit into anything but really I fitted nothing. The problem with "false identities" is they never worked very long so I would flit around doing this and that, never really belonging or dealing with the root problem. Today, I have learned that these outward things do little to define who I am, and can hinder more than help. Over time I have been able to build inner confidence by surrounding myself with "good" people and learning from them has really helped. The dodgy false friends would just take from me, often establishing my wrong self beliefs. Picking up good healthy life habits is invaluable. Slowly this challenged my destructive ways and I saw changes before my eyes. Finally I made my peace with God and as I joined a loving church, things started to change for the better.

I believe certain life events have patterns. My life tube map reads: first life, stop, abandonment; then all change; new stop, adoption; next stop, bullying; stop, self-harm; stop, eating disorder (anorexia); stop, abusive relationships. All change, stop! Counselling, stop, healing; then lots of going round like on the Circle line; then all change to stop, hope, stop, joy and inner peace; and now finally all change on the line of fruitfulness, purpose and inner wealth. I believe until you make a change within, you can't change without. I had to destroy the victim mentality and change lines. I had spent years cutting off the fruits of self-destructive behaviour, vowing to change for a few months then bingeing when under pressure; now it was time to dig up the root and learn to plant and cultivate good things in my life.

Having a difficult childhood was soul-destroying but learning as an adult to forgive people and myself for all the hardships and mistakes has slowly set me free. The advantages of not suffering peer pressure as a teenager enabled me to develop and advance educationally and individually, but at the expense of under-developing interaction with other children. I have struggled to develop lasting and meaningful relationships to this day. I would trust anyone. Failing to recognise a wolf in sheep's clothing took me years to spot, especially when it came to guys. Men would see my weak broken areas and prey on me until they got what they wanted.

I have lived my life in show business (as a dancer/model in my 20s) which is perfectly suited to dysfunctional people – developing a "persona" instead of being oneself, a lack of boundaries, crazy extreme behaviour, constant cravings for love and the drive for success were seen as normal and sometimes celebrated. I worked silly hours and went to parties all night religiously, till I eventually burned out and became sick.

Think carefully about whom you share your precious adoption story with. I still cry when I tell people because I am talking about a lovely little girl who suffered terrible things and I wish I could tell her what I know now. In my 20s I would share personal things with people who were nosy or ill-equipped to deal with it, resulting in bad advice or flippant and damaging comments.

Sympathy and empathy are words at different polarities of experience; people can sympathise but have no idea what you are talking about, and yet others can empathise with you as they have lived similar experiences. Recently, I was talking to a guy in a bar who made cruel jokes when I told him about my adoption, as he attempted to get me drunk, but unlike the old me I put him straight and walked away boldly sober! In the past I would have struggled to do this, I would have said nothing and gone home in tears.

I am who I am because I don't fit the "mould" and if people reject me, who cares? Some critics love me, some don't. Overcoming my adoption hurdles has given me strength of character for my career. Stand-up comedy is tough but I have a huge resource of life experiences to talk about and a great understanding of people. Taking all the negatives and turning them into positives is exciting. Now I am healed, give talks, write books and am teaching a seminar on the power of comedy to heal, something I have first-hand experience of! Without it I would be another jobbing comic like everyone else. I wear clothes not many would wear because I love to express who I am. Not conforming has a glorious freedom all of its own. Would I want an easy life? Never! Challenges build character. I still take chances and live free and unafraid.

I view adopted people as being like rare priceless jewels. We are each formed like a tiny piece of unwanted carbon which, as we overcome extreme problems and pressures, will one day turn into a diamond – strong, wise, unique, beautiful and supremely priceless. Then, with more years of cutting and polishing, one day we emerge able to shine into the darkness of many others. As a child I couldn't even mention the word adoption as it held connotations of despair. Now it is the most precious thing I have in my heart. Every nuance of my life, albeit good or bad, is like a facet for light to reflect through, from tears and tragedy to strengths and success. I judge my life by where I have come from and where my heart is today. I have obtained inner wealth and a peaceful equilibrium that some people, despite their outward riches, never obtain, as true wealth has nothing to do with fast cars, a perfect body and millions of pounds.

So what now for me? I embrace the "new me". Learning how to live fully without the dross is weird but wonderful. Freed from the sting of my past I am still bubbly and outgoing but I am now also private and quiet of heart. You could say I've evolved. My past trials have made me the success I am today, like gaining a PhD in life. It is one thing to read books and talk about overcoming and another thing to overcome yourself, gaining the rare pearls of wisdom, compassion and revelation. Now I can hug my friends, cherish my parents, walk with a smile, have a sense of purpose in life and enjoy living. I have a better understanding of how to handle difficult problems and situations. Adoption has given me so much.

I don't have a complex life plan or goals but what I do have is the desire to fully live every moment and be a blessing to others. I consider myself fortunate to be alive. Some things I do maybe non-adopted people will never do: I will always marvel at children who look like their parents; I will always be eternally grateful to my parents who gave me a chance to live and were patient though all my troubles. I will always celebrate my birthday for a week just in case my birthday date is wrong. (Plus, I get more presents that way!) I may always suffer a little from rejection. I may never be able to afford a pair of Jimmy Choos! So my advice is, don't allow people to rush your healing or life journey. It is yours and you are moving forward at your own pace. I still have my days of tears and maybe always will, but like the rain they soon stop.

Many people rush selfishly through life, never having to ask any questions about their existence or face extreme hardships, while through adoption many have had to seek and define their identity like finding buried treasure. I have no genealogy to lug into my future. I have an open road to define as I please and the recognition of the gifts and value of life that is my legacy. I don't understand my journey. I accept it and look back at the narrow path which has brought me to a good place today. I can say, 'It's not how you start, it's how you finish,' and I am far from finished.

I would like to thank all those who have always loved and believed in me, especially my beautiful parents.

Living with uncertainty

SHANEL CUTHBERT

Shanel Cuthbert was born in London in the late 1970s and joined her white British adoptive family around the age of 18 months. Her biological parents are both Persian and, as an adult, Shanel travelled to Iran for the first time to meet her birth mother and various relatives. Since then she has made more than five separate trips to spend time in Iran and explore the culture. Shanel remains in contact with her adoptive mother and family although her father passed away when she was 11 years old. After growing up in Rochester, Kent, Shanel moved to London and still lives there when not travelling. She is currently studying for a Science Honours degree and working on her first book.

*T*here are no rules.

Born in London of Iranian descent, I was placed in a children's home as a baby and then fostered at 18 months. I was adopted by an English family at seven years old. As an adult, I was contacted and reunited with my biological mother who I visited and met in Tehran. I have stayed in contact with her.

When asked to reflect upon adoption in my life, I ask myself, 'How do I make sense of the question?' My clearest answer is 'uncertainty'. Uncertainty is the best word to describe my experience. Being an adoptee is a label with no certainty attached. It's like having a container but not knowing what to do with it. Was it lent, borrowed or does anyone know if you give it back? You're left hanging. Everything is blurry. There is no start and no ending.

I don't think we can point a finger and say "this" was caused or initiated because of x, y or z – not in the emotional spheres. Life does not operate like that; it is too complex an emotional web.

Yet on another level, reading the biographies and stories of other adoptees I feel a sense of familiarity and not so alone. I began to realise and understand that I am not as strange or mixed up as I initially believed, and perhaps there are common reasons for some of the peculiar ways in which I have behaved.

Maybe there are others who understand or associate with my inner confusion. The reasons why I feel incomplete… I cannot even describe what this feels like. Nothing makes sense on a very profound level.

I believe the experience of being adopted can be compared to a colourful palette of emotional drives and intensities extending beyond the normal spectrum. I believe an adoptees' spectrum is slightly different to others.

The levels of emotional intensity and struggles I experience are extreme and powerful compared to those felt by most people. Sure, we all feel the pang of rejection, but why does it swamp me? Why does rejection consume me to the point where my behaviour becomes disturbed or out of control and out of character?

There is something very profound about being an adoptee.

It goes beyond reason to a very primal aspect of oneself. An unstable place where a glitch was triggered in the system yet nobody can find the switch; where a circuit was rewired, changing the system for ever. The numerous battles with myself are the strongest indication of this glitch. It is the external flagging up that something isn't quite right, a case of "we called an engineer but the damage seems to be permanent" type scenario.

Throughout my life I have been drawn to a string of addictive behaviours involving food, drugs, work, co-dependency and anything that provided me with a cushion of avoidance, a way to escape this internal turmoil. Addiction has been my lifelong companion supporting me but breaking me at every step. Does this relate to being adopted? I cannot say for certain. In retrospect, I can say a potential cause of difficulty has been a deep lack of self-worth, one I still don't fully understand. Years of therapy, self-examination and minor glimpses into the void of despair and shame that I seem to carry prompt me to believe this. Ironically, on another level, I feel great.

A personal difficulty for me has been the loneliness of the journey. I am lonely when watching others successfully move on with their lives and jobs, forming relationships and general well-being, and frustrated at my own inability to manage my life, which has been a string of continual self-destructive and punishing actions towards myself. It can be lonely when you don't understand why you are doing the things you find yourself doing. It can be frustrating when you thwart every effort to move on. The toll it can have on your life is weighty.

I have this label "adoption", but I am not sure of its implications. I find myself facing many challenges internally, externally or quite often one leading to another, but I am unsure whether adoption is the root cause.

For years, I went round in circles unconsciously trying to understand what was happening.

On reflection, I look back and understand that I was trying to reconnect to myself. A part of me was submerged yet trying to communicate but using destructive methods and patterns of addiction. Addiction is a way of feeling, an attempt at reconnecting, recapturing or reigniting the lost parts of self that have been buried through the process of trauma.

It is only now I begin to understand what was going on. At the time, I seemed unable to grasp or understand the inner turmoil. Upon reflection, I believe I wanted someone or something external to help by providing some new guidelines.

I believe receiving external recognition of what I have gone through is fundamental to the breaking of patterns and the healing of the self.

So often in my own recovery I have felt huge relief at hearing someone address the issues I have wanted to hear. On an unconscious level, I have wanted someone to apologise and recognise what I was going through. I was desperately trying to locate this within me but couldn't because inside I was fighting with myself.

Self-love can be hard to ignite or maintain when the core inner belief is personal shame and responsibility for what has gone on in our childhoods. Self-punishment becomes a mode of behaviour and the punishing and intensity increase. It can be released when another person gives permission for the cycle to stop, through therapeutic counselling, spiritual progression, insight, or some other means.

Having someone tell me I wasn't to blame or wasn't responsible for my past has had powerful repercussions in my life. Although, on a rational, conscious level, I don't believe I am to blame, there seems to be an inner lock this logic escapes. Even as I write this I recognise the power of forgiveness. Forgiveness seems to unlock a part of our self that needs to forgive the other, normally the part that is hurting.

Children often lack the communication skills to express this inner frustration or turmoil, yet like adults would greatly benefit from hearing words of forgiveness spoken to them. We may not always consciously understand why we are told something but the human psyche operates on many levels, including the non-verbal/reasoning layers, and it is these layers within our psyche that sometimes need to hear such words.

I would never change anything.

In summary, my life as an adoptee has been filled with bumps and bruises and all kinds of self-inflicted injuries.

Learning to take care of myself is a challenge. I am learning how to do this each day. What seems so natural and easy to others has been a constant struggle for me. It seems more natural to want to hurt myself than it does to take care of myself. Even acknowledging this makes me feel slightly awkward.

I could never have grown as a person without the many challenges I have faced. The knowledge and understanding I have developed about life and the self are amazing. People sometimes refer to adoptees as "special" because they were "chosen". I like to think of adoptees as "special" because of the understanding and remarkable insights they have access to. These insights give adopted people a freedom worth more weight in gold than any treasure. There is something remarkable about being an adoptee, something so pure and beautiful that makes us some of the richest people alive.

Sometimes the most devastating experiences can be the most freeing and enlightening, allowing us to be the greatest people, achieve and surmount the highest of obstacles if we allow ourselves to. There is a common thread that runs through the biographies I have read. There is a light, a freedom and understanding that comes from every struggle and the authors all speak of this remarkable truth. This has given me the will to live through every hurdle and to challenge every obstacle. If the path of life I have followed is because I am adopted, I am honoured. Today, I am so happy to have been and to be the person I am.

Wife to husband

JACKIE RIVETT

Jackie Rivett was born in 1957 in Alton, Hampshire. She was adopted at the age of six months through the Catholic Children's Society. It was a successful adoption and worked out well for her. In her later years, Jackie traced her birth family; her birth father had sadly passed away but she has met his other daughter who lives in Arizona and they are in constant contact. Jackie met her birth mother once back in the 1980s. She was born in Ireland but after giving birth to Jackie in England relocated to the US, so all Jackie's family links are in the United States. Jackie's birth mother did what she thought was right for her daughter and Jackie admires her bravery in making a decision that broke her heart, and her tenacity to overcome this and move on with her life. Sadly she died on 9/11.

Do you love me?
Yes.
Why do you love me?
Because you are you.
But I don't know who I am.
I love you anyway.
That isn't enough.
What would be enough?
I don't know but much more, the sky, the universe and everything.
I love you more than all that.
Why?

I want to be loved but I don't know how to accept love, or why anyone could possibly love me. I don't want to be disliked or hated and have worked hard all my life for acceptance from everyone. I want to know how it feels to belong but even though I have traced my birth parents I still do not feel I belong. I don't belong to my adoptive family and I don't belong to my birth family, so here I sit, confused and disappointed. How do you know when you belong, I mean really belong somewhere? As a child I accepted things were as they were and, although I was bullied, it was water off a duck's back. As an adult I carry this burden, this feeling of being a second-hand child and, therefore, unworthy of anything good in my life. Today isn't a good day and tomorrow I will feel better about myself.

Outside looking in

BETH ARCHER

Beth Archer was born in London in the 1980s. Irish by ethnicity, she joined her English adoptive family when she was about six weeks old. She made contact with her birth parents in her early 20s.

Isolation. Freedom. Death. Anxiety. Meaninglessness. These core existential concerns seem intrinsically linked to my personal experiences of adoption reunion. It is said that the initial writing of most authors is to some degree autobiographical. We are compelled to make sense of our own experience; to leave a mark on the world. But the thought of recording my story on this page terrifies me. Will I offend my parents who rescued me from isolation and kept me alive by adopting me as a baby? Will I be rejected for a second time by my birth parents if I throw light on that painful time? And what of my wider family and place in their tribe? Where do I fit in and to whom do I belong? Daring to talk about my truth has always carried a heavy penalty. It means risking rocking the boat and disrupting the status quo, but it also brings potential meaning out of emptiness; finding my freedom.

I believe I was always aware of being adopted. My memories are interwoven with fantasy but the story of "being told" centres around Christmas time when I was a young child staying at my grandparents' home. The house was very large with high ceilings, creaky floorboards and rattling sash windows. It had an eerie, magical feel which bewitched me as a child. Time seemed to stand still there, like being wrapped in a warm comfort blanket far away from the cold reality of life. I recall sitting on the bed in the room I shared with my parents. As part of an extensive family, I knew what pregnant women looked like and I knew who the babies belonged to when they emerged. Then I was told that I had come from a different woman. A stranger. Somebody outside of our tribe. My father told me I was special, a gift from God, I had been chosen from the Lord's top drawer. The unspoken bond between my father and I, the warmth and unbounded connection I feel towards him, make the reality of the reunion with my birth parents and my desire for something "other" feel like the ultimate betrayal.

Even as I write this I am engulfed by a profound sense of guilt and shame. But haunted by an enduring feeling of separation and incompleteness – imagined or not – I am left with an unresolved tension between my own self-identity and what constitutes my kinship network. When I observe my family from the outside peering in, this mysterious fraternity connected by genes and traditions, shared values and history, I become painfully aware of my own separation and regret at ever having been born. I am invisible to all, and yet I have become an inherent part of the furniture. I try to be as they want me to be but I do not know what that is. I am divided, broken, scattered, confused.

In adult life, the issue I struggle with most of all is my inadequacy in the presence of others. Clinging to the despairing prospect that I may face rejection and be cast out, alone again, I try desperately to build a secure place for myself. I may behave magnanimously and then use my good will as a golden ticket to gain acceptance from the clan. I have a perpetual need to prove my worth and earn my seat measured by others' validation of me. I don't expect to be adored but can't bear the torment of being ignored. This ever-present struggle goes on underneath the surface of my smiley, submissive façade and only I am aware of it.

The first story which ever interested me as a young child was the tale of the *Ugly Duckling*. I have been told I would recite the words and then pretend to read them from a book to the neighbours before I even learned to walk. During periods of vulnerability, seeing myself as the outsider has aroused uncontrollable envy of those on the inside. The "included" ones seem to possess a quality of wholeness and integration which is alien to me, and these destructive forces of envy have brought perilous emotional entanglements that create further gaps between myself and others. In my isolation and frustration, I have tried knocking on the doors of my loved ones in an effort to re-open the channels of communication, and then lash out bitterly when they remain shut.

The truth is that I dearly love the family who raised me. They *are* my family. I traced my Irish birth parents and extended blood relatives in my early 20s and was astounded by the similarities between us, but the common history, the shared joy and pain and the experiences which bond people together were missing. Admittedly I had carried unconscious expectations, cultivated over many years of fantasising, that my birth parents might live in a castle surrounded by acres of land. They would welcome me into their perfect family with tears streaming down their beautiful faces and I would instantly feel complete. The few meetings I have had with my birth parents have been frantically spontaneous, full of mystery, elation, disappointment and desire. As though trying to compensate for a lifetime of separation in only a few afternoons, it has been difficult to accept them as real, fallible, separate human beings, now that they exist in a tangible rather than imaginary form.

A dream of salvation, which I had perhaps long repressed, no longer held weight. The realisation that nobody else was carrying a magic wand which could wave away my insecurities disturbed me. Not knowing who my birth parents were allowed me to invent lives for them. On a good day, they were the king and queen of the castle. On a bad day, they were street junkies or dead. For so long I had been living a secret life inside my head, idealising the lives of others, dreaming about a world in which I felt connected, free and at peace, that when meeting my birth parents did not cure my fear of exclusion, I also had to honestly question my fear of belonging.

Culture tells us that belonging to something greater than ourselves gives our lives meaning and purpose, it is the very foundation upon which our whole way of relating to the world evolves. When a baby, joined to its mother physically, mentally and spiritually, comes into the world the parents act as guides and vital carers, without whom the baby would usually not survive. If they are uprooted and transported to a new set of caregivers – a mother who has not carried the baby in her womb for nine months, others who are not inherently attuned to the baby's needs or nature – the experience is bound to be traumatic. Babies look for mirroring from their primary carers in an instinctive attempt to feel acknowledged and secure. If early trauma goes by unresolved, issues around trust and attachment may persist throughout the lifespan. This is what Nancy Verrier calls the "primal wound".

The life I live today, 27 years after my birth and four years after meeting my birth parents, is very different from the path I had vaguely planned in my younger years. Delusions of grandeur and visions of a fairytale life that could have been were killed when reality confounded them. Likewise, the despair I felt growing up that my life was a horrible mistake has dissipated. I have become more open and more fully present, and this has afforded me a freedom I could never have anticipated. My habitual tendencies to beat myself up, defensively withdraw from others or obsessively search for reasons not to trust them, can erupt in darker moments. I aim to bounce back into shape like elastic by turning my attentions to more universal concerns. Connecting with nature, other people and animals helps my perspective shift. I see life as a creative rather than destructive process, but I do recognise the energy we do not invest in creating may be wasted in destroying. Comparing myself to others and searching outside of myself to gain a semblance of affirmation and validity never seems to fill the void. Parts of me may feel naturally drawn towards people who confirm my negative self-concept and share my fears that the world is a threatening, unsafe place, and the danger is that my fragile sense of self can become enmeshed with them.

Ultimately, I think we all carry a sense of deprivation, even if it is deeply buried, and we all shut off or deny more vulnerable, painful parts of ourselves in order to sustain our mental health. In my case, I am yet to find a quick fix to my long-held insecurities. All relationships present potential risks for repeating familiar destructive patterns and all bring different challenges to the fore, but with every obstacle opportunities arise, even if they are difficult to distinguish. After many years of doubt and confusion, I am gradually assimilating my personal experiences into my work and life path.

Release

BETH ARCHER *

Anxious and confused I lie on the bed,
two blankets covering my legs,
the heat is becoming uncomfortable
but I do not remove them, I do not free myself.
I am used to discomfort.

I zone out to the sound of the children playing in the room next door,
the roar of traffic in the background.
Crystal Palace played earlier, I recall, but the sirens have stopped now.
The sound of a helicopter echoes through the night sky.
I am at home in Gypsy Hill, lest I forget.

But I am not supposed to be here.
I missed my flight out of London this morning on purpose.
I let it go, along with the relationship with my birth parents who are still
consumed with extreme feelings for each other after all these years;
a game I am too tired of playing with them.

I unwittingly offered myself up as a pawn when I journeyed to meet him
four years ago; that was the first time I realised the life I knew had ended,
and a disturbingly new and unrecognisable me would emerge.
I was 23 but in many ways I was merely an infant.
Flying home prematurely, feeling utterly alone in my skin,
and on the run from a man who terrified me.

That man was my natural father.
He had a kind heart but a terrorising mind.
I saw parts of myself in the schizophrenic fractions of his mania,
like glancing in the mirror and facing the devil's reflection,
he was my real-life Bob from *Twin Peaks*,
my alter ego, my darkness and my inner demon.

From the moment we met I felt I knew him like I knew my own shadow.
The amalgamation of our dark sides, both compelling and repelling at once.

I followed him into coffee shops where he introduced me as his daughter.
I trailed along to the pub where he sat drinking *Guinness*,
and sat beside him in church during Sunday mass.

I listened to his music, read his literature, lived under his instruction.
Witnessing his life from the inside of his self-created prism,
I saw how my life could have been and the person I may become
if I abandoned myself in the way he had neglected himself,
withering away in his squalid bed-sit.

When I received his telephone call a few days ago I knew that
something was wrong. He had changed his mind about my visit.
He said I had turned the world against him. His prism holding him hostage,
and his mind telling him I was to blame.

In a mysterious way his paranoia has set me free.
Like the perpetrator who allows his obsessive jealousy to drive away
the object he feels he cannot live without,
I have been released from the chains of his suspicion,
to let go of an unalterable past. Armed with knowledge of my heritage
I have been liberated to take possession of my destiny
and to face my demons alone.

Your secret

CATH STAINCLIFFE

Cath Staincliffe was born in 1956 of Irish parentage and adopted at seven weeks. In 1997 she was "reunited" with her birth mother and seven full siblings (her birth parents had gone on to marry) and they have formed close relationships. RTE television made a documentary about her adoption and reunion. Cath is an award-winning crime writer, creator of ITV's *Blue Murder* and author of the *Scott & Bailey* novels based on the popular ITV show. She has also published a novel, *Trio*, which follows the lives of three babies born in 1960 and those of their birth and adoptive families. The following poem was previously published in *She Says* (Crocus Books, 1988). Cath lives in Manchester with her partner and family.

People back home never knew it had happened
A year that's all, nothing unusual
No one will tell, nobody knows.
Nine full months you laboured, bore me
Six brief weeks you nursed me, named me
Clothed me, cuddled me, topped and tailed me
Watched me squall and sleep and frown
Saw my black eyes turn to blue
Caught my first wide windy smile
Noticed what I'd got from you
Sang me songs, rocked me rocked me
Whispered long sweet sad farewells
Let me go, left me, lost me
Kept a photo tucked away.
Now I wonder should I seek you
Knowing that you can't find me
May the secret now be spoken
Is it best to leave it be?
Surely you'll remember, wonder
Each year on that autumn day
How my way goes, what my life is
How I've turned out, as they say
And I would love to know for certain
Where you are and how you go
And most of all I want a picture
For there's a face I want to know.

Cast on

ANWEN LEWIS

Anwen Lewis grew up on the south coast of England after being adopted at birth into a family with five other siblings – all boys. Originally born in London to an English mother and Jamaican father, Anwen's aspirations as a child were well met as a transracial adoptee, other than the desire for a sister. Her cultural experience began to be broadened in the early 1990s on arrival in Manchester to study composition and she still lives there, now with a family of three children of her own. Anwen began writing poetry in 2005 and used this medium to help navigate the rollercoaster of reunion with her birth family in 2007. Her poetry collection, *How To Weave Time* (Crocus Books, 2011), documents this period in her adoption journey.

20th June, 12pm
it's *just* happened

cast on my black doormat
embroidered in unfamiliar hand
a windowless white envelope ticks
amongst the bank statements
supermarket vouchers and quarterly
subscription to the musicians union

through the tour bus tiredness of the
motorway night drive
unletterheaded type swims into focus
spinning unexpected sentences
cruelly brief to be so life changing

was I born in…
during the early part of…
no urgency in reply…
use the SAE provided…

tears slip and splash on the
welcome mat
the details re-submerge
in disbelief
I was, so I did

reply by return
prick the portly red postbox
dither, drop in the stitch
then twist on my heel in retreat

it looped back by phone call from the agency
a birth parent has been making enquiries
the matronly well-meant contralto
rises excitedly with every phrase:

your mother's been registered
to make contact with you,
for over ten years, and you've siblings too –
oh, and it's your dad who
was the one who was black
he's still about and wants in on the act!

STOP
I cease her jubilant babbling
I stand immobile, slip and splash

I can't hear any more
from a stranger who knows
more about me than I do.

I fix a trip, so they can
tell me face to face
where mine came from

Jennifer's story

JENNIFER JONES

Jennifer Anne Jones was born in 1949 in Barrow in Furness, Lancashire (now Cumbria). Her birth parents were Jean and Ronald Robinson, and her adoptive parents Peter and Elizabeth Ena Jones of Llanfairfechan, Caernarvonshire (now Gwynedd) in North Wales. She has searched for her birth family and met her birth mother and four siblings. She also discovered that her birth father had committed suicide and she has a dead sibling. Jenny keeps in touch with her "new" family, including many nephews and nieces through visits, phone calls and Facebook. She now lives in Bristol with her husband.

Where shall we begin? With a room in London, somewhere in Bloomsbury. The year is 1949, the month July. I imagine the décor being functional, wartime, maybe the walls are cream, the chairs wooden. My prospective parents are waiting nervously. They have travelled up from Wales by train, probably from Bangor, or Llandudno Junction. They have with them an empty carrycot, and a shopping bag full with baby paraphernalia – a shawl, bottles with formula, gripe water, nappies, maybe even a soft toy, although at six weeks I would have been much too young for that. If they didn't bring it, they would have thought about it. Maybe they stayed in London overnight since they were well off at that time. Maybe the Strand Palace. I think I remember that being part of the story.

We must remember this is a story; it can't be a factual account since the main players are missing: my parents, my baby self and the adoption society officials. It is a story which has been told to me many times over, in various ways appropriate to my age at the telling. The first story was about my parents going to London and choosing me, among all the other babies. (I imagined maybe six cots, but was never curious about the unselected occupants.) They looked maybe at two babies before me, but they didn't look any further once they saw me.

They were so excited that my dad, prone to colic, drank all my gripe water before they even reached the rendezvous. I can imagine the old-fashioned railway compartment, but I don't remember being told much about the journey. Ena and Peter Jones were probably so excited and anxious over baby Jennifer Anne that they couldn't really remember that much. They took a taxi back to their home in Station Road, Llanfairfechan, North Wales. I was going to grow up Welsh.

Ena and Peter had married late for the time – he was 28, she 33. Theirs was a wartime wedding with Ena wearing a smart suit and what I came to know as "wedding shoes". Anyway, at the age of 39, after moving to Llanfairfechan, she fell pregnant. Sadly, her baby girl was stillborn. She told me it was months before she shed a tear.

My parents became a part of the business community and social life of the village. They knew a teacher, Connie, at the local private school for girls who advised them to adopt. Maybe she'd seen girls at the other end of the adoption process and it was familiar to her – or maybe she just saw adoption as the best solution to their grief. Connie became my godmother.

So I lived in Pretoria House, in a flat above the shop with a balcony at the back overlooking a stream. The house was on a road that ran down to the sea, and Ena and Peter took me out first in the pram and later the pushchair. They were proud of their little girl. I can still remember the feeling of those walks on the promenade – just being built in 1949–50. The light, the smell of the sea take me back to an emotional state I can't characterise in adult words.

Later we moved to Colwyn Bay. This house was further from the sea, but had four bedrooms, a south-facing lounge at the back with a veranda over the garage. There was a very long garden, with three apple trees and gooseberry and redcurrant bushes at the bottom, next to a railway line, where the Irish Mail ran to and from Holyhead, morning and evening. I turned five just after we moved.

When I was six, I came down with TB. My parents opted for treatment at home – bed rest for months, followed by a very gentle recuperation. Even today, I can almost enjoy being ill in bed. This must go back to the web of security that my parents wove for me, while ensuring I had enough to keep me amused and mentally active. I remember paints and drawing, books, a huge jigsaw of a beach scene, and a very bulky portable radio on which I listened to the Monte Carlo rally, under the bedclothes. My dad took my temperature every day, and weighed me once a week. No question they loved me.

After the best part of a year, I was allowed to go back to school and joined a class I hardly recognised. The first lesson must have been arithmetic. I was lost in long division. My re-introduction to school wasn't going well. My mother went to see the headmaster and I was put into Miss Jones's remedial class. This was the making of me, education-wise. It was a very small class with about eight pupils, most of whom could have been described as "backward" (then) or "having special needs" (now). I lapped up everything Miss Jones could teach me and even enjoyed school at this time.

After Miss Jones' success in turning me into an educable child, I was fed back to "proper" classes, given my mum's old Parker 51 pen (I never realised what a gift that was; my teacher disapproved) and got on with the business of learning. By 11+ year I was promoted to the "A" stream. This was a hard year, not academically but socially. I didn't make friends easily and now I had a whole new class to deal with. My class teacher was scary Miss Allen, who we thought was 100 years old – she might have been less. In hindsight, she was an intelligent woman, a bluestocking, and she probably gave me the attention I needed. I made it though the 11+ and into the "A" stream of the local grammar school.

All this time, I was comfortable and familiar with the knowledge that I was adopted. Where babies *really* came from was all a bit vague so I thought my story was as good as any other, and a good deal more precise!

Now, I am going to jump forward a long way to 1976. I am working at the BBC on contract, and there has been a change in the law allowing adopted adults to learn about the circumstances of their adoption. Part of my "adoption story" was that I had been adopted through the Church of England Adoption Society and remembering this, I was able to access my adoption file. There was my birth mother's name, and really not much else – a letter, I think, written by her to Ena – or maybe one from Ena to her. The adoption worker explained that the young women they saw in those days usually concocted some "cock and bull" story to cover the role of the father. Dead airmen were popular. My file was no exception, she said, although there was some legal constraint on how much information could be given on the father. The upshot was I now had enough information to find my original birth certificate and my birth parents Jean and Ronnie's marriage certificate at Somerset House. Later that year – or maybe by now 1977 – my then partner, Terry, and I went to Ambleside. We found the church where Jean and Ronnie had married and their entry in the register. It was a small jump to find Jess Crossley, my maternal grandmother, on the Electoral Register and we went to her front door and knocked. To this day I don't know whether through good or ill fortune, she wasn't in. I was speechless by this time, but we tried the neighbour, who confirmed Mrs Crossley lived there, and that she had a daughter, Jean, who had children. Terry passed us off as distant relatives, which I suppose was true. She gave us Jean's phone number, which I never used.

Some months later I did return to the Lake District and drove through Broughton Mills. I had in mind to at least stop and look around, but at the last minute, when I realised how small it was, my nerve failed me. Suppose I went into the pub. Suppose I looked like my birth family? Suppose I was recognised? Well, I wasn't quite ready for that. Like many adopted people, I felt it was disloyal to my mum and dad to go and look for another set of parents! There are many more reasons too, quite deep and complicated ones.

There is a small tail to this story. Terry was looking for me that weekend, and thought I might have gone in search of Jean. He made a phone call to her home. I am not sure with whom he spoke, or what was said, but I wondered if that had triggered anything – almost like a message from another world.

I am sure Jean and Ena were required to exchange letters, although I have no evidence of this now; it is so clear in my mind that I am sure it happened. I think Jean referred to me as 'baby' and to me this was an indication she had already hardened her heart, built her defences, against her baby girl. She had set herself on a path she had to follow. (It seems to me now she had to build an emotional bunker in which to hide from this baby, lest she fall in love, as mothers mostly do.) In the same letter she mentioned she was pregnant again, with her new baby expected in June 1950. So, I concluded Jean and her husband were building a family, and it was probably best they were left alone.

In hindsight it is difficult to remember exactly what my early fantasies were about my birth mother. She had little substance. I could have been left in the crib by fairies, transported from another galaxy by aliens… and a number of stories could be mine. With the 1960s my birth mother became more of a heroine, standing up for her sexuality in a masculine world. It was around this time Ena told me about the young woman, the nurse, who she had seen in the adoption office, glimpsed in another room, sure, at least in hindsight, it must have been my birth mother.

The post-1976 fantasy was very different. Now the young heroine had become pregnant – a careless celebration of the August Bank holiday was a favourite idea – but there were reasons why she and my father couldn't marry. Maybe they weren't in love, or maybe he was married, or maybe she didn't even know who he was. Enter the knight on the white charger in the shape of Ronnie (for now I knew the name on my birth certificate). He already knew her; they were going out, they probably had a sexual relationship. But there was a devil's bargain. I imagined he had proposed marriage to Jean, but had no desire to raise another man's child. That was the price she must pay. Her mother, Jess, would have colluded, and she walked up the aisle, in white, the pregnancy concealed. She and Ronnie set up house in Barrow, the nearest anonymous town, where she could easily move neighbourhoods, go unchallenged when the baby disappeared. For a long time, part of this fantasy was that she and I would have been together, in a kind of maternal bubble for the six-week compulsory period before the adoption could take place. It took a very long time for me to recognise I must have been at home with Ronnie too.

The Jones family is an interesting one, but not a close one. All the older generation are now gone – the uncles and aunts – now it's just us cousins and their offspring, and some of them are estranged. There was/is an adopted cousin. She is Ghanaian but we have lost her. My parents died within a year of each other, in 1990, aged 82 and 78.

I am proud I grew up Welsh, with Welsh parents, cousins, aunts, uncles, stories, legends, and sayings. There were clear benefits to being adopted. I could grow up to be anything I wanted, and I suppose I did.

My pathway to peace

RON MCLAY

Ron McLay was born in Glasgow, Scotland, in 1961 to a Scottish mother and Kashmiri father. He was placed in an orphanage at birth and adopted by a Scottish family six months later. The family emigrated to Australia when he was eight years old. He found his birth mother when he was 30 and his birth father at 43. Ron was brought up as a born-again Christian by his adoptive parents and returned to his faith at the age of 39 after struggling for many years with addiction. He has travelled extensively, including two years in Israel, and has visited orphanages in several countries with his Church. He works as the IT Services Manager for the Australian Human Rights Commission and completed a Masters in Management – Information Technology in 2009. Ron is married to Sarika and is the father of Rebekah and Avigail.

I was born Lal Shah Taylor in Glasgow, Scotland in 1961. My birth mother is white Scottish and my birth father Kashmiri. I am of Kashmiri/Indian appearance with dark skin and black hair. My adoption into a white Scottish family and my renaming as Ron McLay has had a lifelong impact on me. It has thrown up many challenges but has also enriched my life experience and given me many wonderful moments.

Racism and racial shame

I emigrated to Australia with my adoptive family, a month short of nine years of age. Prior to leaving the UK I had not experienced racism. However, arriving in Australia while the White Australia policy was in force, meant there were few minority ethnic children in my schools. I was racially taunted and physically attacked from my first days. It was frightening. My adoptive parents were unable to support me because they lacked understanding of racism and the issues faced by transracially adopted children. They merely advised me to ignore it, thus leaving me to deal with racism without support.

Racism continued throughout my schooling, although as the years passed, Greeks and Italians began appearing at my schools and I was accepted by them. I had few white Australian friends. Throughout my teenage years I suffered from an identity crisis exacerbated by my non-white appearance whilst living in a white society; my adoptive parents had inadvertently chosen the whitest part of Sydney to live in (where the Cronulla race riots were to occur many years later) and, consequently, I was usually the most noticeably minority ethnic child in my class. Incomprehensively, I became racist myself.

I felt like I was a white soul trapped in a brown man's body. Racist attitudes were inculcated into me by the white society around me, the kids at my schools, by radio, TV, newspapers and within my adoptive family. I looked down on others who had similar features and colouring to me. I cannot recall meeting a Kashmiri or Pakistani person whilst growing up. I relived the shame of my origins each time an enquiring person looked askance when I told them I was from Scotland. I then felt compelled to tell the story, as I knew it, as a sort of ritual self-humiliation.

Meeting my birth parents and healing from racial shame

I tracked my birth mother down within three days after beginning a search for her whilst on a short trip to Scotland. It was a kind of spur-of-the-moment thing. Meeting her for the first time was something I will never forget. It felt like I was an observer rather than a participant. I knocked on her door. The first thing I said was, 'Hello, my name is Ron McLay but you'll probably know me better as Lal Shah Taylor.' She collapsed, started crying and asked for my forgiveness. I watched in amazement as her anguish played out in front of me.

The majority of my Scottish family was not keen to meet me. I eventually met three of my uncles and one of my brothers but I let the relationships diminish. There was a quotient of shame associated with me, understandable given the circumstances of my birth. My mother claimed at my birth that I was the product of a sexual assault while she was married to her first white Scottish husband. I do not share any features in common with my Scottish family – in fact I felt like an alien amongst them with my Kashmiri appearance and taller height. However, they made a real effort to make me feel a part of their family. This was especially true of one cousin who I have remained in contact with. She is of a similar age to me and we seemed to click with each other. I struggled to feel a part of them due to all the differences, plus there were derogatory comments often made about Asians (Indians and Pakistanis) and this made me uneasy.

As a consequence of my mother's addictions and mental problems I have been unable to form a lasting relationship with her – in fact, at our last meeting a few years ago, I had been staying with her for six days when she suddenly became very angry with me and threw me out of her house. Although very painful at the time, I understand that her actions stemmed from her own problems.

The question of the shame surrounding my ethnicity was resolved for me when I met my father and my Kashmiri family. It was a wonderful healing, cathartic event that has affected me profoundly. While I was with them, I had to keep telling myself not to become so "ethnic" that I lost my Scottish/Australian identity. I even felt racist towards whites, temporarily – as an outworking of inner feelings. In truth, I am part Kashmiri, part Scottish and part Australian. However, in appearance I am Kashmiri and I was (happily) lost in the world of Luton where my father lives in a large Kashmiri community. I was anonymous. I cut my hair very short and wore a stud in my ear to became more Kashmiri in appearance.

I immensely enjoyed being the centre of attention in my father's family. They treated me so well. My two sisters were lovely and so attractive. It was strange to be surrounded by so many brown blood relations; everyone made comments about who I looked like. One of my sisters, in particular, played a major role in helping me feel part of the family just through her similarity to my daughter. She also appeared to admire me. The other sister was similarly attentive and I felt terribly flattered. It felt strange on the one hand, but it also felt *really good*. The brother I spent the most time with was similarly kind and loving to me. It was not too long before I felt as close to this brother as I've ever felt to anyone.

The few days I spent on this first trip were a wonderful blur of other family members and friends who travelled from different parts of the UK to meet me. The contrast with how I had been received by my maternal birth family could not have been starker. On the one hand, I was an unwelcome reminder of my mother's behaviour but in my Kashmiri family I was very welcome.

My father's English was not good so we did struggle to communicate but he would often giggle and smile when I was around, and he was obviously very happy I was there.

I spent a lot of time getting to know my sisters and brothers. Being with them, I felt connected, a part of the family. Seeing all these brown faces around me felt good. I realised I had lost a lot through growing up half-way across the world. That is not to say I didn't have a good home environment and good adoptive parents. Rather, it was the loss of racial identity. My shame about my ethnicity stemmed from the total lack of Kashmiri role models.

I recall one particular meeting with my oldest female cousin, a beautiful and intelligent woman. She said to me that because I was the oldest son and she the oldest daughter of my uncle, I could have been her husband. I nearly fell off my seat. It was a wonderful moment of affirmation I will never forget and yet, for me, it was tinged with sadness at the symbolism of the loss of a life I could not reclaim.

I have been blessed to meet both my birth mother and birth father. I am aware many adoptees don't get to experience reunion with either birth parent but this need not be an impediment to "wellness". Neither, as my own experience demonstrates, is it necessary to have a completely successful experience of reunion. Meeting my birth parents was a positive, life-changing experience and ended the great mystery about my origins that had haunted me all my life. I no longer wonder who I am. I have peace about my identity.

Relationship with adoptive parents

I had a very poor relationship with my adoptive mother. During my teenage years I felt she treated me differently to her two natural sons and I rebelled. We fought over the years and my adoptive mother suffered a mental breakdown at one stage as a result of the fighting. On occasions she would tell me she wished she had never adopted me – that she hated me. She tried to kick me out of home several times. I can see now she was the convenient target for my grief at the loss of my birth mother. I also recognise my acting out behaviour was intended to test her love and this was a pattern I took into all my adult relationships with women. Contrastingly, I had a much better relationship with my adoptive father. In fact, I used to idolise him. He was very patient with me and, at one stage, when I had attempted suicide, took his holidays to spend time with me as I recovered.

After meeting my birth father my relationship with my adoptive mother improved. I attribute this to my continued recovery from alcoholism and making a successful connection with my father. There was also a significant moment in my relationship with my adoptive mother following a phone call with her. I asked myself, why am I trying to change her to think like me? From that moment our relationship improved.

Alcoholism and drug addiction

My alcoholism and drug addiction are related to my experience of adoption. I began to drink alcohol at the age of 15 and continued to drink and take drugs until the age of 39. I ended up in detox units and psychiatric wards. I was arrested under the Australian Mental Health Act and resuscitated in casualty wards after drug overdoses and suicide attempts. Thankfully, I was to have a spiritual experience in a detox unit when I was 39. This stopped the cycle of addiction. A voice spoke to me. It said I had chosen to be a victim all my life but if I handed my life over to God everything would change. From that precise moment the desire to drink, which I had had for 25 years, was taken away. Nine years later it has not returned. From that moment I joined a 12-step programme that has remained a major part of my life.

Bonding with my daughter

I have always struggled with the concept of love. It is only really through my daughter that I began to understand love. I was estranged from her for several years as a result of my alcoholism. Once I became sober she eventually came back into my life and I began to learn how to love her. I made a number of mistakes when we first met again – one was to tell her too much about my life. Today, love for me is thinking and caring about others in practical ways such as making sure I stay in contact with my daughter, daily if possible, and listening to her without telling her what to do.

Relationships with women

I was insecure in my relationships and marriages and, fearing rejection, tested my partners continually. Inevitably, I would sabotage these relationships until they ended with being proven right – I was unlovable, I was flawed. I enjoyed feeling sorry for myself. I saw myself as the quintessential victim. Self-pity, sad songs and tears, these were part of my experience for many years. I constantly sought reassurance from my partners. I was unfaithful and chased other women, including my friends' wives and partners. I have been married three times and had more than 20 other relationships. I was seeking love and approval, looking for unconditional love – something I felt I'd never experienced, yet craved. Over the last decade, since becoming sober, I have stopped this behaviour. I have met and married Sarika and together we recently welcomed Avigail into the world.

My faith

My father and family in Luton are Muslim. My birth mother is Protestant. I was brought up Pentecostal, a born-again believer in Jesus. It was my 12-step programme that revealed God to me. I discovered that He is a God of love who cares about me. For me that God is the same Jesus I learned about in Sunday school but had rejected in my teenage years. I have had to let go of the old belief that God abandoned me in the orphanage, and instead see Him as the One who was always there looking after me. I learned to forgive through my faith and my membership of the 12-step programme and this has become my lifestyle. God is my ever-faithful friend and I live to do His will – to help other alcoholics with their recovery.

The resources and people who have helped me

At my first meeting of the Intercountry Adoption Support Network [3] (ICASN), I met and discussed my adoption with other adoptees. I was amazed to find

---

[3] ICASN is an Australian network linking organisations related to intercountry adoption and supporting adoptees and their families – see www.aican.org.

others were interested in my story and I could identify with their experiences. It was the first time I had openly discussed my adoption. I also sought counselling from a number of psychologists and a psychotherapist, and derived value from these sessions including dealing with the sexual abuse I suffered from an adoptive uncle. I have read books on adoption but one publication was particularly significant in my journey: *The Primal Wound* by Nancy Verrier.[4] I found her book insightful and I cried through many of its pages. Her premise, that a baby is wounded when separated from its birth mother, rang true for me.

Advice for other adoptees

Seek out all the information you can concerning your origins but do so at an appropriate age and while receiving counselling. It was ending the mystery of my origins that helped me to reconcile myself. Networking with other adoptees is also important and affirming. It is vitally important to share your story with others who will understand you.

---

[4] See Footnote, p 49.

More than just a survivor

VIV FOGEL

Viv Fogel was born in 1948 and adopted at ten months old by traumatised Holocaust survivors and this experience formed her. Years of psychotherapy – and later training to become one – helped her to repair the damage of a broken attachment and to function in the world with trust, entitlement and a resilient sense of self. Making art, writing and teaching also helped. Viv has painted murals in Hackney, taught art in Islington, been a screen-printer, community worker, poetry events organiser and performer. Her poems have been published in various anthologies and magazines since the mid-70s. From 1980 to 1982 she was one of the Evettes, a feminist performing quartet. For over 25 years, Viv has worked as an integrative psychosynthesis psychotherapist and supervisor. She gives seminars, writes articles and teaches therapists energy psychology techniques such as EFT, a form of meridian therapy. Her daughter has taught her how to mother.

My birth mother, Jenni, whom I traced and met in the late 90s, had moved to the United States when she realised that she had "lost me". She died a few years ago. She had a son, my half-brother, ten years younger than me, who has his own family and children. For him I was the missing piece of the puzzle. My birth mother kept her secret for 50 years and when I finally made contact with her, she did not want to know. Her heart had been closed off and protected for so long. Gradually I chipped away at it, a light holiday postcard here, a birthday card there, photos of my daughter, her grandchild, with her child's handwriting to 'Dear grandma' … and slowly, slowly, her heart began to soften and open. Eventually, we began to speak on the phone. Transatlantic conversations – her US drawl made me smile. 'Waal – I gotta go to the john now – so long…'

And then, just as I was about to go over and meet her, her heart gave out. I could not help but blame myself – yet again – as the cause of her misery. She remained in a coma for months and when she finally emerged, her brain was damaged by the cardiac arrest.[5]

My birth father was her married boss, long since dead. He contributed some payments for my clothes and food in the nursing home; I still have the receipts.

---

[5] I have written about my meeting with her, in an article called 'Motherlove', (ReVision.ing, 2002)

Shortly before he died, my adoptive father, whom I adored, handed me a wadge of correspondence between the unofficial adoption "agency" and himself and his wife, the prospective adopters.

Apparently I was a non-thriving baby (depressed?) whom they, as prospective parents, feared might be brain damaged, so I was moved to another nursing home where the quality of care and attention I received was much improved. I grew plump and rosy, passed the "intelligence" tests and was cute enough to be adopted! By then I was ten months old. Some of those early trauma memories (embodied almost at cellular level) surfaced with a vengeance when I gave birth to my own baby daughter. *For many adoptees, the birth of their own child will be both re-traumatising – and transformatively healing.*

My adoptive mother was a Jewish immigrant from Vienna. She had left school at the age of 14, although she was very bright, to work as a seamstress and help support her family. She escaped to England just as Hitler was coming into power, on the advice of a young SS officer who befriended her. She managed to bring her brother, his wife and her youngest sister over, but her favourite brother, a jazz pianist, shot himself and her parents persuaded her to leave them behind. They perished in Auschwitz.

She worked in service as a maid (her younger sister was young enough to go to school) and later as a machinist in a small clothes factory. She never forgave herself for those she left behind. She became mentally unstable and depressed, even undergoing ECT (electric shock treatment) whereas today she might have received counselling. She told me the Nazi doctors had butchered her and so she couldn't have babies. I believed her. Now I see this as a metaphorical truth, not fact.

She hurled some cruel and unforgiveable statements at me as I turned into a teenager, which I duly internalised, and no matter how much therapy you do on these things, you never quite forget them. I imagine today she would probably not have been allowed to adopt. I don't think she meant to hurt me, but in her "bad" moments, her bitterness and self-loathing seemed to be projected onto me, the "stranger" in her midst, and I became, then, the object of her hatred, fear and abuse. It was almost as if I became the "Nazi tormentor". 'You must have been born from the Devil,' she would scream. That affected me throughout my early life. I was convinced I was somehow different – and "bad" – and that somehow I had to make it up to everyone around (including "God").

Adoptees are skilful adaptees. 'No child of mine would act as you do!' I was trying to be this new phenomenon: the teenager. In the early 60s this meant hanging out with friends in the local coffee bar, talking about existentialism and French films. I wore black polo-neck sweaters, panstick lipstick and thick eyeliner, hidden behind a fringe. I was into Miles Davies and the Beat Poets. I didn't do sex or drugs until my early 20s but she was still suspicious. When she "came back down" she would smother me effusively with apologies. I never trusted her – and on reflection, I can see that she was probably bi-polar.

In contrast, my adoptive father was a rock, an anchor, my lifeline. He stood by her but I knew he was on my side too. I still miss him. He had a wicked sense of humour and was a good listener. Stubborn too, and fiercely proud of me. I was his daughter and I felt his protective love for me. He had been in a concentration camp (Buchenwald) until a wealthy relative paid money to get him out. He still had the number tattooed on his inner forearm, still had the memories and horror stories. He was one of the lucky ones.

So both my adoptive parents were immigrants with "survivor guilt" and I lived and internalised that feeling. For many years I successfully made it my own, this belief that I was not entitled to live. As well as my particular Holocaust backdrop, this sense of guilt and disentitlement is a familiar one for people who have been adopted. *Many adoptees feel un-entitled, that they should not be here.* For some, this may be experienced pre-birth, in utero, from a womb that is hostile or fearful of carrying them.

On the positive side, being adopted has formed me. I am not just a survivor but I thrive.

I am resourceful and resilient, and transform and heal through being creative. *Many adoptees have an urge to be creative, to "make their mark" in the world – and this is a strong motivational drive.* It's as if we need to get hold of the world, and say, 'Look at me. I'm here and I have a right to be, so see me, acknowledge me, love me.' We want to shape and form a world for ourselves that we were once powerless to shape. Being creative means literally to make our own "worlds".

I believe that the years of transpersonal psychotherapy I received from my late 20s and into my 30s, and then training to become a psychotherapist myself, helped me repair the damage of a broken attachment, and to function in the world with trust and a strong sense of self.

Finally, my choice

LIZ WILDE

Liz Wilde is a life coach specialising in coaching adopted adults. She is also the author of 16 books, including the e-book, *Why Didn't You Want Me? How To Heal The Pain Of Being An Unwanted Child* (available at www.coachingtheadopted.com). It covers common emotions experienced by adopted people including rejection, anger, fear, abandonment, shame and guilt, and offers advice on how to deal with them. Liz was born in London in 1963 to an English mother. Her father was Spanish and her mother had met him while helping her parents run their bar in Benidorm. Liz was adopted by British parents at six weeks old and after years of searching, beginning at 18 and continuing into her 40s, she is now in contact with both sides of her birth family.

My natural mother really believed she was giving me a better life. She already had one child from a broken marriage and wasn't yet divorced. My father, being a married man in 1960s Spain, was unable to marry her (a divorce would have ruined him), so my grandparents packed my mother back off to England to do the right thing. She was never the same again. I will always feel some guilt for this fragile woman's descent into an abusive second marriage, poverty, agoraphobia, and finally death from heart failure at 52.

Because yes, I did have a better life. I was brought up in a comfortable middle-class family where no one shouted. There was no violence in my house. No late-night phone calls to the police. No stealing cans of baked beans to feed the family. No depression or despair. My parents were professionals. They had important jobs and talked about current affairs at the dinner table. We went to Sunday school and had a big garden to play in. My father kissed my mother goodbye every morning and ate his dinner at home every night. If they argued, they were careful to do so behind closed doors. My adoptive brother and I had a quiet, uneventful childhood. I should have been happy, yet something inexpressible was missing.

It wasn't my parents' fault. They showed their love with ballet classes and trips to the park, with extra tutoring and Brownie camp. My mother gave up work while we were young, and I never once came home to an empty house. But from the moment she sat me down on her knee to explain how my mummy had not been able to keep me, I had a wound inside that no amount of nurturing could heal. It didn't matter that my mother showed me every day that she loved me. I chose not to see it. All I could focus on was that my "real mummy" had been able to give me away. I had a brick missing in my foundations and no one could replace it but the person who had taken it away. But that didn't stop me looking in all the wrong places.

I had many boyfriends who promised to love me forever, but I didn't believe them. The merest hint of apathetic behaviour and I jumped ship to feel those initial fireworks again. I could never relax around people who cared for me, ever vigilant that they may change their mind at any moment. I always had a back-up plan, someone waiting in the wings should I need an escape route. If there was one thing I knew for sure, it was that I would never, ever risk being abandoned again. And with each new enthusiastic suitor, there was always a chance that they would love me better. Because that's what you believe when you're adopted. If I was with my real mother, she would love me *more*. What more meant, I didn't know, but I was sure it would melt the fear inside me.

A chance encounter led me to talk to a life coach and her message amazed me. What if we weren't locked into our behaviours for life? What if we had a choice? I was certainly getting bored with mine: over-reacting to the merest hint of rejection; drinking too much to numb the pain. I had built up a wall of self-preservation and no one could see over the top. I pretended not to need anyone, and incredibly, people believed me. I was the heart-breaker, the one no one could tie down. When all along I craved (and feared) the very security I claimed to despise. It was not a comfortable place to be.

So I signed on for a two-year diploma with Coach U, the largest life coaching organisation in the world. As part of my training, I had my first experience of coaching. Up until this point, my adoption had been a shameful secret, something I kept to myself ever since my closest junior school friend had threatened to tell the whole of 3B. The fear of being different had kept me quiet for another 30 years. So when I told my coach I thought all my problems stemmed from being rejected by my mother as a baby, she was able to distance my story from the reality. I was not rejected, she told me. The decision had been made before I was even born. How could I be rejected when I didn't even exist?

I applied to see my adoption file at Westminster Council and there, in an overstuffed, battered folder, was written proof that my mother had never rejected me. There were letters from the agency urging her to sign papers so my new parents could proceed with my legal adoption. The agency wrote of 'this charming couple' and 'their distress'. My mother wrote back of her 'torment'. Here was proof at last that I had been wanted very much indeed.

But there was still work to be done. I had 40 years of fear ingrained in my subconscious. Of never being able to trust that someone loved me enough not to leave. If I had been allowed to see my file at 18, who knows how different my life could have been? But years of self-preservation were never going to disappear overnight. So I set about changing the script. I made a collage of documents that I had managed to wrangle from the council social worker. She saw no irony that these flimsy scraps of paper meant more to me than anything I owned, yet would sit in a dusty vault for another 40 years. I'm sure she eventually handed them over simply to get rid of me. I also filled my home with framed pictures of all my parents, not just the two who had brought me up. This was about being proud of being adopted, of being the person I am. Up until then, I had been ashamed.

I learned more coaching skills and began to question my automatic responses. I had been operating on auto-pilot from the belief that my mother had not wanted me. A belief that wasn't true. I began to stop myself in that painful moment and investigate my frightened mind. Is that true? Is that person really rejecting me, or does it just feel that way? What else is possible? What would I prefer to think? How old am I when I feel like this? Now I'm an adult, could I actually be *safe*? I learned my Achilles heels and turned them around. 'I am unwanted' became 'both my mothers wanted me very much'. 'I will be abandoned' became 'no one has ever abandoned me'.

Through coaching I also began to see the rackets my mind had been running. I had picked up the belief that I needed to please others to be loved. So I wrote, 'I do not need to please for people to love me' and stuck it on my computer. My self-preservation was finely tuned to the merest hint of danger. I expected people to hurt me, so that's what I saw. 'No one is deliberately trying to hurt me' was a huge revelation. I had post-it notes everywhere and read them every day. I stood in front of my collage and read my mother's words every morning. I thanked my natural father's photo for my Spanish colouring and my mother's for my big smile.

And slowly my brain began to rewire itself. Just like learning to play a musical instrument, the more I began to think in different ways, the more those ways began to get easier. Even more slowly, I started to really *feel* them. Rather than it being merely a logical, head-over-heart thought, I would look at the letters from my mother and actually feel her love. I would look at the letters detailing my adoptive parents' distress, and feel the longing behind their words. It was and continues to be the most wonderful feeling because now I know for sure that the fear I have felt all my life is no longer relevant. I have always been loved. I just chose not to notice it. Now as an adult, I can finally be as secure as anyone else. It is finally my choice.

Mixed blessings

LIZ SIBTHORPE

Liz Sibthorpe was born in 1948 in a private nursing home in south London. She is of white and African-Caribbean parentage. Considered "unadoptable", at 12 months she joined her adoptive mother, a single working woman who later adopted a further five children of various ethnicities. Liz has contact with her paternal birth family and her half-brother and sister, as well as her birth mother and a half-brother. She is close to her three adopted sisters. Liz is an independent member on two adoption panels and lives in London. Her previous published writing includes *The Nurse's Children* (Authorhouse, 2005); *Finding Myself*, a children's story based on her own experiences; the poems, 'Warning to adoptive parents' and 'What will you tell your adopted child?' in *In Search of Belonging* (BAAF, 2006); and *Family and Identity: Something that never went away* (AAA-NORCAP, 2009).

In our home we had several much used expressions. One was "mixed blessings". That is how I would describe many of the challenges and opportunities I have experienced. Opportunities could turn into difficult situations while some challenges which seemed insoluble never completely defeated me.

As I look back on my life I can see how adoption influenced some of the choices I made. I now know how my half-siblings grew up and what life in the children's home would have offered me. I was adopted at two years old and brought up with five siblings of different ethnic and social backgrounds. I was given physical opportunities but also saddled with many social and emotional challenges.

I was expected by my adoptive mother (and the well-meaning adults who saw adoption as a noble act and considered our adoptive mother a person to be much admired) to value the opportunities I had been given, but I couldn't always do so. One of these opportunities was that my five adopted siblings and I, who were all classed as "unadoptable", had been offered a permanent home rather than growing up in care and being forced out into the world at 16, with no family or financial support.

Undoubtedly I was provided with good food, a warm house and adequate clothing. There were annual holidays to the seaside, music lessons and extra tuition to pass the 11+ examination. I recognised these as privileges to some extent, but I knew that most of these opportunities would have been available to me if I had stayed in the children's home.

That said, the chance to attend the local girl's grammar school wouldn't have happened if I hadn't had an adoptive parent who rarely took no for an answer. I missed my first choice and was offered a place at a comprehensive school many miles from home. All the arguments were gathered and launched at the local education authority until I was given a place at the local high school where my adoptive mother had always intended me to go. I learned that it was worth persevering and fighting for what you believe in. I was encouraged to take advantage of good schooling and extra-curricular pastimes, sport and music, but this was a mixed blessing. I could take part in these activities as long as they didn't impact too much on my home responsibilities or clash with the strict religious code of behaviour that forbade cinema and theatre visits.

My adoptive mother taught me to fight for the rights of disabled people. The words 'if at first you don't succeed, try, try, try again' irritated me as a child, but have stuck with me and spurred me on to meet certain challenges. One of my siblings had a physical and speech impairment and would have had limited educational opportunities if our adoptive mother hadn't fought for him to attend mainstream school. I suspect the example of determination to fight for the best for others, especially if they are underprivileged, was part of what led me to work with socially deprived children when I qualified as a teacher. It also gave me the courage to take up voluntary work in South Africa and later, to care for children in a respite centre.

My choice of career also came out of my anger at the injustices I felt I suffered in our home, the harsh punishments and being forced to do housework while my friends were free to play. From a young age, despite being told I was loved, I felt a lack of physical love. I was in constant fear that I would get things wrong or unwittingly displease our adoptive mother and then be unfairly punished. I still can't bear to see children neglected or abused in any way. I carry the emotional scars from my childhood but these have made me determined to improve the lives of any children in my care.

My decision to live and do voluntary work in South Africa in my late 40s was partly due to a deep need to discover something more about my father's background. I was told he was African but received no nurturing of my African heritage. If I wasted time daydreaming or forgot to have a proper wash I could be accused of some spurious bad African trait. Our adoptive mother viewed Africans as lazy and not as intelligent as white people. She was keen for me to hide as much of my black identity as possible, including keeping my hair in tight plaits until I was in my teens so that it looked straight and tidy. I was confused about my identity and didn't feel physically attractive, but I was also proud of my African roots. I wasn't taught to use make-up and I had to dress modestly. This caused me to feel ill at ease in social gatherings for much of my adult life. Now, I worry little about how I look. I have my own dress style, I rarely wear make-up and I let my hair grow a little wild.

Like many adopted people I have felt driven to find out where I come from. One huge challenge of being adopted before 1976 was the law, which prevented adopted adults from contacting their birth families. I was born in a private children's home that published an annual booklet of stories about the mothers, children and adoptive families. I knew that these booklets and further details about my siblings and I were concealed in our mother's room. The advantage of having an adoptive parent who worked full time was that we were left unsupervised for many hours, so I was able to access this hidden information. This little knowledge was tantalising and I was determined that when I was older I would discover exactly who my birth mother was. It took me until I was in my mid-30s to start the search and then another 15 years before I met any of my birth family. Many barriers were put in my way, not least my adoptive mother's fear that I would reject her when I found them. Eventually I overcame these obstacles and made contact, first with a cousin in my father's family, and through her I met my half-brother, sister and their families. Later I met my mother and another half-brother.

Certain challenges became opportunities even while I was a child. I learned early in life that to avoid punishment but still enjoy some activities I had to develop the ability to deceive and hide my true self. I perfected the skill of getting jobs done quickly in order to enjoy a book, watch TV or listen to forbidden pop and rock and roll music on the radio, which was all the more exciting because it was forbidden. I think now that the skill is better described as survival. It was another "mixed blessing", knowing what I wanted in life and to some extent knowing how to achieve it.

Being a child who daydreamed, drew and read voraciously was difficult in the family I lived in. We were subjected to the protestant work ethic as soon as we could reach over the edge of the kitchen sink. I could have read for hours every day and I never had enough paper for my drawings. I dreamed of going to art school and becoming a medical artist, but this wasn't deemed acceptable. My adoptive mother assumed I would follow in her footsteps and take up a nursing career. Determined not to be forced to conform to her expectations, I opted to train to be a teacher and enjoyed teaching for 18 years.

Our family was assigned a local authority social worker. She made statutory visits but never seemed to see what really went on: the harsh rules, hours of housework, the punishments and the child care we were forced to carry out. Sometimes one sister and I planned ways of alerting the authorities to our situation but we never found anyone we trusted enough to listen to us. I became distrustful of authority figures, sceptical of those who said they would help us, and deplored the adoption system that abandoned children to unsuitable families with no monitoring. Until relatively recently, I didn't consider adoption to be in the interests of children. I think the excellent long-term counselling I have received, my satisfaction in finding my own birth family and the changes in adoption legislation have helped to moderate this view. I now do something I could never have imagined: I sit on an adoption panel considering the suitability of prospective adoptive parents.

A "mixed blessing" is a term I can use to describe my own identity. If I was lucky I would be referred to as a "coloured" child. More often I was called "half-caste" by adults while my tormentors at primary school would call me "nigger", "gollywog" or "blackie". When I was out with my family it was a constant challenge to know where I fitted in. I didn't look anything like the sibling next in age to me, who is white. That caused us both problems as we were often seen together but could never be taken for sisters. In some ways, the fact that we could attribute our difference to adoption was useful. We were not expected to be alike.

I grew up in a very white area. Until I was ten years old I was usually the only minority ethnic child at school and in our social circle, except when our holiday brother was with us. I was pleased he joined us each holiday. He was of African-Caribbean and white heritage. He looked more like my brother than any of my siblings until we were joined by a baby boy of Asian and white heritage and then, a few years later, by my youngest sisters, both of African-Caribbean parentage. Throughout my life I have valued diversity and known that outward appearances, though important for identity, are not a barrier to loving and living together. Being adopted by someone who didn't actively value diversity nor understand our need to be introduced to our cultures meant I missed out on learning about my own African heritage. I was immersed in a narrow Protestant brand of white middle-class culture. My interest in black music, dance and African culture was not nurtured. It left me confused as a teenager and later, with a longing to catch up on lost opportunities by listening to music that came out of Africa and reading about apartheid in South Africa and Black Power in America.

From early on in life I knew that my birth mother was blonde and blue-eyed and that I wouldn't have been able to stay with her family because, with my black curly hair and olive-coloured skin, I would have stood out. That made me sad but I took comfort in the knowledge that my father was of African descent. I liked to think that I might look a bit like him. In my 30s I met one of my cousins on my father's side and obtained photos of my birth father. For the first time I could identify certain features of mine with theirs. It was the most wonderful moment. From then on I felt completely comfortable with my physical appearance. Any worries I'd had as a child about looking different became a source of pride.

Birthdays were a challenge for me as I grew up. As a teenager and young adult I realised that my birthday was a sharp reminder of the mother who had given me up for adoption. I learned that in my case "given up for adoption" meant that she had made the choice between me or the family she already had. At the beginning of each autumn, as the date of my birth drew closer, I thought about this mother figure who had not chosen me. I was angry with her and slowly developed a theory: she was selfish and could have aborted me and saved me from the trials of my life and the uncertainty of who I was. For many years those thoughts crowded my mind whenever I dropped into a period of deep depression. Over the last decade I've been helped, through counselling, to accept myself as a child and an adult. I now appreciate how much my adoptive siblings, birth siblings and friends love me and want to celebrate my birthday, and I can let them do it for me.

I'm not sure if being adopted was the cause of my lifetime struggle with depression or merely a contributing factor. Mental health difficulties afflict all families, including my birth family. However, I think the lack of physical affection, the narrow Protestant Christian lifestyle, confusion over my identity and the fear as I reached adulthood that I would never be free of family responsibilities did have an adverse effect on my mental health. In my early 20s, when my adoptive mother was in her 60s, she decided to apply to adopt my youngest two siblings. She wanted me to be joint adopter, but with the help of college tutors and friends I managed to resist. My love for them didn't diminish but I knew that if I had accepted legal responsibility for them it wouldn't be my choice. For much of my childhood I had been unable to exercise choice, but this was one I had to make for my own mental health. It caused me deep heartache but I have never regretted my decision to remain a sister to my youngest sisters rather than their mother. With all the pressure to help bring up my younger siblings, I had little energy to pursue my own relationships and didn't set up home with a partner or have my own children.

There was no way I could pretend that our family unit was normal. I was embarrassed at having to call our mother figure "auntie" because I longed to have a conventional mother and father. In the 1950s there were few children in single-parent families and most of those I came into contact with were with their birth mother or grandmother. No one else I knew had brothers and sisters from such a variety of backgrounds. Apart from scrapping with one sister, I loved my younger siblings and felt loyal and protective towards them. We shared similar challenges and presented a solid front to the world. I often imagined I would have had an easier life in the children's home; every holiday we were joined by a boy from the home and his life was more carefree than mine.

The dichotomy I experienced throughout my life, of wanting to fit in and yet not wanting to conform, and of battling against authority, is still with me. I was embarrassed that I had been adopted by a single woman. I lived with racial taunts from older children throughout my primary school days because I looked different, but I never wanted to look "white". I took a perverse pride in my difference. It allowed me to be awkward and rebellious at school. Now it shows itself in a stubborn resistance to being pigeon-holed. I have learned to stand up for what I believe is just, to argue my case reasonably and to align myself with the underprivileged and oppressed in a socially acceptable way.

For many years the word "adopted" was an anathema to me. I cringed when it was mentioned in any context, even in the Bible where Christians were called the "adopted children of God". I railed against a society I saw as giving permission for childless people to fulfill their need by adopting other people's children. I strongly disagreed with replacing an adopted child's first name as well as surname. I never accepted my new name although I had to learn to write it and answer to it. I partly overcame this by shortening it and encouraging my friends to use nicknames for me, though I never legally changed my name back to the one my birth mother gave me.

I am in the older age group of people who were adopted and stripped of their original identity. I would recommend those who have had their name taken from them to obtain their original birth certificate and reclaim it. It is evidence of who we were when we were born and may be the key to opening the door to search for birth family. I would also advise adopted people who have had difficult placements to be honest and not pretend, out of fear of hurting their adoptive parents' feelings, that their adoptive family was perfect. I understand that it is common to try and live up to parental expectations, but attempting to be what an adoptive parent wants has the additional burden of taking away identity and denying your own heritage.

If you struggle with uncertainty of identity, depression and other mental health issues I encourage you to seek professional help. For many years I allowed adoption to define me as a person and for the negative experiences to blight my life. Without skilled help, strong friendships and finding out about my birth family I wouldn't have come to terms with those challenges nor would I have been able to write this.

What if...?

VANESSA GEBBIE

Vanessa Gebbie was born in Torquay in the west of England in May 1952, daughter of a student nurse. Brought up by a Welsh family, she has worked for the Ministry of Defence, in human resources, marketing and as a journalist, and is now a writer, editor and writing teacher. Her novel *The Coward's Tale* (Bloomsbury, 2012) was selected as a *Financial Times* and a *Guardian* readers' Book of the Year. She is also an award-winning short story-writer and author of two collections: *Words from a Glass Bubble* and *Storm Warning* (Salt Modern Fiction, 2008). Vanessa's stories have been commissioned by literary journals, the British Council, for BBC Radio 3 and BBC Radio 4, and are widely anthologised (see www.vanessagebbie.com). Married with two grown-up sons, she lives in Sussex.

I have always been a writer. I even published a new national newspaper once – written in biro, published in my bedroom in a print run of one. I was six. I recall moping about and writing ghastly poetry as a teenager. I wrote silly stories in my 20s for my young son and his friends, and even sillier sketches in my 30s for my own friends' birthday cabarets. Then I was actually paid real money in my 40s for a few years of local journalism.

I only started writing serious fiction later on, at roughly the same time as I began a search for my roots in 2003/4. I am now well published with a couple of books out there, another on the way – and I don't think it is a coincidence that my best work so far appeared at the same time as I was tackling a difficult personal journey.

Looking back now, I am able to compare this creative work with the actual story that was unfolding, and I see the very real supportive role my writing was playing in helping me come to terms with my own situation. But I was not conscious of that role as I was writing.

You will have to take my word for it that I did not and do not "set out" to write about adoption. But being an adopted adult underpins who I am, and the resulting bewilderment, displacement, loneliness and a constant search to "belong" therefore permeates what I do. Add those feelings to the knowledge that strong fiction (work that resonates and touches the reader as opposed to "page fillers") comes from deep inside the writer, tapping subconscious layers, and I was bound to tap into those issues. It's nothing new. The creative writing guru Dorothea Brande described these processes in the 1930s. I must have been tapping into my own experiences rather well, for the writing I did while searching for my family produced some great work – stories that won competition after competition, and ended up in my first book.

I hasten to add that I am not (I hope!) a bunch of directionless neuroses. I had a very happy and stable upbringing, and have been married for over 30 years, with a wonderful family of my own. But it is important to be self-aware, and the process of exploration of difficult issues through my imagination – giving those issues to invented characters and allowing them to react in a fictitious context – was both liberating, important and in retrospect, therapeutic (with a small 't'!).

Perhaps it would be useful to look at a few of those characters, to see the issues *they* were tackling. One of my favourites is Spike, a young Welsh garage mechanic in a story called 'Cactus Man'.[6] Spike wants to know his "real name" for his wedding. In what he assumes will be a simple conversation with his social worker, he discovers far more then he bargained for, and the fallout follows.

Without giving the story away, I can tell you this: I wrote 'Cactus Man' after I went through the process of applying for my own complete birth certificate in 2004, and like Spike, I too was discovering far more than I had bargained for. Writing that story, giving my own experiences away to a character far removed from myself, gave me permission to look at what I was uncovering, allowing me to explore my feelings safely thanks to the distance afforded by fiction. What happened to Spike couldn't hurt me, could it?

All I *thought* I was doing was fictionalising a conversation that had really taken place between me and my own social worker (a lovely lady who is now immortalised, with a different name of course, several times over). But actually, the story of Spike continued as I was writing it, far beyond that simple conversation. It continued itself into a second half of the story in which the character responds himself to the very "what if...?" I was exploring.

What if my birth parents were "bad" people? What if I was the product of rape or incest? Would I be the same person, or would that knowledge change me?

---

[6] 'Cactus Man', 'The Kettle on the Boat' and all the characters mentioned in this account can be found in the collection, *Words from a Glass Bubble* (Salt Modern Fiction, 2008).

Now, you will have to take my word for something else, especially if you are not a writer of fiction. Some work just "takes off". It takes on a life of its own and the writer is almost incidental – just a set of fingers on computer keys or fingers holding a pen. You could argue that the conversation with the social worker is hardly fiction at all, that I was just transposing direct experience. But the second half of that story? Where Spike has to come to terms with what he discovers, and then has to find out if that knowledge changes him as a person… that section arrived from nowhere. A bit of magic. Straight from the subconscious, I suppose. I was exploring my own fears. What if…?

I always knew that I was adopted. When I was younger, I used to make great mileage out of it: 'I am different, aren't I lucky?' I would announce to anyone who would listen. But actually, I didn't want to look too closely at the questions that underpinned my life. Who was my "real" mother? My "real" father? Why did my mother give me away? What if she hadn't? What if she'd changed her mind about the adoption, right at the last minute…?

For a writer, having a life underpinned by "what if…?" is a real gift. The root of fiction is a writer's ability to ask *what if* all the time – to invent happenings, characters, settings is a real joy, and I had been playing at *what if* ever since I can remember.

Here's a well trodden *what if* from my childhood:

What if my real mother is actually the Queen, and what if she comes visiting our town, and what if she recognises me and asks for me back? What will I do? What if I decide to go back with her and be a princess? What will my mummy and daddy do then – will she let them visit?

What started out as a daydream would end up in tears as I invented a scenario in which I was displaced again, and would be traumatised by a fresh separation. Funny, isn't it? But you see, that's all I'm doing now really. Stories like 'Cactus Man' are simply me acting out the *what ifs*, just as I used to as a child (minus the Queen!).

One of the things I have not done yet consciously, and will when I am ready, is explore more about the role of the birth mother, *my* birth mother, in the equation I have discovered about my own adoption. It's not something I've focused on and I suppose there is anger getting in the way. Bewilderment.

But again, just as I allowed a fictitious character to experience my own uncomfortable journey of discovery, so have I already explored loss from a mother's point of view in fiction, many times. I'm no psychologist, but there must be a reason why many of my most successful stories have at their centre the loss or death of a child.

What is success? A piece of work that has won a competition, or been published somewhere difficult. That's one answer. But actually, success is also something I feel myself when I write. If I am moved by a story as I write it (and I'm the inventor, remember?) it must be allowing me to express some emotion. Maybe an emotion I am not otherwise letting out. Something hidden, even from myself?

I've created several women who have lost children. And far from those characters being (as one might expect if I am angry) flawed women, powerful and controlling – they are ordinary, decent women, beleaguered by life, experiencing tough contexts, conflict aplenty. Look at this lot:

There's Batty Annie who lost a son, Dai, in an accident 30 years ago, still searching for his soul in a disused railway tunnel. (Freud would have a field day!) There's Eva Duffy the Irish postwoman who lost two-year-old Declan to asthma years ago, who talks to a plastic statuette of the Virgin Mary. (Just another mother who lost a son, on one level…) There's the synaesthete, May, and there's Shelley, a young single mother from a high-rise flat, both of whom lose baby sons.

Notice the lack of lost girls? Fiction is lovely – you write what is most comfortable, you explore what you can in the best way for you. And obviously, I didn't feel comfortable looking too closely at women who lost girls.

I know from conversations over time with many friends who are adult adoptees how bewilderment is the overarching emotion we feel – we, the ones who were "left behind" as I like to put it; as though it was a simple act of abandonment, as simple as leaving unwanted baggage at the side of the road. You see how immature my definitions are? I am still that small child at the side of the road, somewhere in my being, even though I am a woman over 50, a mother, wife, businesswoman, author, teacher – and many other labels as well. It's important to acknowledge and respect what we feel, I think. Only then can we begin to understand.

I did allow myself to explore a child's bewilderment in a story. But again, I used the distance afforded by fiction, a fictitous character, to give me permission to do so. I became a six-year-old Inuit girl called Qissunqac, whose parents don't have enough food to keep her. The story, called 'The Kettle on the Boat', follows Qissunqac's final journey with her parents, across a lake. I remember crying as I wrote this story – and I still can't tackle it at a reading event. The sight of the writer in a heap of tears on the stage would not exactly be good entertainment!

I think that sums up where I am in my own journey. My fiction has been one of the biggest treats – one that has helped me to explore, albeit unwittingly, all sorts of facets of my life, and specifically, my own journey through the maze of adoption.

I now know how important it was for me to examine my own issues, and to stop hiding from them. To stop pretending that everything was OK, and that I had no hang-ups. They were holding me back, weighing me down – whatever analogy you want to use.

My fiction continues. The work I'm doing now explores the lives of a group of men who are held back by family events in the past. My journey carries on, and my fiction both feeds and supports that journey.

I teach and facilitate writing now, and have done so for some years, teaching adults, school students, and university students. I have worked extensively with disadvantaged adults (meaning the homeless and those struggling with addictions – but I do hate the terminology).

I teach exactly as I was taught myself, trying to help my students to open themselves up to their own words and feelings in the search for the strongest, most vibrant resonant words. In teaching and facilitating, I try to share this gift I enjoy so much, this thing that can both create, liberate and fascinate.

I do not require writers to read out what they do, being acutely aware of how hard it is. But more importantly, because if we know we must read something out, we censor ourselves instantly. It is funny though – establish trust, and most people want to share. Those who don't, that's not my province. But if I can help them to open up and explore their feelings for themselves, then that's great.

I did not censor myself when I wrote the stories mentioned above. I just wrote. The characters came and acted out their stories. And it is only now, looking back, that I recognise where those stories' roots are. The roots are in my own bewilderment, my displacement, my "loss", my coming to terms with it all.

I am eternally grateful for two extraordinary gifts: my writing ability, such as it is, and most importantly, my experience of adoption. Given the choice, I would not change a thing.

SECTION 3

RITES OF PASSAGE

30-minute interview (this time next week) *Catherine Chanter*

Telling her (*Christmas*, 2009) *Catherine Chanter*

Jacques *Caroline Smith*

Meeting Evelyn *Cath Staincliffe*

Our day *Therese Ryan*

Returning to Peru *Milagros Caroline Forrester*

Positive/negative *Nikky Norton Shafau*

Defined by my adoption *Julie Beater*

Swimming up the sun *Nicole J Burton*

Prepare for surprises *Sarah Frances*

30-minute interview (this time next week)

CATHERINE CHANTER *

12.45	I will find a space in the multi-storey car park and pay.
12.50	I will check in at reception, saying I am a little early. 51 years early.
12.55	I will sit on a blue couch, watching strangers taking their lunch break.
1.00	I will notice the delay, even after so much delay.
1.05	I will recognise Kyla. Apologetic. She has no need to apologise.
1.08	I will perch in a room with low chairs, blinds half drawn and tissues.
1.10	I will acknowledge an explanation of process and legality.
1.15	I will explain where I am coming from and why, without irony.
1.30	I will reach out my hand and take what is known and unknown.
1.35	I will turn down the opportunity to ask questions of my own.
1.36	I am holding my file. I am deaf. I am dumb.
1.39	I will take the leaflets and contact (contact?) phone numbers.
1.40	I will say thank you and maybe see you again. Goodbyes.
1.45	Someone will come back to this car, having paid the price for a ticket, for the barrier, for the way out, of these multi-stories.

---

[4] For Catherine's bio details, see p 16.

Telling her (*Christmas*, 2009)

We are in the kitchen at Christmas, stripping the turkey, scraping remains
Of parsnips, wrinkled like fingers, into the dustbin, mother and daughter.
Two things congeal in the sink in between us, waiting to be washed up.
Cancer and adoption. We are both a little soaked ourselves. Outside, the
snow is sallow, yellowing where the house lights meet the evening; inside,
the timer prompts us.

You know I told you, I begin, about the whole birth mother thing,
Well, I've done it. She dries the glasses with linen woven with faces of
children, never believed you could use a machine for that sort of thing,
cheating, she called it. She says she's happy I've done it. Will you tell your
father about it? I say maybe later. She smiles, holds the glass to the light and
the towel to her eyes.

Jacques

CAROLINE SMITH

Caroline Smith was born in July 1968 of white British parentage. She stayed with her birth mother for ten weeks, joining her adoptive family in September. Caroline grew up happily, one of four adopted children, and her parents were always very open about their adoption. In 1997 she had an Adoption Contact Register match. Without any intermediary support, it was a rocky start. However, Caroline met her birth mother in 1998 with whom she still has regular contact as well as other members of her birth family. Her adoptive parents were supportive of the reunion. Caroline recently discovered that her French birth father died in 2004. She has located his daughter in Paris and has recently exchanged letters and photos with her. Caroline has two sons and lives in Yorkshire. The following piece was first published in *Something that Never Went Away* (AAA-NORCAP, 2009).

I see him sitting there at a café table, looking out to his beloved sea in a small fishing village in Bretagne.

I watch him for a few moments, taking him in, wondering what he's thinking.

He looks so calm and peaceful and I realise that my nerves have gone, even the excitement has faded and I feel calm and peaceful too.

Here, in front of me at last, is this man, an old man now, who I have thought about often over the years and whose face became known to me in a photograph just 12 years ago.

As I approach, he looks up and our eyes meet, I realise he cannot easily stand and instead he takes my hand as I sit down – such a simple gesture that means so much. There are no words, just tears and trembling smiles. The photo I have was taken 40 years earlier, he is 80 now but that twinkle in his eye is unmistakable, that smile, the one that I have often smiled back at, is a familiar one.

I fear my French will desert me in this moment but strangely it comes easily. The silence is broken with his first words to me: 'You look like your mother.'

'I know,' I tell her softly. '*And* like you too,' I add more proudly than I intend to.

We fall silent as he looks out to sea again and I wonder if he is thinking about my birth mother, the woman who I have come to know and care about over these 12 years. I have brought photos of her and me together, and with my two boys, her only grandchildren. He studies them closely.

I tell him about my family, about the holidays I spent as a young child in La Rochelle, his home town. It seems important that he understands my love of his country and how I have always felt at home rather than on holiday whenever my feet touch down on French soil. His relief is evident when I explain how my adoptive parents, in spite of any private fears they may have had, generously accepted and supported my decision to trace my birth parents. I tell him that I know they would have liked each other and how my parents welcomed my birth mother into their home, and how I've been welcomed so warmly by her family, especially by her husband and her brother's family.

My French friend Peggy joins us a while later and translates when my French inevitably begins to fail me and his English falters. And so the afternoon passes. She has been with me on this journey for many years and has unselfishly understood my need and desire for a French connection, not just for myself but for my boys too. To share this day with her is special beyond words.

It is a perfect reunion and one I had not dared ever to imagine before now. And of course it can be perfect because this reunion did not take place in Bretagne, in fact it did not actually happen at all. The truth is that it only ever takes place in my imagination. I realise it is how I am dealing with the recent discovery that Jacques died in August 2004. Maybe it sounds like an odd thing, to imagine the perfect reunion now – but what I realise is that no one and nothing can make it untrue or less than how I have wanted it to be. The sense of loss seems to come over me in waves. It is not like the profound grief and sadness I felt when my adoptive father died. This is about the loss of the hope, knowing for certain that we will never meet. I cannot tell you or him why I waited until now to look for him, so the sadness is also about the lost opportunity to reassure him that he has often been in my thoughts. I feel so fortunate to know that he was a well-liked and well-respected man and I know that in time this fantasy reunion will become a comforting "memory".

What I also know is that this is not just a story about me, my adoptive parents and my birth parents. I know that I have been lucky, whichever angle you look at it from. To have had loving and much loved adoptive parents and family is a blessing. I know the journey with my birth mother hasn't always been smooth, due I'm sure in part because my approach to her was an independent one, so there was no caring and experienced intermediary to support and guide us in those turbulent early days. However, it is a relationship I treasure very much. This journey for me is not just about adoption though, it is also about friendship, love, acceptance and understanding. I know how it feels to be on the receiving end of a sceptical look, a questioning comment or a mute silence that speaks volumes when I have talked about the search for my birth relatives. To have experienced the generosity of spirit and kindness of heart, to be able to confide and trust in others to guide me when I have not been sure how or even if to proceed further, is precious and what has brought me this far.

I have come to realise that over the years certain people have come into my life for a reason, when the time is right, and just a thought, a reflection or a shared story is enough to trigger the certainty; the moment has come to understand better, search further or use my personal experience of adoption in other ways.

I would be lying if I said there hadn't been difficult times but I have no regrets.

I have often thought about putting pen to paper but just never found quite the right motivation. Having in a sense lost and found Jacques now, I have, as is human nature to do, taken stock of how fortunate I am and so I dedicate this not just to him but to every friend, relative and colleague who has accepted and supported my yearning to know and therefore also touched my life deeply.

Meeting Evelyn

CATH STAINCLIFFE *

If this were a christening
I could bring silver spoons, bootees, blessings

If this were a wedding
I could bring rings and confetti, promises, cake

If this were a funeral
I could bring wreaths and condolences, memories, tears

But this rite of passage is not bound by tradition
No customs to follow, no correct etiquette

So I will bring poems that speak of my passions
And photos and papers recording the past

And we will swap smiles of sweet recognition
Trade tears for all of the time we have lost
Hold fast to each other, the hug of reunion
Completing the circle
Together again

* For Cath's bio details, see p 108.

Our day

THERESE RYAN *

Our day is approaching.
I expect a blue moon
A meteor shower
A double rainbow
A spectacular sunset
A celebration of the heavens
When we meet again.
But I will be happy with
A skipped heartbeat
Sweaty palms
An inner cry of recognition.

* For Therese's bio details, see p 55.

Returning to Peru

MILAGROS CAROLINE FORRESTER

Milagros Caroline Forrester was born in 1979, in Arequipa, Peru. Adopted at the age of 16 months by a US/Argentine mother and an Irish/Austrian father, she was raised in London. She has three sisters and four brothers, two of whom are also adopted from Peru. Since writing this piece, Milagros's adoption journey has taken an interesting turn. She searched for her biological family with the help of a local television station in Peru, leading to a short documentary. Since then she has become connected with other Peruvian adoptees from all around the world and it has been a huge learning experience. Milagros is currently maintaining and developing relationships with her birth siblings. Her adoption has been an extremely challenging and rewarding experience.

Returning back to my homeland had always been in my thoughts and desires since I was very young. It was never a question of "if" but rather "when" I would go back and with whom. Peru seemed far away in terms of distance but never in thought.

Ever since I can remember, Peru has been a familiar topic of discussion at home. This is how my birth culture was introduced to me – through books, documentaries, art exhibitions and personal stories of my parents' experiences in Peru. Although growing up being transracially and transnationally adopted was difficult, one of the most rewarding aspects is the journey I have taken through learning, loving and appreciating my Peruvian heritage. My parents' introduction to Peru was amazing. They had travelled around the country several times and my mum had studied, lived and worked there. They were able to communicate a very positive understanding and encourage me not to think less of Peru due to her economic situation but understand that she has a lot to offer me. They emphasised that I should never forget about where I come from and to begin to explore and grow from this whole experience.

Getting to know about my culture has been imperative for several reasons. Growing up never having met a Peruvian, I wanted to put all the pieces of my life together. It got to the stage where hearing and learning about my culture through secondary sources wasn't enough; I needed to take a more pro-active approach. My parents' decision to adopt my two brothers and I from a country they knew and loved enabled me to return to Peru with a sense of positivity, optimism and a realisation that it would be an enriching experience.

It has been over ten years since that first visit. I have been to Peru many times now and know it better than any other country. It has taken many visits to understand Peruvian society and customs, to travel to different regions and to build a strong connection with places. I feel very comfortable in Peru and parts of some cities already feel familiar. I am used to the altitude of the Sierra (highlands) and the long incredible bus journeys, and I have lived with Peruvian families and other people. By returning to my country of origin I have re-established links and made Peru a major part of my recent history.

I have never met anyone biologically related to me; the closest I have are my adopted brothers. Although we are not blood relatives, we share a common history and experiences that are unique to us and only we can understand. Trying to make sense of the first 17 months of my life seems like a long and impossible journey. With no concrete information like a birth certificate, learning about my birth country has been the way to piece together my heritage and early childhood.

Growing up, I never came across people who had been adopted, let alone transnationally. My understanding of adoption was through my personal family experiences. I thought transnational adoption was uncommon in England as I had never met another transnational adoptee. Meeting others through the Transnational and Transracial Adoption Group[1] was an extraordinary experience. I was very curious to know about their relationships with their birth cultures and what growing up was like for them. These shared experiences have enabled me to understand adoption in a wider context and to realise that establishing a connection with one's birth country can be difficult and may not happen until later in life.

I have always had a Peruvian passport and have had to apply for British citizenship. However, I felt that only when I had an understanding of what it meant to be Peruvian and had returned to Peru several times, would I consider applying for British citizenship. Living in London has been beneficial to me. Had I been brought up in North America, where there is a large Latin cultural community, my experience would have been very different – I have never had to face stereotypes of Latino people.

I have always been proud of my "race" and know I look Peruvian. As a

---

[1] See under 'Useful organisations/websites'.

foundling, not knowing any information about my background, my inherited features are very important as they link me to a particular group of people. Therefore, perhaps subconsciously, I have focused on understanding my birth culture.

When I returned to Peru I began to consider who I was and to question which traits I have inherited from my birth parents and which were learned from my adoptive family. Being able to identify these traits has given me a greater sense of identity.

Usually I am quite a cautious person but when it comes to Peru I am very open. It has become a place where I can think about things and assess situations, and where I can fully relax and contemplate life.

For transnational adoptees choosing to return to their birth country, my advice would be to think about the kind of experience you would like. I decided to do voluntary work with a local charity and worked for two months in a technical college in the hospitality sector. Working and living with Peruvians from the start helped me to settle in and relate to the people. It also meant I had to speak Spanish.

Although I myself have never searched for my birth family, time and money permitting, I would allow several visits before you begin your search. Going back to your country is to experience an entirely new environment and I recommend that you have some knowledge of its history, culture and people before you set out. With this behind you, communicating and establishing a relationship, perhaps with birth family, may be easier. Just visiting the country is emotionally very draining. Also, remember, a lot of the experience of searching depends on one's experience of "difference" and what kind of exposure you already have had to your birth culture.

For adoptees who have thought constantly about returning, understanding the experience, including what you have learned about yourself, may take several visits. Each time I have travelled to Peru has been different and I never knew when I would return. It all depended on what I needed to do and when I was ready. For instance, during my first visit I met my social worker but it wasn't until the fifth trip that I went to the orphanage where I had lived as a baby.

Now, when I go to Peru I feel sad that I am not returning home or to relatives. When I was younger it was not a problem; everything was new. However, I realise that this situation is not going to change and I am reminded of the fact that I am a foundling, which can be hard to accept. I love going back to Peru. I feel that I always have to be constructive in my relationship with the country in order for it to grow.

I often think about what it would be like to live in Peru but this demands a serious amount of thought. For the moment, I have decided to communicate with fellow Peruvian adoptees who have settled there. In addition, I have decided to enhance and further my education and understanding of not only Peruvian but also other Latin American cultures by visiting a variety of countries in the region.

Positive/negative

NIKKY NORTON SHAFAU

Nikky Norton Shafau was born in 1985 in Nigeria. She came to the UK with her birth family and joined her adoptive family at ten months old, being legally adopted at the age of nine. Now based in Manchester, Nikky is involved in the arts and runs her own social enterprise, Identity Detective, encouraging people to explore themselves creatively (see www.identitydetective.co.uk). Nikky would love to hear from anyone who would like to join the journey.

Lately,
I'm feeling cold.
I'm burning old photographs just to stay warm.
And whilst I shiver,
inhaling my memories' smoke,

My dense pupils fuel the fire.

Sundays
Have started to make me feel old.
I get up before I need to get up
And go carpet skiing in my slippers
And question what life would be like without a cup of tea.

I ponder
On the people I have lost,
Hoping they have found

Hoping
They
Have
Found.

Knock knock knock, is it for me?
This milk has soured in my tea.

Today
She returned.
I had to tweezer pick the negatives,

Dislocate my disbelief
And pull my nightie over my knees to hold myself upright.
She made 364 knocks at the door but this was my time to answer.

Hello…

Tomorrow
Is
Tomorrow.
I will make a firm commitment now to herbal tea.

My words to her will roll out like a prayer mat,
Giving her time for reflection and pause,
My eyes receiving her eyes framed.

Defined by my adoption

JULIE BEATER

....

Julie Beater was born in England in 1964. Her birth mother was Scottish-Irish and her birth father is unknown. She was approximately three-and-a-half years old when she joined her adoptive family and was legally adopted a week before her fifth birthday. Her adoptive experience has been mostly positive. Julie has some minimal contact with birth siblings. She lives in Berkshire.

....

The significant events/transitions in my life have been complex and emotionally charged. It is hard to be sure how I would have approached them had I not been adopted as adoption is all I have ever known.

My earliest memory of major significance is one of change. I recall waking in my own bedroom in my new adoptive family home and racing downstairs with an immense feeling of euphoria and excitement, waiting for people to arrive to meet me with their arms full of presents, just for me, because I was very special, because I was adopted! The next significant memory is sitting in the car with my adoptive parents being told very seriously that a 'very important man (the judge) is going to ask you if you want to stay with us and all you have to do is say, "Yes!"'

Another significant event again relates to change in my adoptive family dynamics. I recall going to meet my new adoptive brother in the large and foreboding children's home. Unfortunately, I took an instant dislike to him (and vice versa). Of course, there are similarities with a non-adoptive family. A non-adoptive child might resent the birth of a younger sister or brother, and this is often expected. However, one of the main differences is guilt. As an adoptive child, there is often an unwritten rule that you should feel a sense of compassion, empathy and understanding. If another adoptive child joins your new "forever family" it is a cause for celebration and is a "worthy and wonderful magical event". I did not feel this way and remained resentful towards him and towards my family for choosing another child. Sadly, this view was reciprocated by my adoptive brother and we would hurl insults towards each other, out of earshot, such as (me), 'You are second best; they chose me first!' and (him), 'You weren't enough for them!' Another difficulty was that neither of us had the chance to gradually get to know the other over time, as birth children do, since I was eight when he arrived and he was six.

My next significant memory concerns new beginnings: starting school. This memory for me is tainted with fear, shame and confusion – the fear of being left alone again and the shame and confusion of not knowing what those big letters on the wall, the alphabet, meant. All the other children in my class could read them out loud with confidence. Was this the same for everyone or was it traumatic because I was adopted? Again, it is very hard to say but I do recall how school seemed to be a breeding ground for confusion and anxiety. Another example is on the day that my adopted brother started at the same school and the inevitable questions: 'Why doesn't he look like you? How come you didn't have a brother yesterday but today you do?' To this day, I can't recall how I responded but I clearly remember the feelings of confusion, anxiety and fear, coupled with a need to run away, to avoid everyone and block it all out. The need to try to fit in with everyone else prevailed throughout my school career and was, at times, like a cut, irritating but often unnoticed, and at others like an open wound – very painful.

My middle childhood years continued to be just as confusing and complex. I remain convinced that this was due to my adoptive status. For example, a simple request to join the local Baptist church, because my best friend had, was met by my adoptive parents with much apprehension. Instantly I understood that this was due to my birth mother being a staunch Catholic. I was allowed to go, just the once. In order to fit in I conformed, again. Would a non-adoptive child have had the same dilemma, I wonder? Or was it that my adoptive parents had been told not to change my religion?

Adoption pervaded family life. During the long hot summer of 1976 it was arranged that we would go on holiday to Scotland rather than to Spain, our usual and more exotic holiday destination. I had been told previously by my adoptive dad that my birth mother had been born in Scotland. I was aware just how much my adoptive parents hated anything remotely Scottish. Therefore, secretly I was thrilled by the fact we were going to travel to Scotland, both unknown to me yet unconsciously familiar. The thrill of the forbidden! My memories of this holiday are some of the fondest of my childhood years. Somehow being in Scotland just felt completely right, safe and familiar. To this day, Scotland feels like a sanctuary to me.

As an adopted teenager, the issue of identity majored. At times, I was completely obsessed with trying to find myself. I recall sitting for long periods of time, examining my face in the mirror in minute detail, wondering where my brownish (sometimes greenish) eyes actually came from. This may be standard behaviour for any teenager. What was so different was the intensely odd but exciting feeling I would get after staring at my reflection for several minutes, a feeling that someone else other than me was staring back at me – a stranger. Who was this stranger in the mirror? Was it really me? Or was it my birth mother or my birth father? Or a sibling? The feeling was intense and surreal and always left me frustrated at never knowing the answer. Thinking rationally, I could see a slight similarity between myself and my adoptive dad but I knew that this was only superficial; that if someone examined our features side by side our secret would be out.

Not surprisingly, as a teenager, the topic of relationships was often all encompassing. However, for me, I somehow just "knew" to have a sexual relationship without being married would be the most unspeakable thing for my adoptive parents to bear and would mean that I was just like my birth mother. My biggest fear was that somehow I wouldn't be able to live up to my parents' ideal and, indeed, I would turn out just like her as it was in my blood. In reality, up until the age of almost 18 I remained resolutely and determinedly single.

However, the next significant event changed everything forever. At the age of 16 and ten weeks precisely, my life changed dramatically: my adoptive parents and adoptive brother died in a car accident. Thus my "forever family" was no more. Of course, bereavement for any child in such a way is utterly and totally traumatic and tragic, but for me, the role of "orphan" was simply unbearable and completely without warning. The sense of being alone without a family was once again a reality. This time there were no more second chances. One of the most hurtful things was that the phrase "adopted daughter left behind" was used freely and without thought in the local paper during the announcement of the accident. This cutting reminder to myself and to others was extremely hurtful, distressing and completely unnecessary.

Thus followed a period of late teenage rebellion with a vengeance, completely void of any form of parental control. My trust in people and life had been completely and utterly broken. The words "out of control" rang true during the following few years. Relationships began and ended with alarming and increasing frequency. The need to be loved, wanted and to fit in felt stronger than ever, whatever the cost to myself or others. A lack of self-esteem and no self-control, fuelled by a desire to live only for the moment, resulted in a shallow and superficial lifestyle. Trust was something I continued to grapple with. What was the point in trusting people when those whom I had trusted in my life so far – my birth parents and adoptive family – were no longer a part of my life? The safest way to survive was to remain independent, mobile and alone. The mantra 'trust no one but yourself' was always on my lips.

The next significant event was during my early 20s when I decided, after an earlier tentative attempt, to try to locate my birth family in order to gain some sense of peace and an understanding of the reasons for my adoption. After very grudgingly having the obligatory birth records counselling (Section 51 as it was referred to then), my social worker located one of my birth siblings and I found out that I was in fact the sixth child out of seven. This discovery was alarming, thrilling and extremely confusing. At this point, I also discovered that my birth mother had died a couple of months previously from a planned overdose. Her death was something I had never anticipated nor felt prepared for. The feelings of anger, distress and frustration were extremely powerful. At the same time, the need to meet my birth relatives was completely and utterly overwhelming. The initial meeting with all of them was bewildering but also truly magical. There was a real sense of coming home and of finally fitting in and belonging. The spectre of Genetic Sexual Attraction [2] reared its forbidden head briefly at one point, something I am able to understand now and put into context.

The next significant rite of passage is commonplace for many people – marriage. The complexity and typical stresses of planning a wedding were, of course, not unique. However, for me the fact of being adopted was always the unspoken "elephant in the room". Everyone knew but no one made direct reference to my adoption, except on the day itself when a distant adoptive relative chose to confide in a fellow guest that, of course, I 'wasn't a real member of their family' as I was 'adopted'. Yet another unwelcome reminder of my adoptive status.

I had always believed that I would never become pregnant as this had been the experience of my adoptive parents. How surprised I was then to discover I had become pregnant almost straight away! There was also a sense of fear within me that somehow I would be a bad mother; that I wouldn't be capable of loving my baby nor caring for him or her adequately. Of course, the usual questions at the ante-natal appointments are already well documented for adopted people: do you have a history of X, X and X in your family? And the standard answers were what I used each time, 'I don't know as I am adopted.' Despite meeting my birth siblings, I still had very little information about my birth mother's health, other than that she had experienced mental illness,

---

[2] This refers to the phenomenon of sexual attraction between close relatives such as siblings, first and second cousins or a parent, who have been separated during the critical years of development. It is not uncommon in adoption reunion – see Alix Kirsta, 'Genetic sexual attraction', *The Guardian*, Saturday 17 May 2003; www.guardian.co.uk/theguardian/2003/may/17/weekend7.weekend2.

and knew absolutely nothing about my birth father. I recall looking at my son for the very first time and thinking, 'Is this what I looked like as a baby?' How could my birth mother have let me go? The second time around, with my daughter, the questions were exactly the same and remained unanswered.

The next significant event, my divorce, had far less impact on me than adoption. For me, although obviously not for my children, the consequences were relatively minor. However, I do recall a déjà vu feeling as all of my birth siblings had divorced, as had my birth mother – several times. This was in direct contrast to my adoptive family where it had never occurred. Thus, the feeling of being the odd one out reared its head again for a while.

Interestingly, my choice of a career in social work has been influenced by my early and continuing experiences of growing up as an adopted child and adult. At times, this has been difficult emotionally, as well as thought provoking. However, at other times, I feel somewhat blessed to have been able to come out the other side and experience a sense of growth as a person, and finally feel validated from being valued and seen as important.

Finally, looking back, I often ask myself whether, if I could, I would change the past. I always struggle to come to a clear conclusion and probably always will. Yes, if I had control of my history. To grow up in a different family to my biological one is not a choice I would have made, yet it has enabled me to live a very different and more privileged life financially. Would I have been happier remaining with my birth siblings? If I am completely truthful, then yes, I think so in terms of enjoying a relationship with them and growing up to know my birth mother, having a sense of belonging and fitting in. However, such a choice would have meant I would never have known my adoptive parents, never would have experienced a financially stable childhood, nor would I have had access to a grammar school education. All in all, adoption has played an important and integral part in making me who I am. Ultimately, a life without adoption is simply unthinkable. This experience has defined me and will undoubtedly continue to do so throughout my life.

Swimming up the sun

NICOLE J BURTON

Nicole Burton is the author of *Swimming Up the Sun: A memoir of adoption* (Apippa Publishing, 2008), adapted for the stage as *Swimming Up the Sun: The adoption play*. Born in 1956 in Nottingham, Nicole was adopted and raised in England. She learned from her parents early on that her "original" mother was an artist and her father a Jewish businessman. As a teenager, she emigrated to the United States with her adoptive family. Nicole returned to England to search for and be reunited with her original parents at the age of 28. Although they are now both dead, she continues relationships with siblings and other family members. Nicole's story is also featured in the adoption anthology, *Something that Never Went Away* (AAA-NORCAP, 2009). A playwright, Nicole lives near Washington DC. The first three chapters of *Swimming Up the Sun* and the play can be read at www.NicoleJBurton.com.

We adopted people experience special rites of passage as we grow and adjust to the world. Even ordinary rites of passage such as marriage and having children hold special intensity and challenge for us. This is how I've navigated my rites of passage and what I've learned so far.

Growing up

Birthdays are loaded times and they got more intense as I grew up. Birthdays could have been subtitled, 'Happy Anniversary of Your PTSD'. I never knew during the year if my original mother, Eve, was thinking of me, but on my birthday I was sure she was, so my antennae stretched high into the sky like the character from *My Favourite Martian* and I listened for her messages all day long. In my 20s, boyfriends would try to make me happy on my birthday with extravagant parties and gifts, but nothing they could do or buy was enough to fill the hole in my heart. Every birthday began with anxiety and expectations, and ended with arguments and the blues.

I experienced the usual adolescent mood swings but looking back, I see the anxiety and depression I felt was heightened by adoption loss. When I was in my mid-teens, my adoptive parents divorced and my adoptive mother, Moo, to whom I was devoted, became alcoholic. This emotional maelstrom led me to experiment with drugs to mask the pain and to help myself feel "normal". After all, by the age of 16 I had already lost two mothers. I had no idea why my mothers kept leaving; surely, I was doing something wrong. In spite of growing up in a loving family, I felt lonely, rootless and suicidal.

Family history

From the beginning, my adoptive parents told me my mother, Eve, was an artist and my original father a Jewish businessman, both from Nottingham in the Midlands, where Moo was also from. Hearing the details over and over was enormously important to me. These facts – I prayed they were true – were anchors in a confusing, turbulent sea. Moo loved art, literature, music and dance. She took me to lots of performances and exhibitions and in doing so, I felt she honoured my original mother's profession.

My given name was Pippa. It appeared on my adoption order, which my parents kept in a special place in their writing bureau. I often "visited" this document, re-reading my name, my mother's name, and the dates and places of my known past. My adoption order was a touchstone, the only tangible link to the Real Me. Even though no information appeared on the order about my father, Moo told me that because Eve had named me Pippa, the diminutive of Philippa, my father's name was probably Philip. What a joy to find out this was true and how great it was to eventually be able to tell him.

I unconsciously incorporated my birth name into my identity. My adoptive parents named me "Annette." After I emigrated with my family to the United States, everyone I met associated my name with the actress Annette Funicello, who starred in the 1960s beach party movies and began her career as a Mouseketeer on the *Mickey Mouse Club* TV show. I thought her persona silly and fumed under this miscasting until I realised I could change my name when I became an American citizen. At the age of 18, I legally changed my name from "Annette" to "Nicole", and began calling myself "Nicki". "Nicole" retained the French formality of "Annette" but "Nicki" was the short, lively nickname I yearned for. It wasn't until years later I realised my new name, Nicki Burton, had the same number of letters and syllables as my given name, Pippa ------ .

Searching and reunion

I have written at length about searching and reunion in my book, *Swimming Up the Sun: A Memoir of Adoption*, the writing of which was itself a rite of passage. In 1978, I was among the first "graduating classes" of British open birth records. With great trepidation, I applied for my counselling appointment, got through the interview and waited stoically for my birth certificate to arrive in the official brown envelope. At St Catherine's House, I poured through the rows of black, leather-bound volumes for my family members' birth and marriage information, and daydreamed of happy reunions.

Back in the United States, I got permission to search the stacks of the Library of Congress and hunted for phone numbers in the dusty section devoted to international phone books. My search took place pre-internet, when even long-distance phone calls were expensive and difficult to make. Today, reunions happen faster thanks to Facebook, Twitter, internet registries, and private investigators. Yet the speed of connecting may present its own challenges at times; the cushion of time created by old-fashioned communications afforded me a chance to stoke the fire of courage I needed to continue.

Returning to my "home country" meant familiar sights, tastes and sounds, including the comforting lilt of a Midlands accent. Growing up, my adoptive father, Roger, had been in the Royal Air Force and we moved frequently, but my parents never took me to Nottingham. I knew Moo's parents were dead and she had no family there but I still wondered why, especially since she enchanted me with stories of her childhood. I believe she was frightened of losing me and of encouraging my already heightened interest in reconnecting with my original families.

Eventually, Moo moved back to England. Out of the blue, she wrote to me and revealed something she must have known all along: 'Your real father's business is still there in Nottingham; it's Minson's, on Upper Parliament Street.' As quickly as I could, I saved the money for a trip back and arm in arm, we walked together through the front door of Minson's. This act was one of the greatest gifts she ever gave me. It was so important to have her support as well as the quiet approval of Roger.

Of course, meeting one's original parents for the first time is one of the threshold experiences for adopted people. I met Philip first, and he helped me to find Eve; I met them both within a week of each other. What a hallucinogenic experience it is to meet your parents for the first time at the age of 28! So terrifying yet thrilling; every yearning I'd ever felt coming to fruition, every dream-desire coming to pass. And finally, that lonely, lost, rootless feeling began to unknot. I felt my roots take hold, lock in and find ground here on earth. Just. Like. Everyone. Else.

Ethnic and spiritual heritage

I grew up knowing I was Jewish but not having a clue as to what that meant. I never saw a synagogue. I never met another Jew. At times, I thought perhaps they'd all been killed in the Holocaust. While this was absurd, it terrified me to think that I was the last Jew left alive. I asked Moo about the Holocaust, and she gave me a copy of The Diary of Anne Frank to read. When we moved to the States, I finally made my first Jewish friend, and at the winter concert in high school, we sang a Hanukkah song among the Christmas carols. Singing Jewish songs, finding my way into Jewish rituals through friends, I slowly crept closer to Judaism.

A giant leap forward happened when I met Phillip, whose prelude to telling me our family history was this acknowledgement: 'Well, you know that we're Jewish...' I obtained photos of family members by taking photos of photos and by asking for copies and creating my own family albums. Eventually I converted to Judaism, going through the traditional *Bet Din* ritual in which I was questioned by three rabbis and took a *mikva* (a ceremonial bath with special blessings). I joined a friendly synagogue, studying with other adults and participated in an adult *b'nai mitzvah* celebration. After the *b'nai mitzvah*, my rabbi asked me to choose a Hebrew name. After perusing a book of names, I chose *Sima*, Aramaic for "treasure". My journey to Judaism and reconnecting with my family roots remains a treasure to me.

Life events

Marrying, having children, attending funerals and all the other life events we participate in by virtue of being human are extra intense for adopted people. We wonder, 'Who will come, call, or acknowledge us? Will we be included?'

One challenge, particularly after reunion, is how as adults we blend our families together. At first, I felt I had to keep the different family members apart, that their feelings were too fragile to risk the potential discomfort of intermingling. Now, I see the intermingling as a necessity and an opportunity. My adoptive father says he gained – not lost – a daughter when I reunited with my sister Angela, whom he first met at my wedding.

Parenting is another challenging arena. After my son Miles was born, I used to sob with gratitude as I nursed him. Yes, I had raging hormones like all mothers but it was more than that. I felt grateful that I could *keep my baby*. I imagined how Eve must have felt handing her baby over to a stranger and walking away, believing she'd never see me again. I realised how powerful a mother's love is for her child and how painful it must have been to lose me. Now that Miles is a teenager, adoption loss reappears as he separates himself from me and I recognise jabs of the old trauma. How we hate people leaving us.

Eve and Philip never met after I reunited with them. I had begun suggesting a meeting shortly before Philip died of a heart attack; he was only 60. I had one opportunity for my adoptive father Roger to meet Phillip, but I didn't have the courage to make it happen. We were in Nottingham for the sad event of

Moo's funeral. I'd told Philip I was coming and arranged to meet him with my husband at the hotel bar, while Roger was upstairs taking a nap. I wished I could bring my two fathers together but it didn't feel safe. I felt as if I might hurt Roger's feelings. I wish I had pushed past my fears and brought them together. It was the only opportunity I ever had.

However, when my son Miles was preparing for his *bar mitzvah*, I invited Philip's youngest daughter Becca. Despite her intentions, a new job precluded her coming. I'd never met Philip's cousin, Danny, in person but we'd spoken by phone and I decided to invite him, come what may; he'd been Philip's best friend growing up.

To our delight, Danny and his wife flew over and attended my son's *bar mitzvah*; I was thrilled to have real Jewish relatives in attendance! I held a special dinner in their honour at my house and was able to introduce Roger and my stepmother to Danny, Philip's cousin, as a way to make up for the lost opportunity of years before. We do the best we can, and it's enough.

Rites of passage advice

Birthdays: These can be real rollercoasters of loss and hope. Knowing this, create rituals of comfort for yourself. If you're able to, reunite and reclaim your people. Make sure they know when your birthday is and how important it is to you.

Family history: Write it down, every detail of every conversation. Get photos, badger your relatives – nicely. Make yourself a family tree poster with photos of your original family going back as many generations as you can. Create a genealogical wheel and see how many names you can add. Openly acknowledge that you have multiple family histories – hey, you're just lucky.

Adolescence: Read *Journey of the Adopted Self* by Betty Jean Lifton[3] to understand the phases we all go through. Arm yourself and your parents with the fact that being an adopted person is a lifelong experience. Make sure your parents understand adolescence is double-plus-brutal for us. Reunite with your original families (if possible); reclaim and blend what you can to build an authentic sense of self. Don't apologise for your needs, dreams, and desires. It *is* about you. Adoptive parents, take note: it's *not* about you. Be extra cautious around drugs and alcohol; we have extra feelings. It's tempting to self-medicate to deal with them. Get sympathetic, knowledgeable, professional help instead and attend 12-step meetings, if appropriate.

[3] Published by Basic Books, 1995

Searching: Go. Search. Be brave. Get support. Surround yourself with adoption sisters, brothers, mothers, fathers, grandparents and cousins. Get hugs from original mothers and fathers, even if they're not your own. We're all in this crazy social experiment together. Never give up but learn to live joyfully and with acceptance in the present moment. This nutty spiritual balancing act *can* be mastered and will be a great asset throughout your life – it's worth the practice.

Reunion: Write it all down, keep files, don't trust to memory alone. The experiences of reuniting are so intense, you won't recall the details, and they're too precious to lose. It's your story and your life to keep, build, and treasure. Take your time. You have the rest of your life to be an adopted person in reunion. Give your family members the gift of time, too.

Post-reunion: Back to real life. Yes, the honeymoon will eventually be over; enjoy it while it lasts. Get support, especially from your parents. Encourage them to work through their own feelings and fears. Yes, it's *still* all about us.

Blending families: Introduce your parents, siblings, and grandparents. Even if it feels awkward, do it. The opportunity may only come once. It's not the things we do in life that we regret, it's the things we don't do. Be forewarned.

Marriage, funerals, and other life events: Be inclusive. The worst that will happen is that someone says no or can't handle their own feelings. Be courageous, invite everyone. Ask to be included. If they say no, find ways to acknowledge your need for meaning and ask for support from loved ones, such as your spouse/partner, siblings, and friends. It's your life – live it bravely.

Parenting: If you haven't reunited when you have your first child, realise you're meeting and getting to know your first biological relative. Male adoptees often run to adoption support groups and begin the search process when they experience fatherhood for the first time. Read *Mother Me* by Zara Philips,[4] a reunited adoptee who writes movingly about how adoption affects us as parents; and Ann Fessler's extraordinary interviews of mothers who surrendered their children to adoption, *The Girls Who Went Away*.[5] Above all, don't be surprised when adoption loss ambushes you. It's just old feelings being triggered. It gets easier over time. If the feelings persist, get help from professionals or a self-help group.

Rifts: Take a break from relationships when necessary. Expect to be treated

---

[4] Published by BAAF, 2008
[5] Published by Penguin, 2007

with dignity. Ask yourself: Would I let a friend treat me like this? If and when rifts occur, step back but keep the lines of communication open through holiday cards, prayers for well-being, daily blessings for all to be happy, joyous, and free. Take care of yourself. Join or rejoin an adoption support group and national groups that hold workshops and conferences such as AAA-NORCAP and, in the US, the American Adoption Congress. They're not just for the search and reunion period. Focus on helping others search and reunite, and work to repeal oppressive laws and practices. Give of your stock of courage, experience and compassion. Encouraging others will help you feel better when the going gets tough in your own relationships.

Ethnic and spiritual heritage: Explore your heritage as much as you want. It's yours. Exploration may lead to less interest, as it's no longer forbidden fruit, or more, as you connect with deep feelings. Find a way to put your adoption experience into a spiritual context; you were put on earth for a reason. Read the works of Penny Callan Partridge,[6] the American "poet laureate of adoption". Write, paint, sew, sculpt, sing and play your story for all it's worth. It's a precious gift to you, your family members, and the world. You, go!

---

[6] See www.pennycallanpartridge.com

Prepare for surprises

SARAH FRANCES

Sarah Frances was born Susan Duffy in 1968. Her birth mother was from the west of Ireland and her birth father Libyan. Sarah was placed with two families before being adopted by an English family in 1968. They had two birth sons and later adopted another girl. The family broke up in 1977. Her adoptive mother met another man whom she and the children moved in with in 1981, moving to Spain a year later. At 14, Sarah returned to live with an informal foster family, but this broke down and she lived with a different family for another year before joining her adoptive father and stepmother. She then left home, travelled and went to university. Sarah has no contact with her adoptive family but is in touch with both birth families in Libya and Ireland. She lives in Brighton with her partner, Lesley, and Greek rescue dog, Pina Colada. She is presently training in sensorimotor psychotherapy.

My first rite of passage as an adoptee was one I cannot consciously recall: being taken from my birth mother. While my thinking mind can't remember this moment, I believe there is a stored memory of this deep in my body. Babies, I believe, have a certain innate wisdom and when taken from my mother somehow I knew I would not see her for many years and would need to protect myself in the world. In addition, the written and verbal narratives passed to me about my initial adoption have had a powerful influence upon my character and sense of identity from childhood to this day.

The second rite of passage arrived in the official "telling". I vaguely remember my adoptive mother telling me that I was adopted, when I was five or six years old. I remember feeling uncomfortable about being made to sit still and knew I was going to being given some serious information. However, I had already guessed I was different by the way adults talked about me when introduced to family friends; there would be a mixture of whispered conversation and special attention. Following on from "being told", I determined to read about my adoption, which I did when left alone in the house. My adoption papers were in the bottom drawer of a bureau, where anything secret was squirrelled away. I can still remember opening the typed adoption agency letter and reading my birth name for the first time: I really was someone else. As a child this allowed me to build a defence system which protected me when my adoptive family began to implode. I was able to stand outside their system and tell myself, 'I am nothing to do with these people; they are nothing to do with me.' I created a fairy tale, or script, where one day I would find my real family who would accept and welcome me back with great love. This helped me survive the breakdown of my adoptive parents' marriage, but it also left me with fantastical notions about what "mothers" and "real" families were like – ideas I continue to struggle with.

It has been vitally important for me to unearth and own these fantasies I dreamed up as a child. They were useful then but now, years later, they have outworn their use and often undermine my interpersonal relationships, creating ideals which can never be met. I have conditioned myself to stand on the outside of groups and identify as "other". This tracking back to childhood adoptive fantasies can be liberating for the adult who was adopted. By owning the early script there can be an understanding of how the adoptive experience can underscore the present and prevent the adult self from developing and sustaining mature relationships.

Discovering and being told I had another "original" identity left a further legacy: if I really was someone else then who was I? Questions of belonging and self-identity have walked with me ever since. Am I a product of my birth family? Has my "self" emerged from the upbringing and experiences I had in my adoptive family? Am "I" an autonomous being of my own making?

While these questions have often left me feeling confused, bewildered and alone, they have also been a source of great richness. I have had to dig and excavate, for as an adoptee, nothing can be assumed or taken for granted. This search for "I" seems central to the human condition and the subject of centuries of literature, art and philosophy. As adopted people, we are compelled to question who we are and in this way are given a great gift in life.

My third rite of passage was the decision to trace. I decided to start seeking my birth mother when I was 22. Very anti-family and with no idea of what this search may lead to, I was not sure why I was searching as I thought all families were useless. I remember phoning social services and being put through to the adoption team. Afterwards, I remember feeling breathless and excited, as if I was surfing the edge of a huge wave. I felt energised and almost surreal, not quite believing I had started this voyage. Looking back, I realise I had trusted in a deep intuition about timing. When eventually I gained access to my adoption papers the social worker told me that if I had left the search any later, it would have been in vain as the details logged on microfiche were almost illegible and the paper files had been lost. My advice is this: follow your instinct. Listen to yourself. No one else can advise you. Understand that you are setting off on a tumultuous journey which will bring many challenges. Honour your own strength; you are a warrior setting off along this perilous path. Once you set out, whatever you find, there will be no going back.

Once you have made this decision it is necessary to obtain your original full birth certificate and adoption papers. When I met my adoption social worker for the first time I remember my palms sweating as I waited to go into her office. She asked me for details of my adoption and urged me to recall as much as I could, stating that such memories are usually reliable. This was good information. When a copy of the adoption papers arrived in the post nine months later it was just as I had remembered reading aged seven. We do remember what is crucial.

When obtaining my adoption papers I had not, however, considered how the original details given may have been inaccurate and deliberately misleading – or pondered why this may be so. If you were adopted in the 60s or earlier, do be mindful of this. Permissive society had only just happened for a few; having a baby outside of marriage still carried terrible shame and stigma. Birth mothers were told they would never have contact with their baby again and the relationship was legally terminated. Birth parents sometimes made up stories to cover their tracks and enable them to disappear and create a new life. These are all things to bear in mind.

When I read my papers, in the presence of the social worker, there was a paragraph from the now defunct adoption agency. It gave an address for my mother in 1980, stating she would like contact with me. This felt like the most important thing ever. A gap in my heart, which I had been unaware of, started to heal. The social worker remained there while I tried to process this information. It was such a private moment. I should have asked her to leave me alone but I was too young to have the temerity to do so. Be aware of the intensity of emotion that the information you may or may not read may give rise to and consider if you want the social worker to stay or go while you read this incredibly intimate information.

The fourth rite of passage was initial contact (as distinct from reunion). While it may at first appear to bring a resolution, it may also throw up as many questions as it answers. For adopted adults who decide to make contact, contradictory and confusing emotions often ensue. When I discovered my mother had asked for me to get in touch with her I immediately called Directory Enquiries and got her number in France. I was 22, living overseas and did not think about the impulsivity of my actions. I am glad I did not; if I had known what lay ahead I may not have called her, may not have spent years discovering my ethnic and cultural ancestry and may never have had a relationship with my birth grandmother. I telephoned my mother. She knew it was me the moment she came to the phone. Both of us were awkward and breathless but talked for a long time. I learnt she was Irish but had been living in France for over 20 years and had a French partner and three children.

The family details she had originally given the adoption agency were fabricated and from her reaction to questions about my father it was apparent she was still hurting from what had happened 23 years ago. She verified he was from Libya, she was from the west of Ireland and I had five uncles and a grandmother still alive. Suddenly I was not English, but an Irish-Libyan who had a mother who wanted to know me, a heap of Irish relatives and a gang of French and Libyan half-brothers and -sisters. She asked me to write. It would be nine years until we would speak again and 14 years until we would meet.

So what advice would I give to other adoptees about approaching initial contact? Be prepared to find out things may not be as they seem. You may have a different cultural, ethnic, religious or class background to how you have been raised. Remember, not everything you read in documentation may be true. Realise initial contact is only the beginning and not the end. It may take years to move onto reunion or lead nowhere, leaving you with unanswered questions about identity and belonging. You may learn disconcerting information about your biological mother and father. Your ideas about self-identity may be challenged and suddenly you may find yourself embedded in another family, who may not take kindly or wholeheartedly to your emergence. You may decide this is as far as you want to go in making contact with your biological mother or father. There may be huge cultural paradigms separating you from your biological family.

I read and researched as much as I could about the period in which my grandmother and mother grew up in the west of Ireland to understand their situation and how that informed my own beginning. I would encourage anyone else to do the same. It allowed me to feel compassion for my mother and understand her life. Intergenerational understanding helped me to realise the link between myself and my grandmother; how my mother's story was driven by her mother's morals and values, and thus my grandmother's upbringing and times informed my own beginning. Difficult life-changing decisions are indeed located in their own time, times we may find hard to understand from a contemporary standpoint.

The journey from initial contact to reunion, a fifth potential rite of passage specific to adult adoptees, may be long and full of heartache. It may unearth unknown needs for a biological mother or father, and reveal a longing to be nurtured and wanted. It may make you feel more lost than you were to begin with. It can be a lonely road if there are few others you can share your experiences and feelings with, but a brave heart must step into the unknown. You are in control of this journey towards reunion and often the slower the journey, the deeper the healing. Ultimately, each adult adoptee follows a unique path from initial contact to reunion. Some reunions may be happy and complete narratives, more often they may be complex and replete with sorrow and grief. This is a journey only you will know how to make. No advice from any professional social workers, friends or partners can change the direction your heart seeks to follow. My own reunion has resulted in the most amazing, healing and hurtful times I have ever experienced. As Yeats said, 'A terrible beauty is born.' [7] Travel safely.

---

[7] From the WB Yeats poem, 'Easter, 1916'

THE MEANING OF FAMILY

My brother *Shenaz Drury*

To have a brother *Rosa*

Runaway *Rosa*

Brother *Rosa*

Mothers *Therese Ryan*

Proud to be adopted *Andrew Barton*

My father *Anna Treasure*

Without question *Viv Fogel*

My father *Viv Fogel*

The meaning of adoption *Joe Jones*

Adoption, family and me *Marie*

The "Doodah" diaries *Deborah Weymont*

In the beginning *Shenaz Drury*

A diverse family life *Jenny Mohindra*

My brother

SHENAZ DRURY

Shenaz Drury was born in 1972 in Asha Sadan, a home for children in Mumbai, India. She does not have any details surrounding her birth family. Shenaz was the first of three children to be adopted by an Indian mother and English father. They brought her to England and completed her adoption in 1973. They then went on to adopt a baby boy and about four years later, a baby girl. Adoption was something that was open and discussed. As a result, Shenaz grew up feeling positive about her adoption story. Unfortunately, her brother did not have such an easy time and after many years of emotional anguish, chose to end his life at the age of 25. Shenaz lives in Surrey with her husband and two adopted children, one from Asha Sadan, and one placed through the Indian Association for Promotion of Adoption (IAPA), also based in Mumbai.

We were great as a threesome when we were young
Out on our bikes, and having plenty of fun
And the times we were naughty and sent to the hall
We'd be conspiring together, having a ball
But as you grew older, your life became tougher
Little do we know the extent that you did suffer
We all tried to help you, believe me we did
But the key to your happiness seemed too deeply hid
You strove for something that couldn't be sought
I hope that in death, this has now been brought
Despite all your struggles, turmoil and pain
We'll never cease to love you, our brother you remain
Your impish grin and deep brown eyes
Will remain in our minds long after goodbyes
We will miss you more than we can say
You will stay in our memories day after day.

Dedicated to my brother 24 November 1973–19 April 1999

To have a brother

ROSA

Rosa was born in the late 1950s and is of white European heritage. She lives in the UK.

These poems are about a brother I lost after his adoption broke down. We are not related by birth.

It is very strange to be a sister and then not be. Nobody has died. Do you say you have a brother or not? I think whatever has happened and however you are related, sisters and brothers stay with you. On some level they never go away and their presence is felt at the least expected moments. Either you meet people who look like them or something in their personality or way of being reminds you of your brother or sister. Sometimes somebody who doesn't look anything like him or her suddenly does something or makes a facial expression and they become your brother or sister for a split second or two.

It's difficult to describe how this way of making sense of the present affects you. It's a form of searching for something you have lost and of re-defining the world around you. It's not generally re-enforced by other people around you. The family photos with you all in them obviously stop when your sibling leaves and a lot of the family memories change over time. You start meeting people who have never met your brother or sister and you can begin to feel like you are making the whole thing up.

Runaway

Hanging teddy bears with red felt pen blood round their necks
Punching humans
Running away
Coming home to wash his clothes

He was young
No one quite understood
His kindness
The places where he seemed like everyone else.

Brother

I was your younger sister
And then I wasn't
I have seen your face
At unexpected moments
Not your character
Just bits of your face
And I have seen your character too
Not your face
But sometimes bits of your character
Can change a face

Mothers

*THERESE RYAN **

Mary

The black and white photo sits on the mantelpiece over the stove in my kitchen. I am seven or eight months old. You are holding me in your arms in the front garden of our terraced house. Huge daisies lean away from white walls. I have blonde curls. I am wearing a white frilly dress. You are 30 years young, and happy. I am laughing, I imagine, at my father who must be taking the photo.

Memories we share: you and me in the jacuzzi. You are nervous. Without your glasses, you worry about tripping, losing your balance and going underwater. You hold onto me as we wade through foaming bubbles to the ledge where we sit together. I know I will treasure this moment in the future. You say you are afraid of your head going under, of floating away on the bubbles. I laugh and hold your hand under the water. Holding onto me you feel safe. Holding onto you I feel safe. Afterwards, we joke in the changing room. I hold your towel around you while you dress.

We go shopping together. I persuade you to try on clothes you think you don't like, until you see them on. We have tea and scones. I know about your life, the pain you've always held inside you. I've watched you put on weight and lose it again, go grey and start putting colour in your hair. I know your scent, your touch. I know your hands, the colour of them, the shape of your fingers, nails, the rings you wear, the freckles and sun spots. I remember you with my father, the rows and hugs, the struggles with money, his death and you a widow at 50. I thought you were old then. Now I'm astounded at how young you were.

I am with you as you lose your best friends to cancer, finding yourself alone again, sad, lost and then, pulling yourself up again. I couldn't know you better. We laugh together. You putting your coat on inside out, getting lost in the new shopping centre, trying to use the mobile phone your grandchildren bought you for Christmas, teasing you about your massage with a handsome Iranian man. I would bet my life on your love for me.

* For Therese's bio details, see p 55.

I have learned from you, the lesson of kindness towards others, a helping hand. It annoyed me when I was a child, the way you gave away your money, your time, our toys and clothes, without explanation. Now I appreciate you did your best in every way. I know how hard your life has been. I admire the way you are still joyful, loving. By the age of 12, both your parents had died. You were living with an aunt, separated from your brothers. I remember you crying as you described what you had lost. You too, had a wrench in your life, live with the ever present pain of loss. Did that loss prompt you to rescue my brother and me from a home, to adopt first him, then me eight months later? You felt lucky that you were not put into an orphanage.

Maybe loss brings people together. I cannot imagine you not in my life. I fear the day you are taken from me, the one person whose love I am always sure of.

You could not be more of a mother to me. Yet, I need to find the mother who carried me for nine months, who gave birth to me. Sometimes the guilt in needing this is overpowering. I feel it's wrong of me to want this, that I am ungrateful, unkind, heartless. I am throwing everything back in your face, as if you haven't been a good enough mother. I am torn in two. This fierce loyalty and obligation I feel towards you; this deep rooted hunger to find her. Am I betraying you? You are strong and supportive. Inside I imagine you are fearful of losing me.

You are my mother. I tell you this when I can. I see your pride. You want my birth mother to see I've turned out OK. You want her to know that you did your best for me, brought me up as best you could, gave me all the love you had. I see your need for this to be acknowledged. You made my life possible, helped bring your grandchildren into being. What would my life have been without you?

A trickle of resentment seeps out of me. A voice from within whispers: 'I don't want you, I want her.' Ferocious anger wells up from a deep hidden place; anger at her, at you, at myself. I am afraid of this anger. I try to squash it down. It escapes in vicious words, dark moods. It retreats. I ache.

My friends turn into their mothers. Some, even as children looked to me like their mothers. I knew how they would look when they were adults. I don't look like you at all. I am told I resemble you in my manner. I like this, to feel I belong.

We speak of my other mother. You are compassionate towards her. Trying to pluck words that will not wound, I explain to you how I feel – my guilt in needing to find her, my fear of hurting you. I'm not looking for another mother. I'm searching, I think, for roots, a beginning, a sense of where I have come from. Sometimes I don't know what I am looking for. You are too willing to understand. Your love for me will accept anything. What I want, you want for me. When I speak of her, I feel I deny you. I play down how important it is to me to find her. Words fail me. A chasm of silence opens up between us. I am torn between the two of you: my flesh and blood mother, and the ghost who never leaves my side.

Nora

Once I visited a museum in Copenhagen. I saw the bog bodies of a mother and her child. The dead child was placed on a swan's wing beside the mother's body. I have another mother. We were together for less than five weeks after my birth in a mother and baby home.

Friends fumble when speaking about you. They don't know what to call you. When some refer to you as my mother, I correct them. 'You mean my birth mother.' I hammer a nail in the fence between us with that prefix. Some call you my "real mother". Who is more real? The mother who carried me for nine months, gave birth to me, and went through the heartache and sacrifice of giving me up, or the mother who has loved and looked after me since I was five weeks old? You and I were labelled all those years ago. Single mother, illegitimate child. Names given to erect a wall between us, to cut us off from each other. Without labels we are simply mother and child.

Some refer to you as my "natural mother". I am uncomfortable with that too. There is nothing natural about giving birth in a repressive institution with the aim of handing your baby to strangers. Naturally, a mother cares for you, loves you, does what is best for you. You have done all this. You gave me up because you thought it was best for me. As a mother myself, I imagine the pain of that sacrifice. The ultimate act of love; to give away your baby because she will have the chance of a better life. I am in awe of your courage, your capacity for survival.

Ireland in the 1960s. They call you an unmarried mother. Your family shuns you. If you keep me, you cannot work. There is no payment for a single mother and her child. You are considered a threat to decent society. The nuns in the mother and baby home ask how you will manage to look after me. They tell you about the good life I can have with a family. They say it will be best for both of us if you give me up. You can start your life again, forget all this ever happened. No one will ever find out your secret. Did you believe them?

Five weeks together. What memories do you hold in your heart from that time? What kind of a baby was I? Do you remember when you held me for the first time? For the last time? Did my baby smell stay with you, the feel of my skin against your cheek? Do you remember looking into my eyes? Did you talk to me? Do you remember what I wore the day you gave me up? What have you done with your memories? Mary tells me I held my father's little finger on the long journey from the mother and baby home. I cried constantly when they brought me to my new home. They paced the living room floor with me at night, dosed me with gripe water for colic.

I have been searching for you for 17 years. Until three years ago you ignored all approaches, your silence a heavy blanket you hid beneath. Then slowly, cautiously, you agreed to have contact. We write to each other. You cannot bring yourself to meet me. We turn away from our pain, I know that now. For you, I am a deep wound over which a thick scab has formed. I stumble from compassion to anger to despair.

I have no conscious memory of you. Yet there is something deep, nameless, that draws me back to that time and to you. The older I get, the stronger the pull I feel towards you. The longer we are apart, the more I need to find you. We are connected by an ever-lengthening cord. I pull it, draw you back to me. Does a mother ever cease to be a mother? Was there a moment when I stopped being your daughter? Was it when you first had the idea of giving me up? When you let them take me from you? When you signed the final papers? The first time you denied me with your words. Am I still your daughter? Are you still my mother?

Your lesson to me: acceptance. Your reluctance to meet me makes me realise I must accept myself. Life will not start when my birth family acknowledges me. I chased after you in the hope of finding a better me. You led me back to myself. You were imbued with magic and mystery at the start of my journey to find you. Now, I must accept you as you are.

This is a story of mothers; the mother who hardened her heart against you, her daughter when you became pregnant with me. She, I imagine, had the final word in your home. She made sure you would not bring shame on her family. She never spoke of me, her grand-daughter. Mary's mother who died on the kitchen floor while cooking dinner, leaving her daughter with an emptiness she could never fill. I carry parts of these mothers and grandmothers within me. They make me the mother I am.

Two mothers connected by their unacknowledged pact of love. One I know inside out. I can tell how she is feeling from the tone of her first word. The other is a phantom, a hazy form sketched by my imagination and the snippets I have received over the years. In their own way they did their best for me, their child. We are all three survivors, bound to each other by invisible threads.

Proud to be adopted

ANDREW BARTON

Born in 1960, Andrew Barton is best known as a celebrity hairdresser renowned for his makeover work on hit TV shows such as Channel 4's *Ten Years Younger*. Named British Hairdresser of the Year and Britain's Most Wanted Hairdresser, Andrew's work is much in demand. With an award-winning salon in London's Covent Garden and a signature haircare range distributed globally, his business entrepreneurship is also highly respected (see www.andrewbarton.tv). A dedicated patron of BAAF, Andrew works tirelessly to create awareness of the organisation's work.

Adoption has always meant something quite special to me. Maybe it's because I was told as soon as I could understand that I was special, I had been chosen! As a young boy I ran around the countryside of my native Yorkshire with my friends, up to the usual schoolboy mischief, never thinking anything other than that. I'd come home covered in mud or thirsty after a summer's day and Mum was always there to look after me.

As I grew up, I realised that adoption was very special indeed and it was more about how special my family were (are) than how special I was (am) and how they had been chosen to give a child a second start. I've never been able to think of a natural or real family as some may call it, outside of my family. For me the brother, sister, mum and dad I have are my real family, my natural family. It is they who have cried tears of joy and sadness with me, taken care of me and me them, and always supported me on my life journey.

Yes, of course there were challenges as I've grown up, questions to be asked, and there are still questions that may never be answered. What I do know is that my family have been by my side throughout my life; we love and care for each other and that's all this adopted boy (man) has ever needed.

My experience of adoption couldn't have been better. Adoption has shaped me into a happy, successful individual and one who is proud to be adopted.

My father

ANNA TREASURE

Anna Treasure was born in London in the mid-60s and placed in a children's home until the age of three, when she was adopted by a lone white mother along with a number of children of various ethnicities. Anna is of Jamaican and Grenadian parentage. She lives and works in England.

And where are you?
You are to blame
It was your sperm
That caused her pain

To birth a child
She would not keep
It was your thrust
That made her bleed

And I the one
Clean cut asunder
But why
Do I
Just never wonder
Ever
What's your name?

My perception of original family appears to include only those from my birth mother's side. I wonder whether this is primarily because, to the best of my knowledge and recollection, no contact has ever been made between my birth father and I. Secondly, the evidence suggests that the act of coitus was one of violence that resulted in a woman's pain and a rejected child. The strong, innate, inner force that led me to search for my birth mother has never been present with my birth father. Perhaps, a construct of birth family from my perspective is confined to an unconscious sense of positive human connectedness which, from the beginning, however brief, has only been a reality through the maternal line.

Without question

VIV FOGEL *

1

My mother – the mother who gave birth to me –
pushes herself around in her chair using her good leg.
On good days she does not know me, calls me
by another's name, and asks me about school.
Her dead friends visit her, her late husband,
and she converses confidently with ghosts.
It is the living she cannot bear.

The mother who parented me for 18 years died suffering.
I thought I loved her. I knew I hated her.
I did not come from her – her whale-sick body
with its clammy repellent smell, the medicated creams
she asked me to rub into her. In our ways
we loved and bore each other as best we could
and when she died I felt the loss.

My stepmother – an anxious bird pecking away
at the shattered fragments of her guilt – haunted
by the young son she left behind to die.
She clawed, hoping to fix herself to me,
and raged demented when I shook her off.
She rasped her last breath in torment,
unable to mother him – or me.

My gentle mother-in-law, who tries patiently
to right all wrongs, to soothe her angry son
and calm his disappointed ex. She placates, unruffles,
puts the balm of reason and good sense
onto proud and prickly wounds, whilst her men sit
unplacatable, and judge and blame,
and do not see, and do not move.

* For Viv's bio details, see p 122.

2

My daughter lies sick and delirious –
she has lost her voice. I nurse her,
weak myself, hating her, loving her.
She came from me. I give to her.
There is no question. There is no forgetting.
Mothers nurse their children, protect them,
would die for them. This is understood.

There is no question: we sacrifice.

We give ourselves up, so that we can give.
We have created, so we are responsible.
We put aside needs and postpone dreams:
there is no question.
Do not be fooled – it is not easy
as we struggle and cry
to salvage our selves.

We are the muscle and the backbone,
the solid ground, the silent caretakers,
the invisible backdrop.
There are so many of us –
strong arms to return to.

And so it has always been:
giving birth, holding our tiny men,
teaching our beautiful daughters.
A power so ancient and huge
that She must be repeatedly cast out:
Ashera, Mother Goddess, and Lilith,
Destroyer and Protector of mothers.

And all of us – mothers,
longing to be held,
stroked, heard, known,
to be mothered.

My father

My father sold cigarettes to the Nazis.
Blue-eyed and handsome, he nodded and smiled
through the coffee houses of Berlin,
the cakes and the cabaret, a sweet tooth
and an eye for women. He loved all that.

He told jokes. I read between the lines:
Buchenwald was his camp – but it was no Butlins!
He recalled the officer's belt, his polished boots.

I sat by his bed: a big man grown small,
and stroked his burn-scarred arm.
I traced my fingers along numbers
the same blue-grey as his veins,
as if to unlock the stories
he kept from me.

I wasn't meant to hear of the baby tossed into the air.
of the tiny skull cracking beneath the polished boot.

My father loved to polish: the wooden banisters,
the brass door handles, the candlesticks – our boots,
polishing always polishing. And once, only once,
he upturned the kitchen table, mouth foaming,
as plates slid cracking to the floor.

He died the year my baby was born.
He held her in his arms, just once,
a little awkward, a little shy.
A big man grown small.
The line of numbers grey
as the veins on his thin skin.

I fed him – as once he fed me.
I stroked his baby head and read to him
and made him smile at my jokes,
as his watery eyes were fading.

A year later, on his *Yahrzeit*,[1]
the Berlin Wall came down.

For Itzaak Weinreich 1903–1988

---

[1] *Yahrzeit* is the Jewish anniversary of the death of a close relative at which special candles are lit for remembrance.

The meaning of adoption

JOE JONES

Joe Jones was born in London in 1984 and is of Anglo/Irish parents. He joined his adoptive family when he was nearly eight years old. He was placed with his six-year-old brother, Wayne, and grew up with two younger brothers, also adopted. He has lived in two foster homes and experienced neglect and violence in his birth family and abuse in his foster family (he received criminal injuries compensation). Joe shares a house with a friend near Bromley. His parents live about 30 minutes away and Joe visits them most weeks. He enjoys helping out friends with their decorating and general household maintenance. He was thrilled to pass his moped test and enjoys travelling around south London to see friends. He loves to go to see football matches with his friends and his dad, and plays football for a learning disability team. Joe receives floating support from social services and is happy most of the time.

My family is my mum and dad (adoptive) and my brother, Wayne. I have two "half" (unrelated adoptive) brothers. They have been there for me, stuck with me when I went to prison. My family gets on well. We like doing things together. I argue with my little brother, age 16, about football and cricket. I get on with James who likes the same music as me.

I have mates like M who have stuck by me. He is like family. He was in care and he was fostered by my godmother. He is always there for me.

Family means who you are close to. There are people like my godparents who are like family and a friend I go to see Millwall play with. My old neighbour lets me help him decorate.

Children should not live with people who take drugs or get drunk like my first dad. Their parents should be locked up. If children are taken away they should live with relatives who are clued up. They shouldn't live with strangers.

I didn't want to be adopted but I had no choice. It happened in the end. I got a good home, it was a good place to grow up. My parents took me to swimming competitions and I played football and went canoeing. We had a campervan and went to France, Ireland and Holland. We went to see my godfather in Japan and New Zealand when he got married there.

If I had stayed with my first family I would have ended up hurting them because they are no good and they hurt me. I met my birth dad a few times when I was 20, but he got drunk and yelled at me. I can't be bothered to see him now.

I like where I live now. I have my own bed-sit and there are staff here if I need help. It's in a good area with lot of buses and I can get to see my friends, and my family come and we go out at weekends bowling and to the pub for lunch.

My life is OK and I feel happy.

Adoption, family and me

MARIE

....

Marie was born in 1972 and is of white English parentage. She joined her adoptive family at six weeks old. She has given thought to starting a search for her birth family. Marie lives in Staffordshire.

....

I was aware I was adopted from an early age, maybe as young as three or four. I've never seen adoption as a stigma or a negative. I feel adoption is something to be proud of and not a secret to be pushed under the carpet.

I was adopted as a six-week-old baby in 1972 and was placed with my mum and dad who had married in their late teens and always wanted a family but were unable to conceive. They were going to adopt a second child from overseas when I was about five but this didn't happen. My dad is one of four and my mum an only child like me. Growing up, we had a good relationship with all of my dad's family but as the years rolled on I lost touch with all but my uncle's family in Canada – due to family politics and disagreements. We have good relationships with my mum's family, such as her cousins, but as Mum was an only one, friends became an extension to the family.

I have a great relationship with my parents. I feel our relationship has grown as life has gone on due to a combination of factors: my parents' health, the breakdown of my previous marriage and my parents moving to Spain in recent years. My mum and dad are my mum and dad – they brought me up, supported and guided me, they loved me. I love them unconditionally; nothing could ever replace the relationship we have. They are my parents, and friends too as I have got older.

My mum and I have a unique bond. This is because my mum is also adopted. Mum was adopted to a couple within 15 miles of where she was born in 1946. Again, she always knew she was adopted and had a good relationship with her parents, but sadly she had lost both of them by the time she was 30. Mum had a very close bond with her aunt (who was like a grandmother to me) and although she was curious about her past, out of loyalty to her adoptive parents, she didn't act on it until her aunt had passed away.

A couple of years before Mum reached 50, she approached me to see if I would mind if she began looking for her real family. It was a strange feeling –

happiness and fear of the unknown rolled into one. At this point, I felt I had no need to question my background. I gave Mum my blessing and the outcome of her search was amazing.

Mum had her birth certificate and this showed the house name, road and village she was born in. So one morning she set off to the village, which was only seven miles away from where she was living at the time. Within two weeks we met her brother and sister. They were both adopted to different families. They are approximately 11 to 14 years younger than my mum and they didn't know they were adopted until later life. Triggered by my aunt's parents dying and her sister finding her papers, her sister traced her brother and his adoptive mum, at nearly 40, and told him he was adopted for the first time.

Over ten years later, my mum is still in touch with her brother and sister. I have ten cousins I didn't know about until I was in my mid-20s. It all seems surreal sometimes that we have this new family whom we didn't know about for so many years. Although we don't see of much of them since Mum and Dad moved to Spain, there is still a bond with them for Mum.

We also have a very strange coincidence in that my mother-in-law knew my mum's birth mum. When I met my husband, I told him and his parents about Mum finding her family as she was born in the same village they were from. After chatting further, we found out my mother-in-law used to work with Mum's mum. They used to share a taxi to work from the village sometimes and the really strange thing was that in my husband's bedroom there was a palm plant Mum's mum had given to my mother-in-law as a wedding gift. Thirty years later it was still alive.

So my view on family has changed a lot over the years. The relationships I had with my dad's family, who were my main extended family while growing up, were strange and unkind at times. This was especially with my grandfather who I lost touch with because of religious beliefs and his general lack of care over the years. He was very hurtful to me and my parents in the way he treated us. Also, I was badly hurt by a cousin who broke up my first marriage. After this, in my mid-20s I saw some of my dad's relatives as people I didn't want in my life. This was a great transition period for me as I stepped away from people I didn't feel cared for me the way I cared for them. I concentrated on what I felt was right with friends and family rather than doing what I felt obliged to do.

My interpretation of family now isn't just the typical blood/genetic family. My family are my mum and dad, my second husband and his parents, and I have my new maternal family, my mum's existing family and some of my paternal family. My family is also my close friends who I love with all my heart; they are the brothers and sisters I never had while growing up. These are the people I love unconditionally and I class as family. I know they will be there for me and show me the same love and respect. This is more than friendship because I feel I am treated with more respect and love by them than I ever was by some of my relatives.

The reason for getting involved in writing this has been another transition in my life. Over the last eight years or so I have begun to think more and more about my birth mother. Before, I had thought of her – birthday and Christmas and landmarks in my life – wondering what she may be thinking or what she was doing. I am a strong believer in fate and I think there have been signs recently to trigger me starting to search.

My mum has always said that if I wanted to search she would support me. I have already been told all she knows about my real name, my birthplace, and the reason for my adoption. So far this has satisfied my desire to know, but as I get older I am craving more information. Good or bad, happy or sad – I feel I need to know. My mum's mum made her destroy all my paperwork when they adopted me – I know Mum regrets this.

So, I am thinking of taking the first step. What do I do, where do I start or, more importantly, what do I want to know? Years ago, I used to think I would be happy to find out who my birth mum is and to stand across the street from her just to see what she looks like, gain an idea of whether she had more children and what she did in her life. I also wanted to know medical history as it's strange at times not knowing.

My belief now is that I want to know why I'm here – a million and one thoughts go through my head. I've watched the programme *Searching for my Son* [2] recently and I've seen a woman who looked and had mannerisms like me on a TV show and who also shared the same name as my real name – which was really strange. This could be merely a coincidence or is it the fate I believe in? On the *Searching for my Son* programme, there were two teenage mothers who explained what it was like for them when, due to social pressures, they had to give up their boys in the late 1960s. I've thought about the mother's side and I guess the circumstances could have been the same for my mother.

----

[2] *Searching for my Son* was broadcast on Channel 4 television on 18 December 2006.

On the flipside though, the thoughts I have are not just of a teenage accident. Could I be the outcome of something more sinister? It's very strange not knowing because you can easily surmise so many reasons for your adoption. Due to this, I've recently started a diary about my feelings, so before I start searching I can think about the bigger picture. I've never pictured running open armed and shouting 'Mummy,' as I don't feel that is what I want, but I would like to meet her, to know her and the story of the start to my life, whether it is good or bad.

So, in the near future, I will begin my search. My first point will be to speak to Mum and Dad and my husband to let them know what I'm doing. Then what next? Where do I turn? Who do I speak to? How long will it take?

My hopes are initially to get answers to the simple questions like medical history, but then I would like to know so much more. There are lots of questions I'd like to know the answers to, yet I realise deep down that I may never get all the answers I want. I am not frightened of rejection by my real mum and I am not looking to replace Mum and Dad in any way. I am open-minded as to what my search may or may not find but as I approach 40 I feel I should start sooner than later.

Looking back over my life so far, I see adoption as a positive in my life and my mother's. We are proud to say that we are adopted and it has been a wonderful experience for us both. Being adopted gives you another take on "families" and where you are in life and relationships. I think it is important to treasure those who you love and the ones who give you love and care back – whether they be friends or family – and that a link by blood or being brought up with your blood relatives doesn't matter at all in relationships. My mum's brother and sister are proof that being adopted separately has not affected their relationships as siblings after years apart. And what about me? Well, I would like to think by the time I'm 40, I will have some more answers but I don't want the search for them to eat up my life. It's fate and what will be will be.

The "Doodah" diaries

DEBORAH WEYMONT

Deborah Weymont was born in 1956 and placed in a children's home at six weeks. She was fostered twice before being adopted, aged six, into a large family with four birth children, several adoptees and a number of foster children. She is mixed race (her mother was white English and her father from Bangladesh) and was raised in rural Oxfordshire and Exmoor, North Devon. Deborah trained as a teacher and an art therapist and has worked in special education in London and Bristol for over 30 years. She currently works for a charity with bereaved children as well as in schools with children at risk of exclusion. Deborah is also a practising artist and exhibits her work regularly. Deborah and her partner live and work in Bristol, and have four grown-up children and two grandchildren, all living locally.

The birth of my grand-daughter, Pella, has forced me to change the way I think about myself – from someone who is defined by separation and loss to someone who is instead defined by my connections and the gift of family.

Maybe it is because my birth mother abandoned me when I was six weeks old that I literally "find myself" reconfigured in the presence of my grand-daughter. Perhaps I feel and see her with such intense clarity because of the way she seems to fit so snugly into the dark space of my abandoned baby self.

What follows is part of a letter I wrote to Pella as we were preparing to welcome her with a postscript written later for this anthology. I hope she will read it one day but it's about me really, not her. I hope it will help Pella understand more about her own sense of family, her roots and the foundations upon which my relationship with both her mum (my daughter) and herself is built.

Monday May 25th

Dear Pella,

Today you haven't been born...but someone (you) is moving in your mummy's tummy and we think it won't be long now. We are all waiting patiently for the moment when you decide you would like to meet us. "We" means your dad Sam, Millie your mum, both sets of grandparents, your uncles, aunts and all the many other people in our family and friendship group.

You will be very welcomed and very loved in our family. I imagine you will have brown eyes and a chubby face. I also imagine the fact that you are one-eighth Bangladeshi will be encoded in your genes rather than expressed in the way you look. The same as your mum who is a quarter Bangladeshi. It might seem trivial to mention this but you see I grew up in a family and community where no one looked like me and even though I know you won't have brown skin it's important to me to remember your biological inheritance.

I think you will be healthy because Millie and Sam have been so careful to nurture you "in utero", both emotionally and physically but – and I felt this about your mum too – if you are poorly or "different" or disabled you will still be most welcome in our home. Our love for you will be unconditional and without prejudice.

We have been preparing for your birth for a long time now. Your mum and dad asked me to be their birth partner early on in the pregnancy. It's difficult to explain how important this feels and what it means to me. It's like another milestone in my journey to my self. It also confirms for me that whatever mistakes I have made as a parent (and there are many), I have got some things right. I never had the sort of intimate relationship with my adoptive mother where I could have asked her to be with me at my daughter's birth.

Your mum and dad have attended a special birth preparation course and trained themselves in positive thinking, visualisation, relaxation and meditation techniques. Every night they read stories and talk to you – just as if you are really in the room (which I suppose you are!). Your mum and dad wish for you to have a gentle, soft and trauma free entry into the world; but if that doesn't happen I know we will simply love you back to a safe calm place.

All this excitement feels so different from how my grandmother would have felt as the day of my birth came closer. In her eyes, my mother (her daughter) had "sinned" twice over. First, she had had sex before marriage, which in those days was something a woman was shamed for. Second, she had slept with a black man, a Pakistani man – something she would have been shunned for.

Shunned and shamed, my mother was sent away by my grandmother to a Christian centre for "fallen women" where she gave birth to me in secret. Just at the point when my birth mother and I needed my grandmother most we were pushed away from her, our family and our community.

Pella, this was a long time ago, before we had a vocabulary with which to deconstruct the lies, secrets and crimes of race, sex and empire. So it's hard for us to understand now, why my birth mother declared 'father unknown' on my birth certificate. He was not unknown. She had had a relationship with him that lasted several months and only ended when she got pregnant and my grandmother threatened to disown her. Putting 'father unknown' on my birth certificate is like a type of ethnic cleansing to eradicate the sex she had probably enjoyed with him, his existence and half of my genes. He was not "unknown" to the adoption agency either. They openly described him in the negative and racist language of the time; in one report as 'cunning and slippery'. But why would someone who was unknown, cunning and slippery send money regularly to the children's home I was placed in, until the time I was placed for adoption aged six?

I like to imagine your great grandmother and great grandfather were in love. I find comfort in the idea that if I had been conceived later in the century their relationship might have been acceptable to your great-great-grandmother.

Until last night I was unsure how ready I was to be your grandmother. It's been hard to think about or give space to face the uncomfortable feelings that get stirred up when I think about your birth. Now, in these last two days I have taken time to try and understand what this is about.

What I have uncovered by looking deep within myself is a simple but painful truth I have been avoiding. My presence at your birth throws the absence of my own female ancestry into sharp relief. Once again, as indeed throughout my life, I am feeling the absence of both my mother and my grandmother. At moments like these I feel like I do not have what is needed to fulfil the role of daughter, sister, aunt, mother, and now grandmother. But something has changed.

At the same time, I realise that I am also unsettled by the fact that I seem to have re-written my "script". I am not living the life I thought I was destined for. The story I have always told about myself is changing. I have a family. I have roots and I belong. Suddenly in this last 24 hours, I not only face my loss but also reject it as part of my core identity. My identity is not fixed, it has shifted. I feel a little "lost at sea", seasick perhaps, with a sensation of needing to hold on tight. But I don't have to. I can choose to let go of the identity I have established for myself. The world lurches to a new perspective.

I am not simply someone who is defined by separation and loss; I am also "found" by my belongings and family. And so it is that I can now say that I really do feel ready to welcome you Pella, into my life, and assume my role and responsibilities towards you as a grandmother – with hope and with gratitude.

Postscript

"Doodah"

Pella, it has been agreed that I will be called "Doodah"; not Granny, Grandma, Nan, Nanny or Nanu but a strange hybrid of a word that comes about from the set of connections and social family I have built for myself with a Bangladeshi man, his partner and children. Dadu is actually the Bangla word for paternal grandmother while Nanu is used for one's maternal grandmother. My friend's youngest daughter had difficulty pronouncing Dadu and called my friend's mother "Duda" (which I in turn always heard as "Doodah"). It was Duda who helped me to write a letter to my birth father and who connected me to bits of myself that were previously inaccessible. Sadly, she died three months before you were born and did not meet you. It is in her honour, with my friend's family's blessing that I am to be known to you as "Doodah".

In the beginning

SHENAZ DRURY *

The day we first met you, you were so very scared.
You were brought in to meet us all dressed and prepared.
You stretched open your arms and looked straight at me
My heart just melted, I hoped we would become a family.

We then could meet you one to one.
You screamed and wriggled, for you, not fun
To be left with two strangers who hadn't a clue
Of how to hold, comfort and to look after you.

We came and saw you each day for a week,
An hour spent cuddling, cheek to cheek.
You gradually relaxed and warmed to our touch,
Yet your eyes remained scared – it was all too much.

We had to leave you after five days, it seemed so unfair,
To come back home as if we didn't care.
I couldn't bear leaving you yet I knew you would be fine.
I wanted you home but knew it would be time.

Five months on we could come back for you.
Our paperwork finally sorted and through.
This time we could see where for two years you had lived.
We met all your carers and learned what you did.

We saw you were close to those who were there.
You seemed settled, loved and responded to care.
But you didn't want to know us and when we came close,
You rushed away far, frightened and morose.

We came to collect you after lunch one day,
You hadn't a clue what was heading your way.
Your whole life was to be turned upside down
By two strangers who scared you right from day one.

---

* For Shenaz's bio details, see p 174.

As we said goodbye to those who had cared,
Who had saved your life when you were sick and scared,
I couldn't help think back to 34 years earlier,
To my parents collecting me in a manner similar.

You fell asleep on the journey back.
You were not aware you were never going back
To all you had known for 820 days
And the people who had got to know all your ways.

For the first few days you clung out of fear.
You screamed and went rigid, not letting us near.
We persevered through those days, you and I.
Our bond grew stronger and less did you cry.

You hung on to me with desperation and hope,
Unable to trust, not sure how to cope.
But gradually you saw your daddy and me
Were not so scary as first seemed to be.

You started to trust and learned how to play,
To run and to jump, and have your own say.
We are amazed at how settled you seemed to be
As our beautiful, loving daughter, with star quality.

You have come through so much in your life to date
I am in awe at your strength and resilience to fate.
I want you to know we will love you forever,
Through good times and bad we'll always be together.

A diverse family life

JENNY MOHINDRA

Jenny Mohindra was born in Edinburgh in 1969, given up for adoption at a few days and placed into a white English family at seven months old. She grew up in several different countries, spending the most time in Australia. The discovery of her birth parents when she was 30 also revealed her mixed parentage (Scottish and Indian), as well as the fact that she has two full siblings. Jenny now lives in London where her birth family also reside.

I always felt like an outsider in my family, totally unconnected and just different. Family to me really meant my immediate adoptive family as for most of my childhood we lived abroad and therefore away from any relatives. So that was me, my older brother (my parents' "natural" child) and my mum and dad. If you looked at my brother and I, you might think my brother looked like our mum and I looked more like our dad as my brother and mum had brown hair and fair skin and my dad and I would both tan more easily and had dark hair. It used to amuse me when some people would say my brother and I looked totally different while others thought we definitely looked like a brother and sister. I used to think that surely it took more than looking like one's family to really belong to them. I never really got on well with my brother. My perception of our growing up together was that when we were little we used to fight and punch each other a lot; then, as we got older, the punches turned to verbal arguments and, then older still, we learned to ignore each other.

We lived in England for a few years when I was quite young, not far from some aunts, uncles and grandparents from both sides of my family. I don't remember seeing them very often, usually just special occasions like Christmas, which is how it was when we lived overseas, only then it wasn't every Christmas, just when we came back to the UK. My mum was the youngest in her family by many years and so I don't actually remember meeting her father, my grandfather. My only recollection of her mother was when I stayed with a maternal aunt when I had chicken pox as a child and my grandmother was also staying there. I do remember my father's parents, having spent several Christmases at their house. I never detected much closeness between my father and his parents, so with the limited contact that I had with them, I didn't feel that they were really part of a family which belonged to me. Knowing I was adopted made me think that all these people were relatives but none of them mine.

At one stage my father became interested in researching his family tree and took upon the task with much enthusiasm. He tried to share this passion with me but why would I be interested in a bunch of people I had no blood ties with? It was one thing to know that the family I was growing up with had no such connection to me, so why would I want this rubbed in my face by seeing a whole bunch of people who had nothing to do with me? As he was only researching his ancestors, my mum could see my point of view.

I left home when I was 19 and moved to the other side of Australia on my own, just before my 21st birthday. I knew just two people in Sydney but wasn't really daunted at the prospect of starting afresh since I didn't feel I had left many friends behind. After spending much of my childhood away from my relatives in the UK, moving away from my parents (as they had done from theirs with my brother and me) felt like a natural progression. Settling in a new city was fun and exciting, made more so by my "coming out" and discovering the friendly gay lifestyle that Sydney had to offer. It was Mardi Gras season and I had arrived! I started dating my first girlfriend who had lots of gay friends and every Friday and Saturday night we would have people over for drinks before heading out to the golden mile of Oxford Street. Hellos were kisses and hugs, darlings and loves. Going out meant wearing sequins and bright colours, which all equated to fun and lightheartedness. We all dressed like this and we all belonged. Everyone seemed so friendly and affectionate and I embraced this crowd. We talked of Mardi Gras being our Christmas. We would never alienate or cast out anyone. I loved this quick assimilation into my extended "new family".

Girlfriends came and went but I did have an ongoing friendship with a gay man who continues to be my friend and who has felt like family for a long time. Not having any blood relatives made me feel that I could choose new family as I desired. I used this self-elected ability to define my family as I tried to make up for the one I didn't have. Was it purely coincidental that we met on Christmas Day, the day usually reserved for families? That was a good Christmas. I'd spent earlier such days alone or at so-called "orphans'" Christmases where fellow gay people with no family to go to would spend the day together. I resented Australian society for making such a big deal of this time. To me it was just another day on the calendar but one where I was made to feel like an outsider or a reject since I didn't have any real family in the city where I lived and I had no desire to cross the country to see my (by this time) estranged adoptive family.

Seeing the families of my girlfriends over the years gave me insight into what other family circumstances could be like. I was surprised to observe the closeness of siblings – the physical affection of hugs and kisses for hellos and the genuine care for each other's affairs. I was with one girlfriend for several years and I was quite taken with seeing her brothers' and friends' children growing up in that time. I had never had ongoing contact with any children; in fact, the less I saw of any children the better, as I certainly didn't feel comfortable having them around me and did not know how to communicate with them. I saw them with new eyes, watching how they changed and grew, and became quite fascinated with witnessing these little people develop. Children and families were becoming a less creepy theme. My adoptive family felt a long way away, not just geographically on the other side of Australia but mentally as well. Contact was sparse and I felt more and more detached. Family to me meant other people's families.

I reunited with my birth family in my early 30s. My birth parents had married after I had been given up for adoption and had two sons: my younger brothers. I now had a complete "new" family, one which I could proudly call my own. I couldn't have hoped to meet a more welcoming set of parents, who wanted to include me and make me feel a part of the family. Strange new feelings emerged of being the child in a child–parent relationship but I was an adult and not a child anymore. This also raised internal questions about how I could potentially fit two sets of parents into my life, despite having little contact with one. I tried hard to fit in with this new family but still felt like an outsider for much of the time. Of course, I wondered how it would have been if I hadn't been adopted and if I had had the same opportunity as my brothers to grow up in a family that really belonged to me. I have met aunts, uncles, cousins and a grandparent from my birth family. I do feel more of a connection with them than with my extended adoptive family. However, not having had much contact with them and, therefore, time to develop my relationship with them, has left me with a feeling akin to the gap having been filled: curiosity satisfied, on both sides, but that's all. The sense of belonging to my birth family used to come and go but after more than ten years this feels quite cemented.

I have been able to enjoy spending birthdays and Christmases with my birth family; both my birthdays and theirs. For many adopted people, birthdays can be a reminder of being adopted and not being with one's biological family. For me, this wasn't really so. After I had left home it was always Christmas that made me feel isolated and on my own. I can't say the first Christmas I spent with my birth family wasn't strange for me but the sense of belonging and knowing where I came from overrode any feelings of weirdness! A recent birthday saw me celebrate with a wonderful mix of friends, family and also friends who I consider to be my family. This was a blend of my birth family and my friends, my partner's friends and our friends – from both London and Sydney. Our flat was full of people talking, drinking and enjoying themselves and I felt at home.

I have often felt alone in my life, with no bonds to anyone who I could really call my family. It is perhaps for this reason that I developed such a close bond with my pet shitzhu who I had for almost 16 years. He was there for all that time, always happy to see me no matter what was going on for me – faithful to his owner as dogs are. My partner, I and he were our own little family. Sadly, since starting this piece of writing I've had to have him put to sleep as he became too old and unwell to carry on. I have felt quite lost without him but not alone any more since I am now close to my birth family and also have my best friend nearby as he has moved to London.

In my 30s I decided increasingly to make use of my selected flexibility to choose how my family fitted into my life. Building the new family relationship with my birth family has taken time. There are no guidelines or rulebooks on how I should deal with my unique family situation. One changes as the relationship evolves and the relationship has to adapt too. By being adopted, I think I've been forced into thinking about family – more so than someone not affected by adoption. I always used to question where I came from, whose features I have, both physical and personality wise. I've often wondered whether characteristics of mine have been inherited genetically from my birth family or gained environmentally from my adoptive family. I have been able to answer many of these questions now.

I believe being adopted and being gay have, among other things, made me different. Being different has led me to seek out a diverse family life. This has been challenging and complex at times, but has allowed me to appreciate that the western nuclear family is not necessarily the only family I can embrace.

THE LIFELONG IMPACT OF ADOPTION

Write about an article of clothing *Catherine Chanter*

The father in the shadows *Donald Eadie*

A special gift *Chiquita Rajawasam*

Choices and consequences *Bridget Betts*

The things my mother might have given me *Vanessa Gebbie*

Returning to my roots *Shenaz Drury*

Be there *Pam*

Never not adopted *Zara Phillips*

Mute Bella *Bella Frey*

Be strong, brave and proud *Eleanor*

Write about an article of clothing

CATHERINE CHANTER *

What would it have been, this article of clothing
that you would have left me? You who left
everything behind.

Let's speculate, shall we, you and me
together, both ignorant of the answer,
and of each other?

Perhaps the glove you wore so that you
never felt my skin and I never held your
hand;

or the hat which masked your eyes
from the instinctive gaze which might
have made that act impossible;

or the nightie
and the green gown? Or was it a vest and stained
pants dropped on the cracked lino of a shared bathroom?

I don't know.

Maybe you wrapped me in a perfumed silk scarf,
hoping one day I might pass an old lady
and say,

that scent reminds me of someone
I think I knew once, you tightening the knot round your collar,
neither of us any the wiser.

---

* For Catherine's bio details, see p 16.

The father in the shadows

DONALD EADIE

Donald Eadie was born in February 1939 of English parentage and adopted when he was four months old. He began seeking information with the hope of meeting his birth parents in 1994 but discovered they both had died. He continued to search for more details and texture within the story, which also belongs to his daughters and grandchildren. Donald lives with his wife, Kerstin, in Moseley, Birmingham. She shared in the search and has been affected by it. Previous publications by Donald include *Grain in Winter – Reflections for Saturday people* (Epworth Press, 1999); 'Peace-making in Sri Lanka' and 'The practice of meditative praying', both published in *The Epworth Review*; 'The body – wonder and pain, glimpses of transformation?', published in *Hinde Street* (June 2008); two articles in *The Faith Journey of Impaired Pilgrims* (Sarum College Press, 2007); and a chapter, 'More than Eucharistic liturgies and Eucharistic living', in *The Edge of God* (Epworth Press, 2008).

My experience of the father in the shadows is more complex than I first thought. I have described this as the search for Joseph. In exploring this theme I want to honour the adoptive family whom I know so well and also the birth families of whom I know so little. The questions I live with continue to appear, yet the older I become, the more prone I am to wondering and pondering, to accepting paradoxes and living within the mystery of things. I will interpose within the text some of my *questioning*, my *wondering*.

I am the father of two daughters and grandfather to five grandchildren. My wife Kerstin is Swedish and so I am called *Morfar*, which is Swedish for maternal grandfather. Through the years I have waited for our grandchildren to come out of school both in Birmingham's Moseley and London's Tower Hamlets. Women and men, young and old, parents and grandparents, people of different cultures and faith backgrounds push bikes and prams through those school gates and gather in the playground. Some of us men choose to stand around the edge alone while most of the women stand in the middle talking with each other.

I wonder increasingly about the nature and significance of fathering. What do we bring as men which is distinctive to the formation of our children and grandchildren? What could it mean to be a "real father"? What more has to happen in our society for young men of different cultures to be brought up to cherish their role as fathers?

What can be told of my story? There are stories within the stories and there are parts I choose to keep private. Some things are not mine to share.

My birth name was Robert Peter. Who I am is still unfolding. I was adopted in July 1939 when I was four months old. My younger adoptive brother and I have been well blessed both in our adoptive parents and through a wonderful wider family. We have been loved and enabled to love. Before commencing school we were told together we were both adopted. There was no real information about our origins and for many, perhaps too many years, no more conversation. That's how it was then and it's different now and for this I'm glad.

I have an adoptive father who loved both my brother and I, loved us equally and differently. He walked with us on moors and mountains, awakened within us a love of music, followed us when we played rugby, hockey and cricket, watched over us when we lived through rough times, held us but also let us go. His principle was 'hold on and you may lose them for ever; let them go and they will return.' He encouraged us to remain in the testing places; he spoke with us of intimacy within our humanity and of the deep things in life and death. His words were, 'Don't ever forget that death is natural as is birth and is just as much a beginning of new life.' He found pride in our becoming who we now are. And of course, he was more, much more.

I have a birth father whose shadow increasingly crosses my path. His is a watermark, a subterranean image, blurred and unsettling.

A few years ago, during one of three long periods of convalescence following spinal surgery, I decided to search for my birth mother. I have lived since childhood with fantasies and fears about the mother I have never known and much later in my life moved into a search not only for information but also encounter. With the help of others a fat file was eventually discovered. It included correspondence. Months later I learned both my parents had died, my father in 1963 and my mother in 1975. Many share this particular experience of bereavement and like me have, as yet, found no ritual to focus such complex grieving.

Because of the journey I have made within adoption and my living with a serious spinal condition that has required three major operations, I wonder about the connexion between trauma and the effect on the body. I wonder about somatosis, about emotional trauma and body memory and the effect on the physicality of our body. And I wonder about serotonin, about which I know almost nothing save that there are, within the juices in the brain, chemical neurotransmitters, which can be likened to electrical charges.[1]

But what of the man in the shadows who fathered me but was not a father to me? Who was he? What was the nature of his relationship with the woman who was my mother? The birth certificate provides information about her but nothing, nothing but a blank space with a line through it where the details of my birth father should be. The fat file urged secrecy around my father's identity. Who was this man needing such protection? What secrets were so important they had to be withheld? I was curious, frustrated and bewildered. Later I learned my birth father was a pilot in the First World War, a fine sportsman, a lover of fast cars, a master builder and also a married man with a family. He was described as "a man's man". And his name was Joseph. What was it like for him to have his son given away, the son he never knew? Did he also wonder where I was? Who I had become? Would he have liked to know that I was a sportsman too?

It has taken a long time for me to recognise that I had idealised my birth mother and demonised my birth father. For reasons I can't easily explain, I had never faced the father in the shadows. A few years ago, during an eight-day silent retreat, I dreamed for the first time of my birth father – dramatic dreams releasing within me what felt like an historic volcanic rage. Perhaps I had suppressed and projected unresolved ignorance, fear and anger onto him, twisting him out of his humanity. For me, it was an inner and primal encounter between father and son, a confrontation between man and man.

I wonder about male physical sexuality and perhaps this wondering belongs to the gifts of the father in the shadows. I wonder about the living of a gentle and non- patriarchal masculinity, the humanising of our "rough animality", about a passion which fertilises the desire that lies beyond the heat of human desire, and I wonder about the transforming of our flawed mortality.

And what does it mean now to say that I am Joseph's son? How much of his nature belongs to the mystery of who I am now? For good and ill his blood flows through my veins, his genes are in my body, I am his son, he is my father. 'The relationship with a father and a son is never simple, never over. Death never ends it. The absent father still fathers, still radiates spirit.' [2]

Kerstin has her family roots in the forest areas of central Sweden and

---

[1] For further reading see *Molecules of Emotion: The science behind mind-body medicine* by Candace B Pert (Simon and Schuster, 1997).
[2] Pat Barker, *Regeneration*, first published by Viking (1991)

they stretch back into the 16th century. My family roots are elusive and complicated. I wonder what has been passed on to our daughters and grandchildren from my birth father, in physical appearance and through traits of nature. It isn't easy to speak together of these things but we have begun.

Was it coincidence that Doris, a friend in her old age in Notting Hill, gave me a print of a famous painting of Joseph, husband to Mary and father to Jesus?[3] Doris grew up in a children's home and never knew her father. There are no halos, no angels, just Joseph's form, glimpsed in the darkness, his face lit up through the flickering light of a candle held in the hands of his young son. His body frame is thick, arms like tree trunks, hands strong yet gentle. His face is bearded, weather beaten, radiant, grief stained, forged through interiority. He is the master craftsman, trusted tradesman, Mary's man, love-maker, rough, tender, intimate man. What of his fathering throughout those hidden years? What of his watching over his son's painful acquisition of life wisdom, the fearful learning of where faithfulness could lead? Was it Joseph who taught his growing son to address God, 'Abba', 'Father'? And whom did he see when he looked into the face of his child?

I question if there is such a thing as coincidence. Doris and the painting of Joseph? Our granddaughter is attending a secondary school in the same road in East London as my birth father was born and where he lived his growing years. Our eldest grandson is also called Joseph and naturally works well with wood and with the building of things. These unanticipated, surprising links belong within the meaning of a word we seldom use, the mystery of synchronicity.

I have been nurtured since childhood within a faith based in the Fatherhood of God. I wonder what I have projected for good and ill onto the face of the silent absent one, the mysterious origin of all our relating, whom some choose to call God. What is the nature of the real fathering of the one beyond our imagining?

My search is still for Joseph and for more, much more.

In my ageing there has been time to follow where questions may lead and in my unwelcome limitation and stability time to ponder the meaning of things. I have found great encouragement in the advice given by Rainer Maria Rilke in a letter to a young man.

[3] Georges de La Tour, *Christ with Saint Joseph in the Carpenter's Shop*, circa 1635–40; now in the Musée du Louvre, Paris

'Have patience with everything that is unsolved in your heart and try to cherish the questions themselves, like closed rooms and like books written in a very strange tongue. Do not search now for the answers which cannot be given you because you could not live them. It is a matter of living them. Live the questions now. Perhaps you will then gradually, without noticing it, one distant day live right into the answers.' [4]

---

[4] *Letters to a Young Poet* (1929) by Rainer Maria Rilke, translated by Reginald Snell (1945) WW Norton & Co, 1993)

A special gift

CHIQUITA RAJAWASAM

Chiquita Aprille Ghazi Rajawasam was born in London in 1965 to a Sri Lankan mother and Pakistani father. After two orphanages and foster parents, she joined her white adoptive family at the age of two, becoming Aprille Clarke. Her new parents had already adopted two white children. Chiquita's birth family lives in Australia and Pakistan and she has had contact with them via email. Her birth father is dead but she has met his youngest sister and a cousin. Both her birth mother and siblings on her birth father's side have chosen to cease contact. None of this has been easy to come to terms with, but the understanding of who she is through photos and information has been really positive. For her 40th birthday, Chiquita changed back to her original name and added her birth father's surname. She lives in Wiltshire with her husband and two sons.

My fourth Christmas had officially begun with the arrival of my adoptive grandmother. I remember staring at her in fascination as she carried an enormous black plastic bag and placed it beneath our tree. A present was hidden inside, from an unknown lady. Most importantly, it was a gift specifically for me. This lady hadn't provided a present for my adoptive siblings so I imagined she must have some special connection to me. I hoped with great intensity that this mysterious lady was my real mum.

Suddenly Christmas was more exciting than ever, for surely this was my first present from my birth mum. I was utterly convinced she'd found me and maybe one day she'd come and rescue me. She must know I was unhappy in among these people who knew I loved *Marmite* and bacon yet fed me on bland tasteless food. She obviously understood that I had failed to emotionally connect with these people, even after two years, for they hadn't been prepared for any transitional issues, any racial complexities or my inability to love and trust the new adults in my fourth home.

I stood out in my white family with my big brown eyes, flashing white teeth and dark skin. With my Asian parents, a shy child could have blended in and faded into the background. Instead strangers stopped, stared and asked naïve questions. 'Where do you come from?', 'What big brown eyes!', 'Where did you get her from?' My parents offered my personal adoption details to strangers, leaving me feeling exposed and vulnerable. I wanted to escape. I wanted to hide. But where could I go?

The great Christmas celebration arrived and I tore the ugly wrapping away to reveal a most precious gift. My real mum must have understood I would feel lost in my all-white environment and she had given me a large brown bear. I was no longer isolated in an alien world. My real mum loved me. My real mum hadn't abandoned me. I loved the bear that towered above me and symbolised our re-discovered relationship. This giant teddy absorbed all of my capacity to love. It represented the hope of a very different future.

I cuddled my bear while I waited eagerly for my birth mum to arrive but she never came. Every succeeding Christmas brought more emotional pain because no more presents materialised and the expectation of her appearance faded. The hope that had dwelt deep in my heart slowly died.

Now I reflect back on this experience, I know the lady was just a friend of my grandmother and I had simply read into the situation my own desires and hopes. Unfortunately, it didn't make the memory any less agonising. I couldn't communicate my fears and worries simply because I was too young, so I entered an imaginary world where my dreams temporarily protected me from the painful reality of living as a misfit in an adoptive family.

However, I'm still grateful that, for a short while, I had a teddy who made my life just a little bit more bearable.

Choices and consequences

BRIDGET BETTS

Bridget Betts is white British and was born in England in 1957. She joined her adoptive family at ten days old. Bridget discovered that her birth father had died when she was 16. Members of his family have refused to engage with her. A number of approaches have been made to Bridget's birth mother who has refused contact but recently she has met her three maternal half-siblings. Bridget is an independent social worker and trainer. She is currently working part-time for BAAF, managing the Adoption Activity Days project. She has produced three interactive CDs for use with children: *My Life Story* (2003), *Speakeasy* (2004) and *Bridget's Taking a Long Time* (2004). She co-wrote *Recruiting, Assessing and Supporting Lesbian and Gay Carers* with Gerald P Mallon (2004), wrote *A Marginalised Resource? Recruiting, supporting and assessing single adopters* (2007) and has contributed chapters on life story work to other BAAF publications.

On the day I was born I never had the chance to see myself reflected back in my mother's eyes or face. She walked out of the hospital without holding me, smiling at me, delighting in me coming into the world, without saying even 'hello' or 'goodbye' to me. There was no celebration on the day I made my entrance into the world. She did, however, leave me with a name, Clare. I guess a nurse was left holding me as my mother left the hospital for the station to catch a train back to her home town. There she would pick up her life where she had left it before she became pregnant with me. I often wonder what that nurse felt holding this tiny baby whose mother had left her. I must have searched her face trying to find some connection, some sense of belonging. It would be many years before I saw myself reflected back in another's face. I didn't realise how exhausting it was going to be growing up having no mirror, no echoes of myself in the people around me.

I was adopted as a baby at ten days old. I have always known I was adopted, and for the most part I felt loved and comfortable in my adoptive home. When I left the hospital where I was born and went to live with my adoptive parents, I did not know the impact adoption would have on my life. Being adopted didn't matter in the first few years of my life and early childhood, but it did eventually.

Since then I have had different versions of the event in my mind or hovering somewhere at the back of it. Like Tracy Beaker, [5] I developed an inner fantasy life. I had always guessed I was "illegitimate". This was something that both scared and worried me. Perhaps it echoed my fundamental fear of not being wanted.

Growing up, I knew very little about my family of origin. The little I knew focused on my mother who had "relinquished" me. As a young child I felt I should be grateful for this as it meant I was "chosen" to be part of my adoptive family and therefore "special". But my inner experience was one of abandonment and rejection. The game of 'Let's pretend' had seeped into my consciousness. Just as my birth mother had walked back into her life pretending nothing had happened, I was pretending I had no history, life or identity before I was adopted. My adoptive parents had always told me, in tandem with the fact that I was adopted, that I was 'theirs and theirs alone' and 'what we are and do now is of most importance'. I guess my "adopted" self was consistently valued and affirmed. My roots and origins, the "other" me, I now realise was thus subtly, repeatedly dismissed. I didn't understand at the time but I was living in a dual reality where my genetic self was being denied in order to live in the present. I wanted to please, to belong and be accepted.

I was constantly figuring out how to be, and I became a master of disguise. I was for the most part a compliant child, outwardly confident and popular with my peers. However, I kept the other part of me secret, the part I never saw reflected back, and in that way I kept myself safe. Inside I felt helpless, angry and needed to find ways of being in control. I could not risk being abandoned or rejected again and found ways of adapting outwardly in my family and relationships with others.

My adaptive behaviour led me into marriage and children. I had strong messages growing up as the eldest girl in our family that grandchildren were hopefully going to be part of the extended family. I had a boyfriend, Sean, throughout my teens who I became engaged to on my 18th birthday. This relationship was very important to me as I wanted to belong, to have a place. The relationship did not survive the transitions we both subsequently made – me to university and Sean to employment.

---

[5] This refers to the main character in the *Tracy Beaker* books by Jacqueline Wilson, a highly successful children's series following the ups and downs of ten-year-old Tracy, sent to live in a children's home on account of her mother's "neglect". A lovable, naughty character, she survives with wit, imagination and resilience, fuelled by fantasies of another, better life. First published by Corgi Books in 1991 and also made into a long-running BBC TV series (available on DVD).

At university I developed a close friendship with Debra. Over time, I became aware I wanted more from that relationship but I knew that if I had ever articulated this it would have ended our friendship. We were both involved in the Christian Union; I had become involved with the Church in my teens. It was a community to which I felt I belonged, its boundaries and expected code of conduct helped me to feel safe. While I had friendship and companionship in my relationship with Sean during my teenage years, I never felt truly at ease. I had kudos with a boyfriend and I fitted in. My relationship with Debra shone a light into the shadows of my sexuality. I was curious to know more about this part of me but could I risk blowing my disguise? Was I robust enough in my sense of self to manage potential rejection from family and friends? Being connected and accepted were so important to me, I couldn't risk stepping into the light. I retreated to the shadows and after finishing my degree and training as a social worker, I developed a relationship with my future husband, John, who had been part of the church community in which I had spent my teenage years. We married and 18 months later our first child, Richard, was born.

My parents were delighted to become grandparents. I sensed this helped them in some way to come to terms with their own infertility. I was also delighted to become a mother. For the first time, I saw myself reflected back in my son's face; it was a powerful and moving experience. For the first time, I had a living connection to my genetic self. I delighted in all the ways he was similar to me, especially when others affirmed those likenesses. Motherhood also gave me another fixed marker in my identity, alongside being female, married and a social worker. These markers gave my sense of self an anchor. Two daughters followed: Ruth and Elizabeth. We were a family, a family in which every day I could see myself reflected back. I had a sense of connectivity and continuity.

Creating and becoming a family came at a cost. Having children meant I scrutinised my adopted status in a different light. I began to wonder about my birth mother and why she had walked away. As I enjoyed motherhood, I pondered how a mother could give up her child. I thought more about myself as a baby, left in the maternity hospital for ten days in the care of the nurses and then being taken home by complete strangers. In becoming a mother I learned that caring for a newborn is all consuming, taking all your energy and attention, particularly in the first days and weeks. I realised I had missed out on this concentrated level of care and attention. Who was keeping me in mind during those early days? My earliest memories are of feeling intensely alone and of bright light. I guess I spent a lot of my first ten days alone in my cot, looking at the lights above me. My early experience was minimised by those close to me, they implied I could not possibly remember or be affected by being adopted as I was only ten days old. My inner experience and feelings were not being validated; I was beginning to find this level of denial hard to manage.

I wanted to know more about my birth mother and the circumstances that had led to her decision to place me for adoption. It was still too risky to drop my disguise and risk rejection from my adoptive parents and friends if I took the decision to find out about my origins. I also had to weigh up the gains and potential losses. Was this about finding the truth? If it was about the truth, could it possibly be the whole truth? Embarking on the journey to trace your roots implies a narrowing of focus to a single origin. However, roots have branches so was this more about finding a story, or a number of stories as no one story is your true past? Discovering more about my story may inevitably lead me to reflect and re-evaluate my sense of self and my existing narrative. Would this be too painful for me and others who were close to me? I wanted to be honest with my family about my decision to trace; there was no room in my life for more secrets.

An impending move back to the city of my birth meant that the decision was made for me. How could I get on with my life and walk the streets there without wondering whether I was walking past my own mother? I had left the city with my adoptive parents when I was 18 months old, and, at the age of 32, I was to move back. My husband, who had been a teacher, had decided to train for the Anglican ministry. As a family we were moving to start a new phase in our lives as John took his place at theological college.

So I began a journey of discovery. It was not an easy journey. It was fraught with difficulty and disappointment. What was written on my original birth certificate bore no resemblance to the person I looked at every day in the mirror. How do I integrate the two?

I had given no thought to my birth father and the part he had played in my being in the world. It came as a shock to discover that not only did he exist; he had considered playing a part in my life. Tony was married with two children at that time, and had a brief affair with my mother when he was stationed abroad with the Royal Navy. I say "affair"; I later learned in a letter from my birth mother that she had never really liked him. In fact, she could not remember his name. She had only gone out with him as her best friend was going out with Tony's friend. My file indicates that he wrote me a letter to have when I was 21, to explain his reasons for placing me for adoption, and that Tony had considered bringing me up in his own family. I have been disappointed not to find the letter despite extensive research. I can only conclude my adoptive parents were given it to pass on to me, and that they have their own reasons for not doing so.

I eventually discovered that my father had died when I was 16 and I never knew. I couldn't help but wonder what I had been doing on the day he died. I had not felt my world shift and change on a day of such significance; his passing went unnoticed by me. A brief 'hello' turned into a long 'goodbye', to a man I hardly knew but was, and still is, a fundamental part of my being and identity. Looking at his photograph, I see myself and my eldest son reflected back in his eyes. My son reflects his grandfather in more than looks: before he had any knowledge of Tony he had settled on a career in the Navy and expressed his desire to attend a university by the sea to study geography, just as I later learned that Tony had done – the power of genes calling across the generations, influencing choices made in the present.

Through an intermediary I contacted Tony's wife, Maggie. I had wondered whether she knew about me as Tony had given much thought to my future and had after all considered raising me in his own family. My existence was a shock to her and her children. I have four siblings on my father's side, two born after me. Maggie then had to re-evaluate her marriage some 20 years after Tony had died. She became a recluse, apprehensive that Tony might have had other children from relationships she did not know about. My half-siblings expressed anger that I had walked into their lives and had such an impact on their mother. They asked for proof that I was Tony's daughter. I made the decision to write to Maggie, giving her some information about my reasons for contacting her and my circumstances, and reassured her I would not again walk uninvited into her life.

The information recorded on my file about my birth mother, Ann, presents her as somewhat 'cold' and determined to 'pursue her profession' as a teacher. Ann wrote to me after I had eventually traced her and contacted her through a friend. She married two years after my birth and has lived in South Africa since the early 60s. Ann explained in a letter to me in the mid-90s the difficulties that she would have faced as a single mother in the 50s. I also discovered that Ann never saw me and that she was told that this was 'for the best'; she needed to forget about me and get on with her life and career. Ann went on to tell me she loves tennis, the outdoors and painting – my own interests and talents are suddenly anchored and have a context.

In the photographs she enclosed I see myself reflected back again: in the tilt of the head and the way she holds her hands. I remember my initial shock at seeing her. In fact my partner, on seeing the photo for the first time, was insistent it was me but was somewhat puzzled by the "frumpy" dress I was wearing!

I have discovered along the way that I have seven half-brothers and sisters. I had given no thought to the fact I may be part of a wider family. This has taken some adjusting to. I am grateful I did not know before I had my own three children that there is a strong incidence of twins on my father's side!

I have contacted my birth mother twice in the last three years through intermediaries, some 13 years after our initial correspondence. I had waited, hoping that she might write. Time passed and eventually I decided I would like to meet her, to find out more about her and to share aspects of myself and my life. Sadly, she denied ever writing to me and has said I have now ruined her life. She expressed considerable anger about this. Ann had not shared anything about my birth with her husband to whom she has been married for nearly 50 years. She had also not told her three children, my half-siblings. After my intermediary contacted her in 2007 she decided to tell her husband about my birth. He was understandably angry and upset to have a secret that Ann had kept from him for half a century revealed in this way. In 2008 one of my intermediaries attempted to visit her at her home in South Africa. Ann lives in an ordinary suburb, her house the only one on the estate surrounded by high security fencing. My intermediary could not even get access to the front door. She did speak to Ann on the phone from outside the gate; Ann refused to let her in, saying she wanted to know nothing further about me and wanted no further contact. I was left wondering what she had done to herself to now deny my existence and any interest in me.

I felt very saddened by Ann's response to my attempted contact with her and her assertion I had ruined her life. I did not feel responsible for it. The consequences of my choice to trace and engage with her has led to her facing the consequences of the choice she made over 50 years ago, to walk away without saying 'hello' to me. Did she truly have a choice, you may ask? Given the culture of the 1950s, probably not. Did I have a choice about the family I was to grow up in? No. We have both had to deal with the consequences of choices that were made for us so long ago and both had to manage the consequences of our choices and actions in the present.

Moving to the city of my birth had a profound effect on me. For a while I was completely disoriented. I couldn't go anywhere without an A to Z; I felt like my arms and legs had been ripped off. My status had changed, I had given up my job as a GP-attached social worker when we moved, and I was the wife of an ordinand and mother to three children. I struggled to find my place. I was also processing the information I was discovering about my birth family and coping with my adoptive parents' negative reaction to my decision to trace. They declared I was "mad" and the children would be confused and upset when they realised they had other grandparents. I had been honest with my adoptive parents as I had wanted to be honest with my children about their heritage and extended family. I did not want to put them in a position of having to manage secrets. My decision to share my search for my origins with my parents shifted our relationship; it became quite strained and I experienced a sense of disappointment and blame. Had they not provided all I needed and been enough for me? Did I not know they loved me dearly, was that not enough? Yes, I knew they loved me but I felt I had betrayed that love by wanting to know who I am. I experienced their reaction as a rejection. I also had to manage rejection from my birth mother and my birth father's family. I felt completely at sea and in danger of losing my anchor, but in a strange way I now felt a sense of freedom to explore my identity, who I am and yet might be.

It was at this point that I met Kate. I recall she stood out to me across a crowded room at a social function. She was married with four children. We became friends and I began to feel echoes of the feelings I had for Debra all those years ago. I knew I could no longer ignore what was a fundamental part of my identity. It was a painful but liberating experience "coming out" to myself, my family and my children. Kate and I began a long journey into a relationship that has spanned nearly 20 years. We have had to manage the grief and pain of divorce and the impact on our children and wider families. It has not been easy, but I felt for the first time in my life that I was living the truth and I had truly come home, both to myself and in a relationship. I no longer had to pretend as I felt I was truly known by another and belonged. I feel I can take my place in history and no longer feel I was a 'mistake'. I know who I am and I am able to live more comfortably between my two families with this knowledge.

Sixteen years ago I made the choice as a social worker to work in the adoption field. I am a great believer in adoption; it still provides the best outcome for children who cannot live with their birth families. I believe we need to listen carefully to the experiences of adopted children and adults in order to help us understand the lifelong impact of being adopted, and the choices and consequences that are unique to it. I believe we need to support adoptive families to celebrate difference and to validate painful and sometimes contradictory feelings their adopted children may experience. We need to help families feel secure enough in themselves to help their children to live comfortably between two families and manage this dual reality that is unique to adoption. Adoption in the 21st century is complex for all those involved. Adoption is not just a concept; it is a profound and life-changing experience for all those whose lives are touched by it.

Postscript

August 2010

'You look like grandma, you speak like grandma, you walk like grandma – in fact it's like sitting next to grandma,' exclaims my 15-year-old nephew Connor in his broad South African accent. Connor is staring intently at me across the table at the pub where I am meeting my half-brother Stuart and his wife Lindsay for the first time. Two weeks prior to meeting him he had moved to the UK from South Africa to live here permanently. Stuart had greeted me so warmly, embracing me with tears in his eyes: 'Hi big sis, I'm your little brother Stu.' Five hours pass in the blink of an eye.

A few weeks later I meet my half-sister Clare who is waiting to greet me as I return from work. She has made the journey from Australia and I can't believe she is standing in front of me. It's a surreal experience. I am looking in a mirror as I see myself reflected back in her face, smile, mannerisms and even the cut of her hair. Clare shares my birth name; it's an emotional and powerful connection that has implications for both of us as we begin to reflect on our beginnings, our relationship and our place in the family.

Fast forward to March 2012 and I meet my sister Shirley for the first time. She has made the trip from South Africa. We fall into an immediate rhythm and as she leaves Shirley comments, 'It's like I have known you for a long time.'

Here we are – all relative strangers – so much connecting us and dividing us at the same time. A shared bloodline but no shared storyline. How do you begin to catch up on so many lost years?

I had been informed by Ann, my birth mother, through an intermediary in 2008 that she had told my two sisters and my brother about my existence and that they did not wish to have any contact with me. In July 2010 I find myself researching the impact of Facebook on contemporary adoption placements. I create my own Facebook account to understand more about social networking. I type in my sister Clare's name as an experiment and there she is in an instant, sitting smiling with my birth mother Ann in the South African sunshine. My world wobbles. Choices and consequences... What do I now choose? I can be in touch with Clare in a click of a mouse. What will be the consequences for the both of us, my siblings, my birth mother and my immediate family if I choose to make that click? Will life be the same again?

I am in turmoil. Two days later I send a message to Clare, presuming she knows of my existence, and wait. Just 12 hours on a reply arrives: 'I am absolutely blown away with this news but very excited at the same time. I have an older sister – and that is such a wonderful feeling – I am quite emotional as I write this and would very much like to get to know you.'

And so another chapter in my life opens. I now know that my siblings had no knowledge of me prior to my making contact with Clare on Facebook. I'm so glad I took the initiative and clicked the mouse on that July afternoon as I now have an ongoing and deepening relationship with my three half-siblings. They have welcomed and accepted me unconditionally for who I am. It will continue to be an emotional journey as we get to know each other and create our own unique shared storyline.

It is a disappointment to me and my siblings that Ann has decided she still cannot have contact with me but is now happy to hear news about me through them.

My concept and experience of belonging and living between two families has taken on a different shape through this experience – it is the dual reality that is unique to adoption. It is indeed a profound and life-changing experience. I am the richer for it.

The things my mother might have given me

VANESSA GEBBIE *

She might have given me birthday
parties, dresses, white
teddy bears

a sugared orange, a taste for bitter
chocolate, the small pleasure of learning to burst
bubble-wrap

a few siblings, something essential
like a name.

She might have given me a rope and pegs,
to hold my tent steady
in high winds.

* For Vanessa's bio details, see p 135.

Returning to my roots

SHENAZ DRURY *

One of my clearest memories of Asha Sadan Rescue Home for Children in Mumbai is not of small children or tiny babies but of a girl about 16 years old asking if I was her sister. I cannot remember how I answered her question and to this day, I still do not know how to. Ten years on from that visit I am back visiting Asha Sadan home, the place of my birth. Although I was only a few months old when I was in the home, too young to remember anything about it, it will always be a part of me and my identity. We had arranged this visit to coincide with meeting up with a staff member who had worked there when I was a baby.

I have been to India four times now and each time I have visited my place of birth with my adoptive family. This time, I went with my sister, my boyfriend and three other friends. I wasn't sure about taking my friends with me. A part of me wanted to share with them as they didn't really understand what adoption meant for me. I knew they would find the visit interesting, learn something, experience something different but, for me, a visit to Asha Sadan is a lot more. It is my journey into my unknown past, my heritage and my home, unknown yet familiar, made by memories of previous visits throughout my childhood and early adulthood.

As I walked through the large wooden doors separating the hustle and bustle of Mumbai streets into the cool entrance, a sense of calm and familiarity prevailed and I instantly recognised the courtyard where photographs had been taken during previous trips. As we were shown around, I was aware of the changes and developments that had taken place since my last visit. The older girls were being taught literacy and numeracy and basic computing, alongside the more traditional crafts. As we were taken into the craft room where girls proudly offered their work for us to look at, I could not help thinking this could have been me. Would I have been proud to show my work or would I have hung back in the corner?

Our tour continued and we were taken to the nursery area where the small children came rushing up to us, trying to grab the sweets we had brought for them, their big brown eyes watching us in fascination. We moved into the

* For Shenaz's bio details, see p 174.

baby room and saw all the tiny bunk bed cots lined up in a row. I would have been in one of those. I tried to imagine what it would have been like, trying to sleep with so many other babies. Would I have been one of those babies who cried all the time or would I have just lain there, calmly observing everything around me? As we walked through the home meeting staff and children, the others asking questions, I half listened while my emotions, feelings and thoughts, often suppressed in everyday life, became conscious in my mind.

Although we only spent a few hours at Asha Sadan, I came away feeling exhausted and emotionally drained. No visit to India is complete until I have gone back to my roots and been reminded how different my life might have been.

Be there

PAM

Pam was born in 1950 of white British parentage. She was seven weeks old when she joined her adoptive family. Her adoption was arranged through the Church which, she believes, encouraged her birth mother to leave her father as he had left his wife and they were living together. Pam's birth father did not know she had been adopted until she contacted him in 2008. She never met him before he died in 2011. Two brothers contacted her but she has never met them or had any contact with her birth mother who died before she traced her. As a child her adoptive parents worked hard to support her but her adoption was never openly discussed and she felt very alone. Pam lives in Wiltshire and has a son, daughter and three granddaughters. She has previously been published in an adoption newsletter.

The family that I lost,
so many years ago,
were hidden by a veil of fears,
I thought I'd never know.
I dreamt so long of finding them,
it all became surreal;
I lost myself in fantasy,
not knowing how to feel.
The years passed by, just dreaming
about my hidden past
but now I know the secrets
and I feel complete at last.
Although I understand the fears
that drove my mum and dad,
if only they had helped me
I may not have felt so bad.
If only they'd been stronger
and brave enough to see,
it wasn't just about their fears
but truly about me.
If they had only held my hand
and helped me search and find,
we may have been much closer,
with confusion left behind.
Instead I've lived my life alone,

not speaking of the past,
but now with friends beside me
I have found the truth at last.
Remember that this child of yours
needs love and tender care,
and above your fears and worries
needs to know that you are there.
With love and reassurance,
with your support and care,
their journey can be easier
and one that you can share.
Don't hide away and put aside
the things they need to know.
Be there for them, be honest
and their love for you will grow.

Never not adopted

ZARA PHILLIPS

Zara Phillips was born in London on 5 November 1964 to a Jewish mother and Italian father. She joined her Jewish adoptive family in January 1965. She reunited with her birth mother and siblings when she was 24 but has never been able to find her birth father. Zara's music career started as a backing vocalist in the 1980s, singing with Bob Geldof and various other acts. She recently collaborated on a song, 'I'm Legit', with Darryl McDaniels (RUN-DMC) to help raise more awareness about adoption. Today she is an adoption activist in the US, campaigning for the rights of adult adoptees to have open birth records. She has also written a memoir, *Mother Me*, published by BAAF in 2008. She is mother to three wonderful children and resides in New Jersey, US (see www.everythingzara.com).

When I think back over the years, I realise how little I understood about the lifelong impact of adoption. It wasn't something that was deeply discussed in the house I grew up in; it was a subject I sensed made my mother feel uncomfortable. I didn't know how to talk to her about it. I became the secret keeper of my true feelings, battling inwardly and quietly on the meaning of what it was to be a child who was given up for adoption, looking on the streets just in case I saw her, the woman who gave me up, but never revealing the depths of my curiosity or my need of wanting so desperately to know my story.

I did not want my mother to hurt and I did not want her to give me back. In my childlike mind I thought I would grow up and suddenly make sense of being an adopted person. I would gain an understanding of all my feelings and with great clarity it wouldn't hurt any more or affect my life in any way.

What I wasn't prepared for is that being an adopted person meant I would always be an adopted person. There would be passages in my life – acting out as a teenager, searching for my birth mother, reuniting, figuring out how to include this new family in my life, getting married, having children – where feelings surrounding being adopted would hit me emotionally so hard I would be left scrambling for air. I would never not be adopted and somehow this always took me by surprise.

I grew up in a middle-class family in a suburb in north London; my adoptive father was a judge and my mother worked as a legal executive. I had an adoptive brother who was two years older than me. I had everything materially a child could want; I went to an all-girls private school and had holidays every year. Yet I always felt insecure and alone; I never felt as if I fitted in with anyone and spent a lot of time living in my head, thinking. I remained throughout my young years as the good adoptee. The only hint something was wrong was my inability to stay away overnight anywhere, the anxiety and panic that took place during those nights at friends' houses and the calls to my mother to bring me home.

Then came my introduction to drugs and my world changed. At first I felt invincible. I began to behave recklessly; I believed the drugs gave me more confidence but the voices inside my head became louder and the self-hatred stronger until the drugs could no longer cover the feelings. I felt so angry all the time and I didn't know why.

My need became greater, a void that consumed me, and I yelled and screamed, unknowingly wanting my mother to fix me, to understand and tell me what was going on inside myself. My mother, unsure of what to do, would sometimes put her head in her hands and shake it.

My drug use ended quickly. I hit rock bottom. I was 22 years old and didn't really care if I lived or not. I took risks with my life all the time and yet, when I had moments of being quiet and looked at the vast sky, I knew there had to be another way to live. I felt a small connection to some source outside myself and I wasn't sure what it was. Unconsciously, I was always waiting for my birth mother to come and find me and tell me she had made a mistake. Within months of giving up the drugs the clarity came: I needed to find my birth mother; I needed to know my story. I knew it would free me.

I began to read about adoption and to grieve the loss of being separated from my mother. I came to understand that society focuses on the good, happy side of adoption yet there was a deeply sad part of myself and the lack of grieving had played a major role in my life. I needed to go to the place of pain to get relief.

Finally, I began to unravel and make sense of the difficulties I had with all my relationships but, most importantly, I began to understand the way my adoptive mother and I related to each other. Our relationship had always been challenging for us and I never understood why. As a teenager I cried and would scream at her in pure frustration, wondering why it didn't work, why I was so angry with her, why she couldn't accept me nor me her. The relationship just didn't flow, there was no sense of ease and it saddened me.

At the same time, I was afraid of being separated from my adoptive mother. I was terrified of her dying and some nights would check on her just to make sure she was still alive. The woman I pushed away I needed to be close to me, yet I didn't know how to do this. It was a constant internal struggle.

I did not tell my mother I had reunited with my birth mother for a couple of years. I was still protecting her from her feelings. I was now an adult, yet I carried this emotional baggage and still couldn't find my voice and be honest about what I needed to do.

I had loved my mother in a desperate needy way, my anger like a ball of fire directed always at her, blaming her in an unconscious way for my being abandoned by my birth mother. All my feelings of insecurity and uncertainty about whether she would also abandon me came out in my anger towards her. I could not let her see me feeling vulnerable about being adopted. I didn't know how to show my pain so I acted out in other ways, hoping somehow she would notice.

When, as a mother, she didn't know what to do, I took this as the deepest rejection one can take, not understanding her frailty as a human being, as a woman, a tired mother with such a demanding child. When I became a mother myself a door opened into a world of understanding and love I had never experienced before, and the unspoken and unknowing feelings I had carried began to make sense. They were illuminated so brightly I couldn't turn from them any more. Each time I became pregnant I felt extreme guilt towards my adoptive mother and by my third pregnancy I didn't tell her for a couple of weeks. I was trying to protect her from her infertility just as I had done my whole life when I was told it wasn't necessary to tell everyone I was adopted.

I knew my mother hurt. I had felt and seen the pain from a tiny girl remembering the time she had an argument with a woman; the woman had yelled down the phone, 'Well, at least I could have children. I wasn't barren like you.' I saw my mother's reaction to a woman who was mentally unsound. I saw her try and protect herself. That night, I cried deeply. I didn't want my mother to hurt like that again.

As I delved into reading about adoption I learned that I needed to grieve. I had carried not only my own grief but both my mothers' too. I cried for all of us, the three women who were connected by my birth, and finally I began to gain compassion for each of my mothers. I began to stop blaming myself for not being the daughter I thought my adoptive mother would have had. I realised I had carried within me a comparison to a perfect biological daughter who didn't even exist.

I understood that those shadows which had lived beside me as I grew up were more real than I had imagined. They represented all the people who were not discussed – my biological parents, my mother's biological children – and we danced around them as if they weren't there. The truth was that they lived in both my mother and myself.

I had to realise that it wasn't my fault I was fertile and my adoptive mother wasn't; it's OK for me to know what it is like to have my own children; they do indeed look like me and it feels truly wonderful. I felt a connection to another human being I had never felt before.

I had to learn to accept that my mother would never have this experience of birthing her own biological child but she had had a different experience, that of raising another woman's child with whom, no matter how hard it was with our bonding, she would fall in love. Even though I carried so much shame and guilt about my behaviour, I did give her joy. She, in turn, mothered me in the best way she knew how with the little information she had been given about raising an adopted child, and that had to be enough. Acceptance began to sweep over me and I was able to feel more a part of my adoptive family.

My mother became quite ill a few years ago and was in hospital for months. Throughout her life she had battled many chronic situations and as a small child, it would scare me and I would worry about her. When we thought she was dying I began to experience panic attacks in a way I hadn't since I was very young.

During my mother's illness I was living far away from her in Los Angeles. I felt quite powerless as I talked to doctors and my adoptive father and brother about her, trying to figure out the next move. Miles away, I began to experience my panic as an adult woman and now a mother myself. I would talk to myself when I felt the panic rise, as a mother does to a child, reassuring myself that if anything were to happen to her I would be OK. I was a grown-up and I could manage without her.

I was so surprised by my reaction; I was a mother of three small children, an adult, and yet I automatically went back into this place of fear and separation. It was a memory my body still carried, even though I had worked out so much of my adoption feelings.

It took many years for the relationship with my mother to change. Even as an adult I had to work at not taking things she said personally. I never felt my mother understood who I was. I think she tried, but we just never fully bridged the gap. What did happen as a result of all the soul searching and reading I have done were moments of accepting her and appreciating who she was, and those moments I took gladly. They helped fill the hole.

We had times where the love flowed easily and freely. I began to understand the complexity of our relationship. I also understood that it wasn't either of our faults. We just didn't know. We were not educated to understand how this relationship would play out.

By the time my mother died in July 2008, from complications following heart surgery, she had for the first time in 20 years of my reunion spoken to my birth mother on the phone. I knew then this meant she finally felt less threatened. I hoped, in her heart, she truly knew she was my mother and that my birth mother could never take her place. I was lucky enough to have sat with her, my father on one side, me on the other, holding her hand and talking to her as she died. I wouldn't have wanted it any other way.

After she died I couldn't let go of her hand. I was looking at its shape, the roundness of her fingers. I realised her hands gave me a sense of comfort because they were the most familiar part of her, those hands that as a child were always in my sight, the hand I held crossing the street, the hands that made me lunch or cooked my dinner, the hands that stroked me when I was feeling sad, the hands on the steering wheel driving me all over town, the hands whose rings I had looked at and played with, turning them around on her finger. I knew then that regardless of how we had fought and cried, and how adoption had affected us both, those hands without words and without the emotional baggage encompassed everything. They were pure love, all the love that she had for me.

Understanding what it meant to me to be adopted has helped me comprehend how I think about life. I never realised how far the two were intertwined. I came to understand how essential it was for me to search and find out my origins. Without my story and the truth, I created fantasies and none of them were positive. I believed I was a mistake and didn't have the same rights as other people. I believed my birth mother didn't want me, I had done something wrong to make her not remember me and those thoughts created my self-image.

Unravelling the lifelong impact of adoption has helped to reveal to me what

I needed to look at. Having my first child had the greatest impact of all. Up until that point, I had always been able to hide from my pain and now here was this tiny baby looking at me. My heart completely opened and a love I was unable to stop came pouring out of me. I could no longer keep the barriers up.

One night, as I gazed in awe at my son, I was talking softly, telling him how perfect he was and understanding deep within myself that babies are true perfection. I knew then that it wasn't my fault that my birth mother hadn't kept me, that I couldn't have possibly done anything wrong and if I called myself a mistake then I was calling him one too.

The way I began to make sense of being adopted began then, lying next to him. It was part of a bigger plan, one I could not understand but I could turn around and be a voice for all those little adoptees who had felt like me as a child. I wouldn't be who I was if I hadn't been adopted and that was a gift.

The work I do today revolves around my adoption experience. I go to support groups and conferences. I laugh with other adopted people and cry deeply. I share myself openly in the hope that I can help one other person in the room, and when people share back and identify with me it gives me the courage to keep going forward.

There are some days when I think to myself, why am I making myself so vulnerable? Why am I talking and revealing so much about myself to all these people? What I realise over and over again is we cannot touch people if we are not honest. We cannot help one another if we are still hiding, so I take the risk and the gifts back overwhelm me. I know today that I was meant to be here and all those years of silence and suffering were leading me to the place I'm in today.

I still have my adoption days where relationships can feel very difficult. I am still looking for my birth father on the street, but somehow this doesn't define me any more. I am able, even with unresolved issues, to get on with my life and this, I believe, is due to all the groups I have exposed myself to. They have helped me to grieve and have clarity.

Grieving the loss has set me free. Becoming a mother and part of my own family, joining the adoption community and talking about these issues has given me the sense of belonging I have always longed for and, for that, I am truly grateful.

Mute Bella

BELLA FREY

Bella Frey was born in South Korea. On 17 October 1975, aged approximately six months, she was found abandoned on a street in Busan and spent a further six months in an orphanage before joining her new adoptive family in March 1976. Bella grew up in Southend-on-Sea with her adoptive mum and brother, adopted from Vietnam. She now lives in south-east London where she co-runs a painting and decorating business. Bella has visited South Korea twice and hopes to return soon to follow up searching for any information regarding the first year of her life.

I am Bella, 35 years old. I have run a painting and decorating business for about eight years. I am a British and Swiss national. I was found in Busan, a harbour town in South Korea, on 17 October 1975. I spent six months in an orphanage in Busan before being taken to Seoul and adopted by a couple in Switzerland. Since the age of four I was raised by my mum in England, with my brother who is adopted from Vietnam.

I have often wanted to have a t-shirt made with this kind of information on.

To look at me, I may be Chinese or Japanese. To look at me I am possibly a student or a cleaner or a nanny. I may speak with broken English.

We can all make assumptions about people based on appearance. How someone dresses is like a social uniform, where we choose to eat, which type of employment we take. These are all choices we make and it is understandable that someone would think I am a student because of how I dress, so be it. I know I am not.

If someone assumes I am Chinese or Japanese, so be it. I know I am not. But this is different to comments about my clothing or my hairstyle or my job choice. We can't choose our genetic make-up, our facial features and skin colour, yet people feel they have a right to pass comment and draw conclusions, in my case generally based on a set of negative racial stereotypes. I often feel like I am walking beside a separate version of me. A mute me, created by all the people who choose to verbalise their predominantly negative assumptions to my face. I call her "mute Bella".

'Chink.'

'Tart.'

'You love me long time?'

'You speak English?'

'How do you chop spring onions so finely like they do in the restaurants?'

'I like Asian girls. You are so polite, and you know how to treat men.'

'Go back to where you came from, evil Jap.'

I feel sorry for mute Bella as she can never say anything in reply. She just turns red and fills up with anger and frustration. I have to tell myself that she is not real, she is a manifestation of ignorance. I am Bella and I can speak with my clear but slightly estuary English. I can tell these people who I really am, but mostly I think they have no interest in knowing about me; they prefer mute Bella.

As a young child, being adopted was just part of life. It was normal for me. It was normal that I had a mum with blonde hair, and that my mum was Mum and Dad to us. I knew I had a loving family unit. My mum, my brother and I were a team. We still are. As a team we deal with life's ups and downs. We struggle and laugh through bad times and enjoy the good times. When I was a child I felt like we were unlike other families for many reasons apart from the obvious one, that none of us looked alike. People would sometimes speak to my mum about us as if my brother and I could not speak English. That made me cross but on the whole, if you had asked me then how I felt about being adopted, I would have just said it was OK. As a child I easily accepted things the way they were.

As a teenager I didn't accept things so readily. I resented the fact that to strangers my family didn't appear as my own. I resented the fact that I didn't look like my peers, I wasn't pretty and boys didn't find me attractive. I resented that people thought my brother was my boyfriend. Yuck! What an awful thought. I resented that as I became as tall as my mum, a towering five feet in total, people would allude to the fact that we might be lovers. Double yuck! I dressed like a tomboy to limit the amount of crude comments that would be thrown my way. I resented the reputation of Asia producing cheap and inferior quality products. I remember seeing an article in a Sunday newspaper supplement about the trade in international adoption. There was a huge double-page spread showing several different babies from various "races" with price tags above their heads. The cheapest was the East Asian child. I resented that I had no cultural traditions to be proud of; I had no famous role models to aspire to; I only had negative media-fuelled stereotypes of East Asian females. I resented not being able to see any faces similar to mine. I couldn't find my features in Chinese movie stars, rare as they were over here in England. I found my face to be alien looking. I avoided my reflection. I lumped all these resentments together and made the root cause my adoption. I felt no pride in any part of my interrupted start in life. I knew it drew strange reactions from people and so I tended to go along with whatever their preconceptions may have been. When asked where I was from I would just say, 'Southend in Essex'. Then they would ask where my parents were from and I would say the same, so they happily assumed I was a second generation immigrant. I found that whenever I decided to tell the truth I would get a mixture of sympathy or awkwardness, which in turn made me feel awkward, so I frequently opted to let them draw their own conclusions.

I was tormented by the lack of attention from boys and drew the conclusion that being a plain-looking Korean in Korea would have been far better than being a plain-looking Korean in Essex, as even the plainest English girls got boyfriends, so I would at least get some interest if I was in Korea surrounded by Korean boys. I thought maybe we were all programmed to only fancy our own racial types, so it wasn't their fault they didn't like me. At some very low points I wished to exchange my family for a boyfriend. Being a teenager was crap. Now, with some distance since my teenage years and hopefully a little knowledge, I realise being a teenager is always crap, adopted or not.

What I needed at that time was some positive ammunition to fire back at all the negatives. I longed to have a history that I could throw out there about mysterious traditions and revered ancestors. I encountered very few children and young adults from minority ethnic groups but I would be jealous of their cultural backgrounds, of the interest it could generate in others. I knew very little about Korea, only that the Olympics were held in Seoul in 1988 and that Koreans had a taste for dogs at the dinner table – sorry, *on* the dinner table! I knew geographically where it was as we had a world map pinned next to our dining table, but I knew nothing of its history, culture, food, traditions or costumes. There was no internet when I was growing up. If there had been, I might have had a very different outlook much earlier. My mum did her best to find out information at the time but reference material was scarce and without access to internet-based communities we were stuck with a big void. That's what my background felt like until, in my 20s, I leapt into the information superhighway and immersed myself in all things Korean.

It wasn't until my mid-20s that I felt a sudden need to connect with my roots. Maybe it was people around me discussing plans to start their own families that got me thinking about my own background. They would talk about wanting to continue their family line, wondering which facial features a new baby would share with them. It wasn't a deep need in me which started me looking, it was more a moment of interest, but once I started I couldn't stop.

Within a few weeks I had sent off for copies of my adoption paperwork from the agency in Switzerland and had contacted the adoption service in Korea. The next two years changed my life and changed me. I found out that being adopted from overseas was not as rare as I believed. Korea has actually sent hundreds of thousands of its children for overseas adoption since the 1950s, and still does. Strangely, discovering this brought me both great comfort and huge frustration.

One of the most significant life-changing moments of my life was meeting other adopted Koreans at an event in Washington DC. Until I had met other adoptees I really didn't know where I fitted in the world. In Washington I met about 600 other Korean adoptees who had grown up in the United States, Australia, and parts of Europe. Within hours of chatting and exchanging stories I felt a true and overwhelming sense of shared self-identity. We exchanged stories about our lives, of growing up in different parts of the world but experiencing the same identity struggles and assumptions from strangers. Mute Bella wasn't anywhere to be seen, but I discovered that many of the adoptees I met felt as if they spent their lives with a similar alter ego walking next to them, but they too had left them all behind for this one time. I immersed myself in the stories these people shared with me and I cried and cried because the feeling of unity and understanding could not be put into words. I was finally able to embrace my identity as an adopted Korean, and I felt an urgent impulse to reclaim my lost cultural heritage. I made steps to finding other adopted Koreans in the UK and eventually returned to Korea for the first time since I was a baby.

Returning to Korea for the first time was enriching but difficult and emotional. It was no homecoming. I found it so strange to be surrounded by Korean faces. I felt weird when I saw the occasional European features, or when I heard English being spoken I felt a sudden bond of familiarity. I felt that Koreans looked at me strangely since I must have been dressed differently, carried myself differently. I offended someone on the subway when they asked for directions and I said I couldn't speak Korean. It was as if mute Bella was with me again but in a different form. This time people were assuming I was Korean, but a whole new set of silent assumptions were assigned to mute Bella, assumptions I could never even guess at as I had no idea what it was to be Korean. The massive social and cultural differences between my birth country and the country I was raised in often shocked me and made me feel uneasy. I was told my skin looked burnt because I had a light tan from the summer sun. Korean women hide from the sun, which I now know would have knocked about ten years off my sun-aged face, having seen Korean women in their 40s who look like 20-year-olds. Make-up counters in department stores have lightening serums where here we would have bronzing products. At a seminar about 'being Korean', Korean adoptees were scolded for not knowing all the words to the Korean national anthem. I was surprised that in the same way people in England would constantly tell me how lucky I was and how grateful I should be to have been rescued from Korea, when in Korea some Korean people told me how lucky I was to have been raised in the west. They said that now I should return to Korea and repay my birth country by sharing the knowledge I had gained growing up in the west. They hadn't thought about the fact that my knowledge of Korean language was limited to a few tourist phrases.

However, the difficulties I encountered were balanced by the positive experiences I had. For each person I met who judged me and couldn't understand my situation, I met other people who were extremely open and giving. I met young Koreans who took a day off work to show me around and people who would apologise to us on behalf of a whole system for sending us away and not keeping us in Korea. I met people who gave me answers to some of my biggest questions by explaining about the structures and strong beliefs in Korean society that could have contributed to me being abandoned. Even though I found it difficult to hear what I was being told, it helped me towards understanding the social pressures my birth mother or family would have been dealing with. In England, if a baby is abandoned on the street it makes headline news. In Korea, it is just another statistic but is still the result of a heart-breaking decision. I learned how the stigma of being an unmarried mother is enormous, even today. Adultery is still classed as a criminal offence, punishable by imprisonment. I began to build a picture of a society that was very different to the one I was raised in and I could finally empathise with whoever made the decision to leave me. This was a big thing for me, as I had battled for many years trying to understand how someone could leave a baby on a street in mid-October. From what I had learned by visiting Korea, I could see that only desperate circumstances could have forced such an action.

I felt enriched learning about the cultural traditions of wonderful drumming, dance and theatre, rituals of marriage, and annual festivities and celebrations. I absorbed all the information possible so that I could relay it back to people as part of the new more Korean me. I am happy now to be able to tell enquiring strangers about my birth country and its people and food. My God, the food! Whether I had rediscovered flavours familiar to me from infancy or maybe just a lucky coincidence, either way I found a cuisine I immediately loved. I now crave Korean food more than European dishes. Though I love other Asian foods too, they are no substitute for the intense, spicy, sweet and vivid flavours of Korean dishes. I now feel as if it is part of my soul. I can't comprehend that I went 25 years without Korean food in my diet.

While I go about my life here in England, I now enjoy topping up my intake of Korean culture. I regularly watch Korean films on DVD and thanks to a thoughtful Christmas present from a friend, have recently started following popular Korean TV dramas. They too seem to feed my soul, even though they make me laugh and cry in equal measures. I buy Korean products via the internet and my car is always blasting out "Kpop", much to the distress of many of my friends. Rediscovering my cultural heritage has made me feel more complete. I can enjoy the good stuff and deal with the more difficult things in my own time.

I think everyone goes through life constantly seeking to define themselves. I feel like I am searching for pieces to complete a jigsaw of myself. I know I am a very different person to the Bella of ten years ago. I have written on various occasions during my life about my experiences of being adopted and each time I begin writing I have developed as a person. My experiences shape who I am and how I feel about myself. A huge change in me occurred after finding other adoptees and visiting Korea because now I can look in a mirror and recognise that my features are typically Korean. I can see that other Koreans would identify me as Korean. I like that. I like that I can exchange thoughts about Korean food, about traditions and places, about famous Korean movies and pop stars. I like that if someone asks me where I am from I can tell them with pride, knowing at least something about the country I was born in and which is etched on my face.

I still don't know my full story, and I still don't have many of the answers I want. I hope to pursue these in another trip to Korea. I hope to visit the orphanage that cared for me until I was adopted and I hope to find at least some information about who I am and why I was abandoned.

As for mute Bella, I don't think she will ever really go away as long as people keep seeing her, but I will keep speaking for her and trying to educate the people who see her and are willing to hear me.

Be strong, brave and proud

ELEANOR

Eleanor was born in Glasgow, Scotland, in the mid-1960s in a mother and baby home. Her adoptive parents collected her when she was six weeks old. She is white Scottish, living in England but Scotland is her cultural homeland. She has a sense of belonging when she goes there. Eleanor has a female partner and they have two children (her partner has had their second son since she wrote her story for this anthology – he has the same donor as Eleanor's birth son, making them half-siblings). She contacted her birth family in her 20s and has experienced the ups and downs of life post reunion since then. Eleanor is a social worker by profession and one of her roles is assessing foster carers. She enjoys being able to contribute to looked after children having positive experiences with committed and insightful carers.

I live in England with my female partner and our four-year-old son. I was collected from a mother and baby unit when I was about six weeks old. Birth mothers were encouraged to stay with their babies, but my birth mother, who I believe was in denial about what was happening, fled as soon as she could. This led to a delay in my adoption being finalised while my adoptive parents' solicitor traced her to sign the final papers. I bring this information from parts of a story I have pieced together over the years. I find the story very difficult to retain. I don't trust my memory, and also, the story has trickled out over the years, which adds to a sense of information missing either because I have forgotten it or it has not yet been told. I only learned of my birth mother's disappearance three years ago when I spoke to my adoptive mother again, recognising that her memory would wane and the full story would be gone forever.

My birth mother ended up marrying my birth father. They had a number of further children together so when I did make contact I discovered that I had full siblings. I made contact via an intermediary when I was 26. My birth mother initially denied that she had lost a child through adoption, but on a subsequent call, she acknowledged she had.

I was born and brought up in Scotland and both my birth parents and adoptive parents are Scottish. I have always seen myself as Scottish and I have a special affinity with the West Coast which is where my birth family is from.

I want to focus on the course my life has taken since I met my birth family. I was at university studying social work at the time and realised that I needed to make sense of my own history before I could realistically support others with theirs. So I bit the bullet. For a while after finding and meeting them I cruised along on a wave of contentment. They had neither rejected me nor absorbed me, and our contact was enough to represent a relationship (I had probably feared being swept away by a new family more than I feared them not wanting to know). I had also, or so I thought, put an end to the angst that had affected me since I neared the age of being able to trace. I had always felt a great responsibility towards my birth mother. (What if she was out there and desperate for me to get in touch, and I denied her that?) On the other hand, I had an entrenched loyalty to my adoptive parents. (How could I betray them by finding my birth parents?) I found this dilemma impossible to solve.

In retrospect, the mistake I made was thinking that the process was completed and my issues with adoption were finally resolved. Perhaps they would have been, had my life not taken the course it did in the years that followed. The other adoptees I have met have been a mixture of people, from those who don't feel adoption has affected them that much to people where it has had a deep impact, who are very "wounded" by it. For me the jury is still out as to whether this is because they have other troubles in life, or if the troubles are a consequence of being adopted. I am not sure if I hold with the "primal wound" theory which seems to write us off emotionally before we even start, but perhaps this is denial on my part. I do believe that many of the negative impacts of the adoption process can be addressed through good adoptive parenting based on love and transparency about adoption issues.

I'm sure my adoptive father loved me but he was often remote, especially in later years; as with many men of his generation, he found it difficult to speak about feelings and emotions. People come to identify themselves as gay or lesbian for many reasons but for myself, I am sure it was that I felt more comfortable with women. I could engage emotionally. I also held a deep-rooted fear of becoming pregnant and finding myself with an unwanted pregnancy as my birth mother had done. Having a relationship with a woman avoided this issue.

It was at the same time I was meeting my birth parents that I was also dealing with the beginnings of a lesbian relationship. The dilemma of whether to find my birth family was replaced with a new one. They had just met me, how could I tell them I was gay? I knew nothing about their values but suspected that at least some of them would find it difficult to accept. I hadn't told anyone else either – not my adoptive parents nor most of my friends. I was no longer on a wave of contentment; instead, I was in a storm of uncertainty about my own identity and my relationships with other people. I recall meeting another lesbian adoptee at that time quite by chance. We spoke briefly about setting up a group for adopted people who identified as gay and were in the process of reunion, but I doubt we would have found many others who were at exactly the same point. She was also very different from me; she was very much "out" and fitted a stereotype of a lesbian woman that would have prompted her birth family to question her sexuality within themselves, if not directly with her. My sexuality, on the other hand, was invisible.

This storm went on for a number of years. My relationship with my birth family ebbed and flowed, until eventually it drifted away. My siblings had their own issues and my birth mother ceased contacting me. I suspect she was still in denial. In hindsight, I can see that I held them at a distance so they could not see this aspect of my life which they may not have liked. Then my birth sister discovered the truth, and the contact lessened even more. She had told me everyone was cool with it but I couldn't be sure. I had either been rejected because they didn't like me or my sexuality, or more likely a combination of both.

At this point I ceased calling myself an adoptee and began calling myself a "double rejectee". As I was becoming more comfortable with my own sexuality and identity, after coming out to my adoptive mother, friends and work colleagues, I was being pulled back by the horrible cruelty of being rejected a second time. I had no real problem with having been adopted as I could understand that in the 1960s young women were pushed in this direction (although the harder, angry part of me said that she/they should have taken responsibility, especially when they went on to stay together anyway), but to have been rejected again… Suddenly my birth mother was not so much a victim of circumstance but cold and uncaring. In my mind, I called her "the Ice Queen".

Living as a lesbian had given me another challenge which seemed inexorably linked with my adoption – wanting and needing to have children of my own at some point. Once I reached my early 30s my fear of getting pregnant was replaced by a recognition that time was passing and I wasn't going to get pregnant "naturally", and I started to research ways of having children as a lesbian. I was very torn. I was unsure about adopting as I thought this would be difficult because of my own adoption. I also very much wanted a biological connection with my child and I longed to experience pregnancy and birth. I was very aware that unless I used a donor known to me (and nobody was leaping out as a possible choice), I would be having a child who would potentially grow up with similar questions about his or her origins. I wasn't sure if I could inflict this on my child. Perhaps they would be fine with it. In the end I compromised. My son has a donor who is contactable when he is 18. He is American as at the time of my fertility treatment the identity of UK donors was kept secret. I had to give any child I might have a choice. We also have a photograph of the donor as well as a letter from him, and lots of factual information. And so it was that one night I went to collect a tank of frozen sperm from a delivery depot and drove it home, ready to be delivered to our treatment centre the following morning, strapped in with a seat belt. It will be a good story to tell him one day.

I then had one fertility treatment after another over two to three years, all resulting in failure. This was the cruellest time of all, when my adoption came back at me with a force. I felt so angry that my birth mother had produced so many children and I couldn't have one. In fact I was the only one of her children who hadn't had children. I felt destined to be alone biologically, as if I somehow deserved this. I don't know if I would have survived had my final attempt not resulted in becoming pregnant. Fate hadn't stopped throwing me around. I bled heavily at ten weeks and 12 weeks, and then my son was given a one in two risk of having "chromosome abnormalities", where I could have found myself having to make decisions about terminating the pregnancy should the "abnormalities" be "incompatible with life". That would have been such a bitter irony – my birth mother losing an unwanted baby through adoption and me losing such a wanted baby through a termination. The very word chromosome brought to mind DNA; I realised with a kind of horror that not only was I not going to have a child of my own while my birth mother had lots of children but I was also going to lose my son through something which may have been hereditary. My partner and I feared miscarriage so much that we rejected all diagnostic screening offered, relying instead on scans, so we lived with anxiety for months until finally I gave birth to a completely healthy baby boy by Caesarean section.

There were so many fears about my son's potential health problems that after a short time with me he was whisked away to the special care unit. To this day, I feel we were separated at a time when we should have been together. It tore me apart. It was winter and the old Victorian hospital I had been transferred to was very reminiscent of what a mother and baby home would have looked like. I remember the raw emotion of separation from him, and the helplessness. I visited him for the first time nearly a day after he was born and as we entered the ward he was in the arms of a nurse, again so reminiscent of my own early hours. It wasn't meant to be that way and it has taken me a long time to come to terms with this and to see that it hasn't affected the bond I have with my son.

One of the other themes of this book is rites of passage and my journey to becoming a mother is certainly my rite of passage. I feel as though I'm an adult at last and I feel whole.

I had the opportunity to do a life story workshop with the Post-Adoption Centre (PAC).[6] I made a sand sculpture of my adoption, complete with my own family of female partner and donor-conceived son and my birth family, with distant dad and caring mum, (and to my delight there was an ice queen character). While I thought my task in life was to carry on as a "double rejectee", that workshop and the optimism and clarity offered by the participants shifted something within me, motivated me to seek the truth of my second rejection and I re-established contact with one of my siblings. I learned that my birth mother had been experiencing early onset dementia for a number of years. Although not fully explaining my birth family's absence, this goes some way to explaining the lack of contact. I decided I had nothing to lose and was secure enough in my own family to ask the questions I had needed to ask, and also to feel some forgiveness. I was able to ask my sister, 'Was your mum a good mum to you?' Hearing she was has helped me to see her differently. I would definitely advise other adoptees to ask for the information you need. You never know when it might be lost. My birth mother has subsequently met my son and the kind way she treated him will stay with me forever. She gave him an illuminated snowman which I absolutely treasure as though it was a gift for me.

This is my story so far. I know "adoption" will continue as a presence in my life. My birth mother and adoptive mother are both ageing and I will lose them both in the future, leaving me on my own (my adoptive family was very small). I'm sure I will maintain irregular contact with most of my siblings, which is a comforting thought. Nothing is set in stone; I have avoided contact with my birth father but last week I received a card from him. Normally I would have ignored it but I think I will reply this time and see what, if anything, happens next.

We have already begun the "telling and talking" process with my son, who knows he has a "mummy", "mama" and a "donor". I am hoping that being transparent and giving him all the information we have will help him with any identity questions he has as he grows up. I know my future may include supporting him to find his donor who he may see as a "birth father". The journey begins again; I never thought I would be part of another such journey.

---

[6] See under 'Useful organisations/websites'.

Even if my son chooses not to involve me or my partner, we are part of a birth parent–donor–child triangle.

To finish, there are a few things I would like to share with people reading this book. Firstly, we could heal some or most of our "wound" through celebrating the partners/family/children/friends/life that we have. We are more than adoptees: we are sons, daughters, friends and family to other people so, although we started out alone at birth, we are not necessarily alone in life and this is something that we are in control of, even if we had no control at birth.

Secondly, we are brave. We had no choice about being adoptees and living with adoption requires courage. I am a quiet person and feel that people sometimes doubt my strength, but when I feel this way I look back at the courage it took to meet my birth mother, and I remind myself that I am a strong and capable person. It also would have taken strength to have chosen not to find her. Whatever we choose to do, strength and courage are demanded from us, and we should be proud of living with what adoption brings.

Finally, there is a lot to be said for living in the moment. I read a book recently where the character was laughing with her family. She said she recognised the moment for what it was – happiness. This made me think of how much of an adoptee's life is spent searching, wondering what is out there and feeling that when we find her, or him, or them, or something else, we will be happy, rather than seeing what we have in front of us.

Useful organisations/ websites

Information

Adoption, Search and Reunion
Website aimed at adopted people, adoptive parents, birth relatives and professionals. It includes a searchable database to help locate adoption records, a searchable database of local authorities, voluntary adoption agencies and adoption support agencies, and information about the legal framework.
www.adoptionsearchreunion.org.uk

Adoption support agencies

Adoption UK
National self-help group run by and for adoptive parents providing information, advice, support and training on all aspects of adoption and adoptive parenting.
www.adoptionuk.org.uk

Adults Affected by Adoption-NORCAP
Provides a non-statutory contact register that holds over 69,000 entries relating to adopted people and members of their birth families. It also provides intermediary services, a locate and make contact service, NHS Central Register checks and access to a search room.
www.norcap.org.uk

After Adoption
Offers information, advice and support to anyone affected by adoption.
www.afteradoption.org.uk

After Adoption Yorkshire
Provides a range of services for adopted people, birth families and adoptive

families including confidential advice, support, a search and intermediary service, support groups, training, and a mentoring and buddying scheme. www.afteradoptiontyorkshire.org.uk

Barnardo's Post-Adoption Services (Ireland)
Offer a range of services including an advice line, support groups, and a mediation service for adopted people and birth relatives who are preparing to meet through the National Adoption Contact Preference Register. www.barnardos.ie

Barnardo's Scotland Adoption Support Service
Provides advice, support and counselling to anyone affected by adoption. www.barnardos.org.uk/fosteringandadoption/fostering_and_adoption_locally/fostering_and_adoption_scotland/sass.htm

Birthlink
Provides a range of services for people separated by adoption with a Scottish connection, including the Adoption Contact Register for Scotland, a searching service, an intermediary service and help locating court records. www.birthlink.org.uk

Intercountry Adoption Centre
Provides an intermediary service for transnationally adopted adults, and hosts workshops, with the Transnational and Transracial Adoption Group, for adults who have an international element to their search for information and/or birth family. www.icacentre.org.uk

Post-Adoption Centre
Provides advice, support, counselling and training for all people affected by adoption and permanency. Services specifically for adopted adults include counselling, an intermediary service and groups. www.postadoptioncentre.org.uk

Adoption Contact Registers

Adoption Contact Register for England and Wales: www.gov.uk

Adoption Contact Register for Northern Ireland: www.nidirect.gov.uk

Birthlink (Scotland's Adoption Contact Register): www.birthlink.org.uk

AAA-NORCAP Contact Register: www.norcap.org.uk

Self-help groups

British Korean Adoptees
A group for Korean adopted adults and their friends which hosts monthly meetings at a Korean restaurant in London.
https://sites.google.com/site/britishkoreanadoptees/

Group for Adopted People
A central Scotland-based support group for adopted people which holds monthly meetings and provides advice on searching for birth relatives.
http://gapscotland.org.uk

Natural Parents Network
Offers confidential, non-judgemental and independent support for birth parents and their relatives.
www.n-p-n.co.uk

Natural Parents Network of Ireland
A self-help group which offers information and support to mothers and fathers who have lost children to adoption in the past.
www.adoptionloss.ie

Transnational and Transracial Adoption Group
An informal social network run by and for transnationally and transracially adopted adults which hosts social events, workshops and has a Facebook page.
www.ttag.org.uk

UK Hong Kong Adoptees Network
A group for Hong Kong adopted adults which hosts bi-annual social events.
www.hkadopteesnetwork.com

Vietnamese Adoptees International
An international network for Vietnamese adopted adults.
www.adoptedvietnamese.org